CRAFTING AUTOETHNC

This collection explores *how* autoethnography is made. Contributors from sociology, education, counselling, the visual arts, textiles, drama, music, and museum curation uncover and reflect on the processes and practices they engage in as they craft their autoethnographic artefacts. Each chapter explores a different material or media, together creating a rich and stimulating set of demonstrations, with the focus firmly on the practical accomplishment of texts/artefacts.

Theoretically, this book seeks to rectify the hierarchical separation of art and craft and of intellectual and practical cultural production, by collapsing distinctions between knowing and making. In relation to connections between personal experience and wider social and cultural phenomena, contributors address a variety of topics such as social class, family relationships and intergenerational transmission, loss, longing and grief, the neoliberal university, gender, sexuality, colonialism, race/ism, national identity, digital identities, indigenous ways of knowing/making and how these are 'storied', curated and presented to the public, and our relationship with the natural world. Contributors also offer insights into how the 'crafting space' is itself one of intellectual inquiry, debate, and reflection.

This is a core text for readers from both traditional and practice-based disciplines undertaking qualitative research methods/autoethnographic inquiry courses, as well as community-based practitioners and students. Readers interested in creative practice, practitioner-research and arts-based research in the social sciences and humanities will also benefit from this book.

Jackie Goode is a Visiting Fellow in Qualitative Research in the School of Social Sciences and Humanities, Loughborough University, UK.

Karen Lumsden is a Lecturer in Sociology at the University of Aberdeen, UK.

Jan Bradford completed her PhD at the University of Edinburgh, UK, and is an independent researcher.

CRAFTING AUTOETHNOGRAPHY

Processes and Practices of Making Self and Culture

Edited by Jackie Goode, Karen Lumsden and Jan Bradford

Routledge
Taylor & Francis Group

LONDON AND NEW YORK

Cover Image: Stitch journal by Clare Daněk

First published 2023
by Routledge
4 Park Square, Milton Park, Abingdon, Oxon OX14 4RN

and by Routledge
605 Third Avenue, New York, NY 10158

Routledge is an imprint of the Taylor & Francis Group, an informa business

British Library Cataloguing-in-Publication Data
A catalogue record for this book is available from the British Library

Library of Congress Cataloging-in-Publication Data
Names: Goode, Jackie, editor. | Lumsden, Karen, editor. | Bradford,
Jan, editor.
Title: Crafting autoethnography : processes and practices of making self
and culture / edited by Jackie Goode, Karen Lumsden and Jan Bradford.
Description: Abingdon, Oxon : Routledge, 2023. | Includes
bibliographical references and index.
Identifiers: LCCN 2022057725 (print) | LCCN 2022057726 (ebook) |
ISBN 9781032313337 (paperback) | ISBN 9781032313320 (hardback) |
ISBN 9781003309239 (ebook)
Subjects: LCSH: Ethnology--Biographical methods.
Classification: LCC GN346.6 .C73 2023 (print) | LCC GN346.6
(ebook) | DDC 305.8--dc23/eng/20230105
LC record available at https://lccn.loc.gov/2022057725
LC ebook record available at https://lccn.loc.gov/2022057726

ISBN: 978-1-032-31332-0 (hbk)
ISBN: 978-1-032-31333-7 (pbk)
ISBN: 978-1-003-30923-9 (ebk)

DOI: 10.4324/9781003309239

Typeset in Bembo
by KnowledgeWorks Global Ltd.

CONTENTS

SECTION V
Place and Belonging 177

LIST OF FIGURES

LIST OF CONTRIBUTORS

Lauriel-Arwen Amoroso, Northwest Outdoor Science School, US
Lauriel-Arwen Amoroso is an educator, writer and photographer who lives in Portland, Oregon. She holds a Doctorate in Educational Leadership from Portland State University. Her work and writing focuses on narrative research, memoir, walking, embodied learning practices, slowness, placemaking and the ways in which people connect to and learn from the natural and material world.

Panya Banjoko, Nottingham Trent University, UK
Panya Banjoko is a poet and PhD researcher at Nottingham Trent University, with a Vice Chancellor awarded scholarship, studying a practice-led PhD rooted in Nottingham Black Archive, the archive she co-founded in 2009. As poet, her poems feature in numerous collections, anthologies, and exhibitions.

Jan Bradford, independent researcher, UK
Inspired by Helene Cixous' concept of 'ecriture feminine', Jan Bradford practices a feminine style of writing to inquire through psychoanalytic, sociological and literary lenses. Her research focuses on intergenerational trauma and maternal grief in working-class communities.

Clare Daněk, University of Leeds, UK
Clare Daněk's AHRC-funded PhD research uses ethnographic methods to consider how people learn amateur craft skills in open-access community-making spaces. She also maintains a creative practice as a textile artist, with particular focus on the minutiae of everyday life.

Jack Davy, Morley College London, UK
Jack Davy has worked as a curator and anthropologist at the British Museum, Horniman Museum, and the University of East Anglia and is currently head

curator at Morley College, London. He specialises in and has published widely on the ethical and informed curation of Native American material culture in Britain, a process which requires constant professional self-examination and improvement.

Simon Denison, Hereford College of Arts, UK
Simon Denison is a photographer, photography critic, and senior lecturer in Critical Studies at Hereford College of Arts. For more information, see: www. simondenison.co.uk

David Méndez Díaz, National School of Theatre Arts, Mexico
David Méndez Díaz is an actor who graduated with distinction from the National School of Theatre Arts, Mexico, with a BA in Acting. He has participated in academic and professional stage productions, short films, and national and international performing art festivals in Latin America and the UK. He began doing theatre in 2012. Since then, he has collaborated on multiple stage projects.

Jackie Goode, Loughborough University, UK
Jackie Goode is Visiting Fellow in Qualitative Research in the School of Social Sciences and Humanities at Loughborough University. She has published a variety of autoethnographic articles in mainstream social sciences journals and is editor of Clever Girls: Autoethnographies of Class, Gender and Ethnicity, published in 2019 by Palgrave Macmillan.

Javiera Sandoval Limarí, IOE, UCL's Faculty of Education and Society, UK
Javiera Sandoval Limarí is a Chilean artist, activist and an ANID-funded PhD researcher. Her work connects, through and within art, experiences of migration, language, mother tongues and forgetting. She also works with AMPLA, a collective of Latin American mothers in London, creating with them spaces to engage in art and in activism.

Patrick Limb, Nottingham, UK
Patrick Limb is a Midlands barrister. His writings on memoir and nature have been published in the online journals of Selkie Press, Little Toller Books and Pilgrim House. He is completing a biography on another Nottingham barrister, F C Dietrichsen, and serves as Chair of Nottingham UNESCO City of Literature.

Karen Lumsden, University of Aberdeen, UK
Karen Lumsden is a sociologist and qualitative researcher. Her research focuses on policing, victims and cyber-crime. She has published two monographs with Routledge: Boy Racer Culture (2013) and Reflexivity: Theory, Method and Practice (2019). She is editor of Reflexivity in Criminological Research (2014) and Online Othering (2019) published by Palgrave Macmillan.

Joanna Neil, Leeds Arts University, UK
Joanna Neil is a course leader for the BA (Hons) Fine Art programme at Leeds Arts University. Her doctoral thesis 'Making the invisible visible: creating spaces for reflexive artistic practices through digital autoethnography', investigated arts and design-based practitioners' phenomenological experiences of using digital autoethnography as a strategy for reflective practice.

Mark Price, St Mary's University Institute of Education, University of Edinburgh Centre for Creative-Relational Inquiry, University of Brighton School of Humanities and Social Science, UK
Mark's writing and research interests lie in the fields of narrative and participatory inquiry and autoethnography, exploring particularly issues of agency, voice, border crossing and boundary spanning. This work mirrors his own professional life changes from playworker, to teacher, to youth worker, to counsellor, to academic, researcher and writer.

Edgar Rodríguez-Dorans, University of Edinburgh, UK
Edgar Rodríguez-Dorans is a qualitative researcher and mental health practitioner interested in the study of identities, sexualities, the everyday lives of LGBTQIA+ people, and the use of performing arts in research. He holds a PhD in Counselling Studies and currently works as a Lecturer in Counselling & Psychotherapy at the University of Edinburgh, UK

Rommy Anabalón Schaaf, IOE, UCL's Faculty of Education and Society, UK
Rommy Anabalón Schaaf is a Chilean PhD researcher in Sociolinguistics, as well as activist and artist. Her interests include language and work, language and gender, art and research, ethnography and social inequalities. Drawing on a social provisioning approach, her research examines processes of precarisation of female labour in higher education.

Aidan Teplitzky, Royal Birmingham Conservatoire, UK
Aidan Teplitzky is a Glaswegian composer and AHRC-funded Doctoral Researcher exploring the creative potential of embodying working-classness in new music composition. Aidan has worked with ensembles, including BBC SSO, Psappha Ensemble, the Glasgow Barons, the Glasgow New Music Expedition and Orkest de Ereprijs.

Chrissie Tiller, UK
Chrissie Tiller is currently undertaking a PhD by prior publication at the Technological University Dublin, exploring her lived experience as a working-class woman born in 1949, in the arts and cultural sector and academia. She continues to act as a critical friend for a number of national and international arts organisations.

INTRODUCTION

Jackie Goode, Karen Lumsden and Jan Bradford

Crafting Autoethnography

This edited collection on the crafting of autoethnography explores *how* autoethnography is made. We surface the *making* by inviting contributors from a wide variety of disciplines, practising in a variety of settings, to reveal, illustrate and reflect on the processes and practices they engage in as they craft their autoethnographic artefacts. The contribution which this collection seeks to make to the field of autoethnography is not to offer a 'how to' primer, but rather, to offer a rich and stimulating set of demonstrations with the focus firmly on *artful making*. In other words, we focus on the *practical accomplishment* of autoethnographic artefacts.

Ruiz-Junco and Vidal-Ortiz (2011) see the dominant form of autoethnography as emerging from the reflexive work being undertaken within sociology and anthropology in the early 1990s. They suggest that several developments coincided in the reassessment of ethnography taking place at that time: the need to value and engage subjectivity within research; ethnographers' interrogation of their own practice in a context of a 'crisis of representation'; Burawoy's (1991) critique of ethnographic practice (defined predominantly as participant observation) as confining its focus to understanding at the expense of explanation; and a reformulation of interpretive paradigms more broadly in the light of critiques arising from the work of feminist, poststructuralist and postmodern scholars. They identify symbolic interactionists such as Carolyn Ellis and Norman Denzin as foundational figures in autoethnography's further development. Enriched by cultural studies, poststructuralism and feminism, Denzin's autoethnographic work highlights *speaking to and for the powerless* (1995, p. 57). Ellis's (1997) focus has

DOI: 10.4324/9781003309239-1

been on opposing realist narratives in favour of 'evocative' accounts. Together, these scholars have:

> ... pushed interpretive narratives to ... the point of leaving the ethnographic method, focusing less on the notions of ethnography as analytical text (Anderson, 2006), and more on the centrality of the 'I' either for political or 'therapeutic' (Ellis, 2004) purposes.
>
> *Ruiz-Junco and Vidal-Ortiz (2011, p. 193)*

Autoethnographers vary in their emphasis on *auto-* (self), *-ethno-* (the sociocultural connection) and *-graphy* (the application of the research process) (Reed-Danahay, 1997). There is also variation in the exploratory strategies they use. For example, Ruiz-Junco and Vidal-Ortiz (2011) identify autoethnography as consisting of: stage performance, poetry, first-person essays, simulated conversations and video diaries. Regardless of genre, all of these strategies and materials aim to challenge a 'scientistic' epistemology that critiques qualitative research from a position that is 'grounded in narrow and outdated assumptions about what it means to be "scientific," assumptions that do not even validly represent actual practice in the *natural* sciences' (Maxwell, 2004, p. 36). There is also variation in the topics which autoethnographers choose and the theoretical framework/s shaping their work. In recent years, for example, autoethnographic narratives have often come from those writing 'from the margins'. These include academics challenging the marketisation and neoliberalisation of higher education and academic life, and authors documenting personal experiences of the social structuring of gendered, classed, racialised, embodied or sexual identities (and how these intersect) (see Addison, Breeze, & Taylor, 2022; Goode, 2019; Lumsden, 2022). Theoretically, posthuman and new materialist narratives have also contributed to the field of autoethnography. As Blyth and Aslanian (2022) observe, posthumanism attempts to question the notion of knowledge by 'decentring' the human, discounting the idea of self and understanding both the human and the 'more-than-human' as mutually productive and 'entangled'. While this may seem antithetical to autoethnography, they cite recent work (e.g. Dickinson, 2018; Warfield, 2019; Wilde, 2020) that explores what happens 'when autobiographical stories are understood as *already* more-than-human' (p. vi).

Autoethnography is a method which attracts both criticism and defence. Atkinson (2006), for example, seeks to undercut claims to methodological novelty by some autoethnographers by providing numerous examples of the long history of auto/biographical bases for ethnographic work. In some cases of autoethnography, he notes an 'elevation of the autobiographical to such a degree that the ethnographer becomes more memorable than the ethnography' (p. 402), with a concomitant lack of analysis of social action and social organisation. This applies especially to exclusively 'evocative' autoethnographies, in contrast to the 'analytical autoethnography' that Anderson (2006) favours. The risk with the former is a form of autoethnographic 'naval gazing' that overshadows the wider social and cultural relevance and insights which the 'storying of the self' can impart. However, some exponents, such as Ghita (2019), have illustrated the ways in which evocative accounts can make visible practices and phenomena that were not apparent before, thereby bringing into question assumed behaviours.

Freeman (2015) considers the point at which autoethnography blurs into other forms of inquiry and genres of writing and attempts to 'do autoethnography' while problematising the whole enterprise (Freeman, 2020). Stahlke Wall (2016), meanwhile, calls for a moderate and balanced treatment of autoethnography in place of polarisation, with room for a range of voices that also sustain 'confidence in the quality, rigor, and usefulness of academic research' (p. 1). Sparkes (2020) offers clarification of evaluative criteria that provides a solid foundation for rapprochement.

With so many clamouring voices, what more is there to say?

One way forward might be to maintain a collective curiosity about the many ways in which an 'autotheoretical impulse' (defined as 'an encounter between first person narrative and theory as an established body of academic thought') (Wiegman, 2020, p. 1) manifests itself. However, for those coming to autoethnography for the first time, it can feel somewhat mystifying as an approach to research, the language used sometimes obfuscatory, the invitation to participate as daunting as it is exciting, until one becomes more familiar with certain linguistic formats. As Denzin (2017) observes:

> … terms slip and slide, fall over one another: critical, embodied, transformative, dialogic, reflexive, participatory, emancipatory, narratives of resistance, plateaus, planes of composition, Deleuze, Guattari, assemblages, affect, nomadic inquiry, rhizomatic, love, loss, praxis, writing as a way of being in the world. Writing framed around acts of activism and resistance. How do we move forward?
>
> *p. 8*

We trust that our contributors bring clarity to their work, thereby illuminating practices and processes that are not commonly described and examined.

Theoretically, this edited collection is inspired by a focus on crafting in its broadest sense, as featured in the work of classic texts such as Sudnow's (1993) *Ways of the Hand*, Sennett's (2009) *The Craftsman* and Ingold's (2013) *Making*. Within the social sciences, this focus on the relationship between 'knowing' and 'doing' can be located within the 'practice-turn' (Miettinen, Samra-Fredericks, & Yanow, 2009; Schatzki, 2001). It is a development that seeks to rectify the disconnection that Gauntlett (2011) identifies in the late twentieth century separation of art and craft in Western culture; one which led to a separation between 'having ideas' and 'making objects' (with the former being ascribed higher status). It is a split, as Dormer (1997) comments, that implies the existence of some *a priori* 'knowing' how to make things; and one that is particularly marked in relation to women's domestic craft practices, where the lower status accorded represents a failure to recognise the complex practices and meanings involved in all craft, including the domestic and amateur.

Within the broad 'practice turn' in the social sciences, knowledge is no longer conceived of as an object of possession, nor as something that pre-exists action, nor as a substance to be applied when and where needed (Gherardi & Perrotti, 2014). Rather, there is a conceptualisation in which the distinctions described above, between *knowing* and *doing*, collapse. Knowing and doing are seen as inextricably connected. For Ingold (2013), making things is tantamount to a process of growth. This growth occurs when there is a 'correspondence' between maker and materials, with each acting on the other. To convert what we owe to the world into 'data' that we have extracted from it, he states, is to:

> ... stipulate that knowledge is to be reconstructed on the *outside*, as an edifice built up 'after the fact' rather than as inhering in skills of perception and capacities of judgement that develop in the course of direct, practical and sensuous engagements with our surroundings.
>
> *2013, p. 5, original emphasis*

Ingold identifies three key aspects of *making*. Firstly, making has a narrative quality, with each action, movement and line building on the last. Secondly, making does not only come about through the exertion of external force on a material but also requires care, judgement and dexterity. Thirdly, making is predicated by the 'field of forces' set up by the relationship between the maker and his or her engagement with the material (see Roxburgh, 2021, p. 161).

Further, the term 'knowing-in-practice' advances the idea that knowing is not only a *practical accomplishment* but also one that is situated in the historical, social and cultural context in which it unfolds. In this way, the autoethnographic knowledge production that we are focusing on in this collection is an essentially social phenomenon, (re)connecting mind, body and hand; art and craft; present, past and future; self and (O)ther(s). As Turney (2013) observes, the 'made' object:

> ... acts as a cultural marker, representative of the making process, of a journey or a time that is symbolic not just of constructive leisure, but of wider relationships, with kin, community and global citizenship. Making therefore makes meaning and acts not just as a time-filler or the expression of busyness ... but also as a means of self-expression, of identity formation and of a means of establishing one's place ....
>
> *p. 136*

Ideally too, as Dissanayake (1994) suggests, there is pleasure involved in making. This engagement with ideas, learning and knowledge contains a pleasure that arises from a sense of being alive within the process of making something exist that did not exist before. It comes from using one's own agency, dexterity, feelings and judgement to mould, form, touch, hold and craft physical materials. Dissanayake characterises this as a *joie de faire*.

For some, of course, 'practical and sensuous engagements with our surroundings' (Ingold, 2013, p. 5) do not represent a departure. It is familiar ground for those traditionally undertaking arts/craft-based making. For example, Bunda et al. (2019) engaged in basket-weaving, painting and stitching as a method of investigating their matrilineal ancestry and recovering a sense of belonging. Dwyer, Beinart, and Ahmed (2019) used embroidery as a way of collaboratively exploring stories of faith and place – making art as making a recovered and reconnected self (see also 'Stitching Together', the 2020 Special Issue of *The Journal of Arts & Communities*). The practical and the sensuous is also familiar ground for those engaged in *analysing* the production of craft-based knowledge (see Barrett & Bolt, 2007; Torell & Ranglin, 2012).

An active engagement with one's surroundings is also fundamental to those grounded in indigenous ways of knowing, like Whitinui, whose autoethnographic creation springs from a desire to ground one's sense of self in 'what remains "sacred" to us as indigenous peoples in the world we live in, and in the way we choose to construct our identity as Māori' (2014, p. 456). Our Western ways of knowing and of world-making, on the other hand, are belatedly being reformed through decolonialising initiatives (e.g. the 'Decolonizing Autoethnography' Special Issue of *Cultural Studies ↔ Critical Methodologies*, 2018); and through reconnecting with what might be described as the sacred in encounters with the natural world closer to home – such as those undertaken by psychogeographers and some sociologists (e.g. Ingold, 2010; Keating, Portman, & Robertson, 2012; O'Neill & Roberts, 2019; Wylie, 2005).

In contrast to recreating ourselves and our cultures through making connections with the natural world, the creation of *digital* identities and social relations continues apace, not least through such phenomena as the marketing of selves that 'influencers' employ via platforms like Instagram and Tiktok. This area of activity has also come to the attention of autoethnographers. Dunn and Myers (2020) argue it is vital that autoethnography evolves 'in concert with the ways our lives have become inextricably tethered to digital technology' (p. 43), raising the question of how such technologies might be used in ways that resist the commodification of the self.

How might we capture such diverse forms of cultural production? And how can we take into account the variety of locations in which autoethnographic activity takes place? In this edited collection, we acknowledge a range of autoethnographic making which includes those working within the academy (i.e. work undertaken by doctoral students and early career researchers through to senior academics) and those working outside of the academy (i.e. in places where professional practitioners are honing their skills by making artefacts that are autoethnographies 'by other names'). For example, some instances of blurred literary genres such as life-writing, memoir, creative non-fiction and autofiction might qualify (e.g. Deborah Miranda's (2013) *Bad Indians*); as would some community-based practices with a social justice agenda referred to as 'craftivism' (e.g. MAI: Feminism and Visual Culture, 2021; Peach, 2020). We can also include walking as a way of generating community-based knowledge-production (e.g. O'Neill & Hubbard, 2010). Methodologically, then, the collection includes but goes beyond 'writing as inquiry' (Richardson & St. Pierre, 2011) to encompass a variety of practice-based approaches.

In terms of academic discipline or professional practice, our contributors are drawn from: sociology, education, counselling, the visual arts, textiles, drama, music and museum curation. The materials and media they use in their *making of autoethnographic artefacts* include: writing and text, performance, film, photography, digital technologies, craft, composing, walking and the making of exhibitions. This range draws attention to the usual primacy of written text as a representation of autoethnographic activity. The written journal article as 'output' tends to be the standard representation of autoethnography in the majority of disciplines, while attempting to navigate and communicate the relationship between written discourse and *practice-based knowledge* may be more complicated. Hemmings suggests that models of knowledge production conveyed through text command greater agency within arts education despite other models and media often occupying more of a practitioner's time (2020, p.1). Igoe (2013), on the other hand, explains how the use of words in her doctoral study at the Royal College of Art in London enabled her to discover what it was she was trying to articulate through her practice. She saw this as a positive outcome due to the fact that it is 'words and commentary that have been missing from textile design, not the thinking and making' (2013, p. 21; see also Quinn, 2020). This dilemma underpins the terrain on which the collection is laid out – one too often characterised by a false binary between thinking and (the) making (of a 'text'). This traditional binary leads to a failure to recognise that, as in Sudnow's (1993), Sennett's (2009) and Ingold's (2013) conceptualisations, the two (thinking *and* making) are inextricably interwoven in *both* 'traditional' *and* 'practice-based' disciplines. Contributors' accounts of their own making practices in this edited collection are intended to open up this terrain.

A crucial component of autoethnography is that it mines personal and/or professional experience in order to throw light on wider social and cultural issues and relations. Therefore, the contributors in this book present autoethnographic artefacts that also illuminate significant issues in relation to topical (and enduring) subjects. These topics include: social class; family relationships and intergenerational transmission; loss, longing and grief; the neoliberal university; gender; sexuality; colonialism; race/ism; national identity; digital identities; indigenous ways of knowing/making and how these are 'storied', curated and presented to the public; and our relationship with the natural world. Together, they offer insights into the processes and practices through which academic and professional practitioners make texts and/or artefacts that connect the individual to the social, self to culture, the personal to the political and private troubles to public issues. Following Appadurai's (1986) notion of 'the social life of things', we were also interested in the 'after-life' of autoethnographic 'things'. Thus, some contributors revisit earlier texts, performances or artefacts and offer examples of 'what happened next'. They illustrate the ways in which autoethnographic projects are only ever provisionally 'finished'.

Finally, what our contributors undoubtedly have in common, regardless of discipline, institutional or organisational location, or the specific materials and media they use, is an *impulse to creativity*, a *resistance* to being confined within an established groove and a delight in making selves and worlds anew. In other words, Dissanayake's (1994) *joie de faire*.

The chapters in the collection are organised into five thematic sections according to the materials and media being used and/or themes covered: *(1) this writing life; (2) making a drama out of it; (3) crafting selves; (4) creating class; and (5) space and belonging.*

This Writing Life

In our first section, Jackie Goode and Panya Banjoko consider how they engage in *writing* as crafting. In her chapter, Jackie Goode conceives of her autoethnographic writing practices as a form of collecting – of fragments which have become dispersed along the way and which she begins to gather up alongside various theorists, novelists and poets. As she chases the White Rabbit, gets stuck in a hole, engages in memory-work, traces absences and examines notions of nostalgia and its meanings, she invites the reader to make their own autoethnographic discoveries.

Panya Banjoko answers Fred De'Aguair's (1996) plea for Black people to write their own slave narratives in order to create their own versions of the past. The simultaneous making of a self and the crafting of poems offers her a means of finding ways to bear witness to history, to intervene in it creatively by giving expression to ignored and submerged voices, and to move towards a reclamation of culture, identity and self-government.

Making a Drama Out of It

In our second section, Karen Lumsden, and Edgar Rodriguez-Dorans and David Méndez Díaz use dramatic production in their autoethnographies. In her chapter, Karen Lumsden presents a performative autoethnography of the higher education managerialist tool of surveillance commonly referred to as a 'Performance Development Review' (PDR). Designed to ensure the accountability of employees, the PDR shapes behaviours/actions deemed to be evidence of 'success' in academia. Lumsden provides an account of the 'backstage work' involved in her attempts to process, write, present and reflect on this snapshot of academic life; and of how the sharing of this confessional story via performance enabled her simultaneously to engage in self-care, mourn the loss of a stable academic identity and learn to value an 'unsettled identity' (Grant, 2007).

Edgar Rodríguez-Dorans and David Méndez Díaz introduce us to 'Arkadium', a dance and theatre group that Rodriguez-Dorans co-founded in Mexico in 1999 with his friend Julio. Over a period of 20 years, they created a community of people of different ages, professions, identities, ethnicities and social classes, all connected through their love for dance as a form of expression and way of being. Julio's death in 2019 prompted Edgar to write 'Mi amigo Giovanni', a play that uses autoethnographic material to create a moving memory of his life. After months of virtual rehearsals during the Covid-19 pandemic, Arkadium premiered the show to live audiences at the Edinburgh Fringe Festival in 2021. In their chapter, Edgar and David discuss how autoethnographic performance served as a method to create, explore and reflect on intimacies that are challenged by aspects of geography, time, discourses and materialities.

Crafting Selves

The third section includes five contributions from authors who use both material and/or digital media in their crafting. We include chapters from: Rommy Anabalón Schaaf and Javiera Sandoval-Limarí, Simon Denison, Joanna Neil, Clare Daněk and Mark Price.

Rommy Anabalón Schaaf and Javiera Sandoval-Limarí explain how the creation of a video and the four artefacts presented in it (a blanket, a portrait and two drawings of trees) was a way for them to 'think with their hands'. On returning to the UK after a period of fieldwork in Chile, Schaaf and Sandoval-Limarí searched for a way to intertwine their personal stories with the stories they wanted to tell for their doctoral theses. They found themselves approaching the process of 'becoming' autoethnographers through the image and the shadow of their mothers, recognising how their experiences with their mothers had shaped their relationships with their participants. In making a video of the reflective processes that arose as they manually created material artefacts together, they not only aimed to create and share a space in which to recognise the ways their personal stories were deeply entangled with the social processes they were investigating, but also to promote the notion that such entanglements form a significant part of academic journeys. Framing their role as female researcher-artists from the Global South making sense of their experiences and work in the Global North, they reflect in their chapter on the decolonial and feminist roots of their approach and offer practices that challenge and subvert what counts as knowledge in academia.

The visual medium which Simon Denison uses (and analyses) is photography. His autoethnographic approach represents a largely new, experimental form of practice in art criticism. He presents a protocol designed to draw out links between the critic's pre-reflexive 'intellectual' (contextually and culturally aware) interpretation of a photograph; their emotional response to it; their memories, experiences, life-story, deeply held values/beliefs; and the ambient circumstances, both material and emotional, of the viewing moment itself. Using the example of a specific photograph to elaborate the process, he suggests what the contribution of 'autoethnographic criticism' to this area of cultural consumption and production might look like. He also discusses the potential difficulties involved and argues that it might nevertheless increase our emotional engagement with photographs and intensify the lived experience of viewing them.

Joanna Neil's work explores themes at the intersection of researching visual arts education, digital technologies and arts practice by engaging in technology-supported reflective processes. Her approach to digital autoethnography involves looking inwards, finding a way to make what has become familiar through routinisation unfamiliar again – a 'deconstruction' rather than a construction of self, a way to understand and develop creative practice in the making of visual art, a way to reconnect with one's work and to regain a sense of authenticity. Even when we are allowed into the process of an artist, she suggests, it is often to see the technical side of them making that work or to access a narrative of how their ideas developed, rather than how they reflect on their work, what the making of the work feels like, or how they make sense of what they do, whether immediately or over time. In her chapter, she explores how technology enables her to experience both a distancing from and a new intimacy with her work, through seeing and hearing what usually goes unnoticed.

Clare Daněk's chapter tells the story of a 'stitch journal'. Her Masters project explored the experience of learning basic woodwork skills. On its completion, she became curious about the experience of learning craft skills alongside others in a shared community space, and this enquiry formed the basis of her doctoral research. The Masters research used autoethnographic methods, largely due to a desire to 'get her hands dirty'. She uses the same approach in her PhD. This desire to 'think with her hands' and to express herself through material engagement rather than via words tapped out onto a screen led to the making of her stitch journal. Her chapter traces the sensory processes in which she engaged: the feel of a threaded needle pulling through fabric, the juxtaposition of a particular colour and weight of thread against a particular colour of fabric, the sensation of using small, sharp embroidery scissors to cut precise shapes from stiff acrylic felt. The images she wanted to create appeared as snapshots in her mind far more readily than the slowly coaxed sentences that were adding up to endless drafts of thesis chapters.

In his chapter, Mark Price engages in an autoethnographic exploration of life-transitions and transformations. When, during lockdown, he left his academic role of 20 years, his attention was drawn back to a statuette of *The Thinker* he had been given as a gift by a particular cohort of students. Over the following months, he used bricolage and découpage to apply assemblages of found texts and images to it, gradually turning *The Thinker* into *The Dreamer*. Here, he makes this 'making process' explicit, evoking the shape-shifting he experienced in the liminal space betwixt teacher and student; researcher and writer; thinker and dreamer. His choosing, re-positioning and applying of texts becomes a personal narrative of becoming; of the layering of identities and of 'arriving' somewhere; but not finishing.

Creating Class

In our fourth section, Aidan Teplitzky and Chrissie Tiller unpick and unravel gender and class-based identities. Aidan Teplitzky uses sound. He incorporates his own experiences and those of others from working-class backgrounds into his *Seven Working-Class Time Pieces* for keyboard and metronome. His aim is to explore the creative potential of embodying working-classness in new interdisciplinary compositions; and specifically, to examine the way in which *time* is experienced by working-class people. It is experienced in a positive way through the affective 'gift of attention over time' and in a negative way, due to the lack of security related to low wages and/or part-time work. In contributing to the making of his own 'sonic persona' (Schulze, 2018), each of his works offers an insight into the lived experience of being working class and how working-classness changes perceptions of time: 'how we cope with precarity and the challenges of sustaining ourselves and working-class ways of being within capitalist society'. He offers an autoethnographic narrative of the creation of these compositions: providing the context in which the pieces were created; explaining the creative process of translating lived experiences into compositions; and reflecting on the finished pieces. In crafting a new compositional contribution to our 'sound culture' (LaBelle, 2010), Teplitzky seeks to mobilise the medium as a vehicle for social transformation.

In her chapter, Chrissie Tiller examines the ways in which interactions of class and gender in educational contexts can continue to operate as disabling even after a long and successful international career. From her beginnings as a clever working-class girl from Leeds, through teaching in the 1970s, leading a Theatre in Education company in the 1980s, setting up and running international networks and training programmes in the 1990s, to establishing the first MA in collaborative and social arts practice at Goldsmiths, London University in 2004, she returned to education as a mature doctoral student, undertaking her PhD by prior publication/practice. Here, through a series of 'Starts, False Starts and Re-Starts', she shares with the reader the 're-making' of her academic self *in process*, as some painful past experiences are reactivated. She is simultaneously crafting a new self *as* she crafts a thesis. Both Teplitzky and Tiller illustrate how autoethnographic practices can be mobilised in the assimilating, synthesising and integrating of past experiences with the ongoing crafting of new identities.

Place and Belonging

In our fifth and final section, three contributors (Lauriel-Arwen Amoroso, Patrick Limb and Jack Davy) highlight relationships between place and place-making and between these and the making of selves, social relations, knowledge, belonging and culture. Lauriel-Arwen Amoroso and Patrick Limb both engage in walking in specific landscapes. Walking as an arts-based approach to doing biographical research (O'Neill & Roberts, 2019) and as a method that brings together a set of place-based theories (Springgay & Truman, 2022) can be seen as the latest in a long line of developments aimed at 'reclaiming' the land in a way that recognises and honours not only our rights but also our responsibilities to it.

Lauriel-Arwen Amoroso shows how she came to a new way of learning through walking – in the Caribbean, along the Camino de Santiago, through the Northwest Industrial Area of Oregon, through the Oxbow Regional Park, the Tyron Creek State Park and on the Kilchis Point Reserve. She describes how her walking practice became an embodied form of research, the realisation of which not only constituted the making of a new epistemology and a new self (a self connected to the land, to her own body and to a deep feeling of awe and aliveness) but also simultaneously gave rise to the *un*making of a self raised with an inheritance of colonialism, epistemic hegemony and disconnection from embodied ways of knowing.

Patrick Limb's story and his commentary on its making is an excavation of the making of human relationships: with place and time; with landscape and birds; between mother and son; between being ill and being alive; and between story tellers, as they shared tales and supported each other 'remotely' during periods when physical human contact was restricted. Through his illustrated 'telling of walks', both shared and alone, there is an exploration of the extent to which people make places and places make people – and a lyrical account of how this can happen.

Last but not least, we look at anthropological museums' roles in the 'making of culture'. Jack Davy tells how one 'non-Indigenous' curator who works with Indigenous museum collections learnt the hard way. Indigenous collections, formerly described as 'ethnographic' and before that as 'tribal', he explains, are those formed from living cultures as opposed to archaeology; and through what used to be called 'primitive peoples', so named because our nineteenth century predecessors thought that by examining the material cultures of hunter gatherers and subjects of expanding colonialism, we might gain insights into our own European prehistory. In this context, he suggests, a non-Indigenous museum curator might be seen more as an assessor, sifting through the looted salvage from a burning building, than as a scientist preserving and curating intact culture. In considering our historical legacy and responsibility, he asks how European institutions use what has survived, to tell *other* peoples' stories (and if it is not too much of a spoiler, to suggest that more often than not, they do it by getting it wrong). His account problematises notions of ownership and belonging and thus reveals the (re)making of a (professional curatorial) self – one who hopes he is learning to 'make culture' better.

In the concluding chapter, the editors review the chapters as a whole, drawing out commonalities and summarising what we can learn from this range of situated processes and practices involved in making and crafting selves and cultures. It is our intention that through the sharing of our autoethnographic crafting of selves and cultures, readers will gain insight into how this 'crafting space' is itself one of intellectual inquiry, debate and reflection and be encouraged to consider their own autoethnographic making processes and practices.

References

Addison, M., Breeze, M., & Taylor, Y. (Eds.). (2022). *The Palgrave handbook of imposter syndrome in higher education.* Basingstoke: Palgrave Macmillan.

Anderson, L. (2006). Analytic autoethnography. *Journal of Contemporary Ethnography, 35*(4), 373–395.

Appadurai, A. (Ed.). (1986). *The social life of things: Commodities in cultural perspective.* New York, NY: Cambridge University Press.

Atkinson, P. (2006). Rescuing autoethnography. *Journal of Contemporary Ethnography, 35*(4), 400–404.

Barrett, E., & Bolt, B. (Eds.). (2007). *Practice as research: Approaches to creative arts enquiry.* London: IB Tauris & Co Ltd.

Blyth, C., & Aslanian, T. K. (Eds.). (2022). *Children and the power of stories: Posthuman and autoethnographic perspectives in early childhood education.* New York, NY: Springer International Publishing.

Bunda, T., Heckenberg, R., Snepvangers, K., Phillips, L. G., Lasczik, A., & Black, A. L. (2019). Storymaking belonging. *Art/Research International: A Transdisciplinary Journal, 4*(1), 153–179.

Burawoy, M. (1991). *Ethnography unbound: Power and resistance in the modern metropolis.* Berkeley, CA: University of California Press.

De'Aguair, F. (1996). The last essay about slavery. In S. Dunant, & R. Porter (Eds.), *The age of anxiety* (pp. 125–147). London: Virago.

Denzin, N. K. (1995). Symbolic interactionism. In J. A. Smith, R. Harré, & L. Van Langenhove (Eds.), *Rethinking psychology* (pp. 43–58). Thousand Oaks, CA: Sage Publications.

Denzin, N. K. (2017). Critical qualitative inquiry. *Qualitative Inquiry, 3*(1), 8–16.

Dickinson, S. (2018). Writing sensation: Critical autoethnography in posthumanism. In S. Holman Jones, & M. Pruyn (Eds.), *Creative selves/creative cultures: Critical autoethnography, performance, and pedagogy* (pp. 79–92). New York, NY: Springer International Publishing.

Dissanayake, E. (1994). *The pleasure and meaning of making.* Great Lakes Regional Symposium on Craft, Detroit Institute of Arts: Detroit. Retrieved from https://www.craftcouncil.org/sites/default/files/2018-10/The-Pleasure-and-Meaning-of-Making.pdf

Dormer, P. (1997). *The culture of craft.* Manchester: Manchester University Press.

Dunn, T. R., & Myers, B. (2020). Contemporary autoethnography *is* digital autoethnography. *Journal of Autoethnography, 1*(1), 43–59.

Dwyer, C., Beinart, K., & Ahmed, N. (2019). My life is but a weaving: Embroidering geographies of faith and place. *Cultural Geographies, 26*(1), 133–140.

Ellis, C. (1997). Evocative autoethnography: Writing emotionally about our lives. In W. G. Tierney, & Y. S. Lincoln (Eds.), *Representation and the text: Re-framing the narrative voice.* Albany, NY: State University of New York Press.

Ellis, C. (2004) *The Ethnographic I: A Methodological Novel about Autoethnography.* Walnut Creek, California: Altamira Press.

Freeman, J. (2015). *Remaking memory: Autoethnography, memoir and the ethics of self.* Oxfordshire: Libri Publishing.

Freeman, J. (2020). Projects with people, participant-coercion and the autoethnographical invite. *Canadian Journal of Action Research, 20*(2), 85–103.

Gauntlett, D. (2011). *Making is connecting.* Cambridge: Polity Press.

Gherardi, S., & Perrotti, M. (2014). Between the hand and the head. How things get done, and how in doing the ways of doing are discovered'. *Qualitative Research in Organizations and Management, 9*(2), 134–150.

Ghita, C. R. (2019). *In defence of subjectivity: Autoethnography and studying technology non-use.* Proceedings of the 27th European Conference on Information Systems (ECIS), Stockholm & Uppsala, Sweden, June 8-14, 2019.

Goode, J. E. (Ed.). (2019). *Clever girls: Autoethnographies of class, gender and ethnicity.* Basingstoke: Palgrave Macmillan.

Grant, B. M. (2007). The mourning after: Academic development in a time of doubt. *International Journal for Academic Development, 12*(1), 35–43.

Hemmings, J. (2020). Textual agency: Pitfalls and potentials. In J. Potvin, & M. E. Marchand (Eds.), *Design and agency: Critical perspectives on identities, histories, and practices* (pp. 273–285). London: Bloomsbury Visual Arts.

Igoe, E. (2013). *In textasis: Matrixial narratives of textile design* (PhD thesis). Royal College of Art, England.

Ingold, T. (2010). Footprints through the weather-world: Walking, breathing, knowing. *The Journal of the Royal Anthropological Institute, 16,* 121–139.

Ingold, T. (2013). *Making: Anthropology, archaeology, art and architecture.* London: Routledge.

Keating, R., Portman, K., & Robertson, I. (2012). Walking the wateryscape: Exploring the liminal. *Journal of Arts & Communities, 4*(1–2), 10–31.

LaBelle, B. (2010). *Acoustic territories: Sound culture and everyday life.* London: Continuum.

Lumsden, K. (2022). Becoming and unbecoming an academic: Performative autoethnography of struggles against imposter syndrome from early to mid-career in the neoliberal university. In M. Addison, M. Breeze, & Y. Taylor (Eds.), *The Palgrave handbook of imposter syndrome in higher education* (pp. 577–592). Basingstoke: Palgrave Macmillan.

MAI: Feminism and Visual Culture. (2021). *Focus special issue eight: Feminist craft.* Retrieved from https://maifeminism.com/issues/mai-issue-8-feminist-craft/

Maxwell, J. A. (2004). Reemergent scientism, postmodernism, and dialogue across differences. *Qualitative Inquiry, 10*(1), 35–41.

Miettinen, R., Samra-Fredericks, D., & Yanow, D. (2009). Re-turn to practice: An introductory essay. *Organization Studies, 30*(12), 1309–1327.

Miranda, D. (2013). *Bad Indians: A tribal memoir.* Berkeley, CA: Heyday.

O'Neill, M., & Hubbard, P. (2010). Walking, sensing, belonging: Ethno-memesis as performative praxis. *Visual Studies, 25*(1), 46–58.

O'Neill, M., & Roberts, B. (2019). *Walking methods: Research on the move.* London: Routledge.

Peach, A. (2020). Made with love, filled with hope. Knitted knockers and the materiality of care: Their impact on the women who make and receive them. *Journal of Arts and Communities, 10*(1–2), 83–93.

Quinn, J. (2020). Reflecting on reflection: Exploring the role of writing as part of practice-led research. *Journal of Writing in Creative Practice, 13*(2), 243–258.

Reed-Danahay, D. E. (1997). *Auto/ethnography: Rewriting the self and the social.* Oxford: Berg.

Richardson, L., & St. Pierre, E. A. (2011). Writing: A method of inquiry. In N. K. Denzin, & Y. S. Lincoln (Eds.), *The Sage handbook of qualitative research* (5th ed., pp. 959–978). Thousand Oaks, CA: Sage.

Roxburgh, M. (2021). Making, problems and pleasures. In E. Igoe (Ed.), *Textile design theory in the making.* London: Bloomsbury Visual Arts.

Ruiz-Junco, N., & Vidal-Ortiz, S. (2011). Autoethnography: The sociological through the personal. In I. Zake, & M. DeCesare (Eds.), *New directions in sociology: Essays on theory and methodology in the 21st century* (pp. 193–211). Jefferson, NC: McFarland & Co. Inc.

Schatzki, T. R. (2001). Introduction: Practice theory. In T. R. Schatzki, F. Knorr-Cetina, & E. von Savigny (Eds.), *The practice turn in contemporary theory* (pp. 1–14). London: Routledge.

Schulze, H. (2018). *The sonic persona: An anthropology of sound.* London: Bloomsbury Academic.

Sennett, R. (2009). *The craftsman.* London: Allen Lane.

Sparkes, A. C. (2020). Autoethnography: Accept, revise, reject? An evaluative self reflects. *Qualitative Research in Sport, Exercise and Health, 12*(2), 289–302.

Springgay, S., & Truman, S. E. (2022). Critical walking methodologies and oblique agitations of place. *Qualitative Inquiry, 28*(2), 171–176.

Stahlke Wall, S. (2016). Toward a moderate autoethnography. *International Journal of Qualitative Methods, 15*(1). https://doi.org/10.1177/1609406916674966

Sudnow, D. (1993). *Ways of the hand: The organization of improvised conduct.* Cambridge, MA: Harvard University Press.

Torell, V., & Ranglin, U. (2012). Knowledge in action in weaving. *Techne Series A, 21*(1), 22–37.

Turney, J. (2013). Crafty chats or whose craft is it anyway? Domestic discourse and making marginality matter. In L. Sandino, & M. Partington (Eds.), *Oral history in the visual arts* (pp. 136–142). London: Bloomsbury.

Warfield, K. (2019). Becoming method(ologist): A feminist posthuman autoethnography of the becoming of a posthuman methodology. *Reconceptualizing Educational Research Methodology, 10*(2–3), 147–172.

Whitinui, P. (2014). Indigenous autoethnography: Exploring, engaging, and experiencing 'self' as a native method of inquiry. *Journal of Contemporary Ethnography, 43*(4), 456–487.

Wiegman, R. (2020). Autotheory. *Arizona Quarterly: A Journal of American Literature, Culture, and Theory, 76*(1), 1–14.

Wilde, P. (2020). I, posthuman: A deliberately provocative title. *International Journal of Qualitative Research, 13*(3), 365–380.

Wylie, J. (2005). A single day's walking: Narrating self and landscape on the South West Coast Path. *Transactions of the Institute of British Geographers, 30*(2), 234–247.

SECTION I
This Writing Life

1

SHORING UP THE FRAGMENTS

Jackie Goode

Introduction

Writing is my medium. It has been since schooldays when I got good marks in English classes. It remained so through the teenage years when I confided adolescent longings to a diary. And through years of marriage when a private journal became a means and a repository for articulating what, deep down, I knew I knew. Then through the 'performance' of conventional academic articles, working and reporting on others' research agendas. And finally, to subverting the genre with my own voice in autoethnographic texts like this. 'Ask yourself in the most silent hour of your night: must I write?' said Rilke (2012, Letter 1). Autoethnographic writing is where I make myself (up), hold conversations and make connections to wider social and cultural phenomena. Writing is my salvation. My comfort and joy. It's the place I come home to.

Collecting and Assembling Fragments

Some years ago, I wrote an autoethnographic article based on interviewing my old English teacher (2007). He quoted from Eliot's (1961) *The Waste Land*: 'These fragments I have shored against my ruins' (p. 67) – which apart from reigniting the same frisson of desire I'd felt listening to him read poetry in class fifty years earlier, resonated strongly for me as a way of thinking of our lives as a series of fragments which get dispersed along the way and which we are constantly collecting up in order to reassemble them into some kind of container in which to hold ourselves intact. It's often difficult to trace the origin of the concepts we accumulate as meaningful to us in some way but I think the way ideas of assembly (and ruin) resonated for me at this point originated long before with notions of dis/integration and coherence acquired from reading Jung (1962) during my social work training. For Jung, 'individuation' is a developmental psychic process

DOI: 10.4324/9781003309239-3

during which: innate elements of personality, components of an 'immature' psyche and life experiences become integrated over time into a well-functioning whole (or, in forms of mental illness, where these elements 'disintegrate'). This was built upon by notions of integration in the learning theories I studied during the teacher training I undertook, in which the reactivation of prior knowledge enhances new learnings (Piaget, 1926). Further echoes occurred when I read Walter Benjamin on collecting. And finally, links were made when I came across the Japanese art of *Kintsugi*, in which the fragments of a broken pot are stuck back together with a powdered gold mixture so that the cracks not only show but also become a record of the life (and beauty) of a mended vessel. All of which is to say that I conceive of my own 'making' of autoethnographic texts as a process of (re) assembling fragments, through acts of memory (or re/membering).

The texts themselves, which have tended towards the 'analytic', even when also including the elegiac (see Goode, 2019), are not necessarily fragmented. Although this chapter might be. I usually chase magpies away from my bird feeders to give the little birds a chance but when reflecting on my own 'making' practices, I feel like a magpie myself. Or one of those infuriating cooks who doesn't use a recipe and, when asked how they make a particular dish, says that the ingredients 'depend of what they've got in' and that the required measurements consist of 'a pinch of this' and 'a handful of that'. Unlike complying with the vocabulary of 'designing', 'data collecting strategies', 'data coding' and 'managing data' in relation to the making of an autoethnographic artefact (as Chang (2008) and Hughes & Pennington (2017) do), my autoethnographic writing is a much more organic process, which only gets 'crafted' into an artefact such as a journal article at a much later stage.

So this is how it goes this morning. I'm 'googling' *The Waste Land* and find a thesis referencing it. It's actually about the poet Anne Carson's *Nox*, in which she mixes translation, memoir, poetry and personal artefacts to create an entire text in the form of a 'scrapbook': 'To express what language cannot hold within itself, Carson turns to the fragment to gesture towards the inarticulatable' (Deighton, 2017, p. 2). Looks promising, I think. I don't know what I mean by 'promising' at this point but I add it to my desktop folder where it becomes part of a process in which a maker purposefully gathers and experiments with magical objects (Fisher, 2021, p. 38); a textual example of what cultural historian Steven Connor (2011) calls 'paraphernalia' – things that urge us to play with them to try to make out what they might be good for.

I see another object (article) (Holdengräber, 1992) that I've placed in the desktop file, on Walter Benjamin's 'collecting' and I re-read it. I've written about material collections in the past but, for some reason I am not at this moment party to, it's the idea of 'redemption' that I take away from the paper. Which gets me thinking (again!) about my long-held preoccupation with the notion of nostalgia and from there to thinking (again!) about loss.

Wholes and Holes

I recall Scott's (2018) paper on the 'sociology of nothing' but don't have it to hand so 'Google' that. In the process, I come across a paper by Meyer (2012) which is also about absences, empty spaces, holes. And *that* takes me back to a poem I wrote years ago, with a hole at its centre, about my older son leaving for university:

The Jumper

Just before he left
he asked me to knit
him a jumper. I thought he'd read some text book on how to help grieving mothers cope with the loss of their beloved sons. Actually he wanted to look like the guy in Trainspotting and to save some money. But it was still the perfect gift. I helped him find the pattern. He chose the wool. Afterwards I worked on it every day: Knit one miracle of life. Purl one pair of bright eyes fixed on you. Knit two arms held out to be lifted up high. Purl the feel of each cushioned finger-
tip creeping round the back of your neck. Knit
warm cheek against yours. Purl big smiles,
shared stories. Repeat each one until known by
heart and then, repeat a hundred times more.
Knit loud music, wicked wit, long lean frame.
Purl one pair of eyes fixed on him. Knit the grip
of love upon the heart. Check the tension and
adjust. Purl the late night sound of the key in
the lock. Slip three breaths and hold in anticipation of precious conversation. Drop several
stitches blinded by tears. Put a hand through
the gaping   hole. Pick yourself up
again and   leave painful memories
on a spare   needle. Count and recount
the stitches.   Silently watch the rows
falling away.   Thick downy wool made the
jumper grow far too fast. I tried to leave it alone.
Tried to make it last. I stroked its softness, too
embarrassed to hold it against my cheek. But the
pull was so strong, the need to be doing something
for him so irresistible that in two weeks, all that
remained was to cast
off.

An empty

shape

waiting

to be filled.

I lay

my hand

on it

in

blessing

Berger (2014) suggests that poetry brings together what life has separated or violence torn apart. It cannot repair loss, he says, but it defies the space which separates by a continual labour of reassembling what has been scattered. Now my mind is buzzing and I have to stop. I love being on this kind of detective trail, though, one idea 'springing' another, 'running through your head in all directions, scampering animals flushed from coverts' to quote Mantel (1996, p. 11). I am Alice chasing the White Rabbit. But now I need to pause.

I get up, walk around, look outside to see squirrels scampering across the lawn in search of somewhere to stash their treasure for winter. I step out to chase them away before they turn their attention to denuding my heavily laden crab-apple tree. The sun is high in the clear blue sky and warm for the day before the autumn equinox. Five leaves on the Amelanchier I planted last week have turned red. Before long the rest will follow and then fall. I lift my face to the sun, stand for a while with my eyes closed, wish there was someone to go somewhere lovely with on a day like this, banish that thought, come inside and make tea. I finished my Reading Group book last night so I can go on to Sally Rooney's (2021) *Beautiful World, Where Are You.* I'm a little way in when, in a letter to a friend, a character quotes Rilke: 'Who is now alone/will long remain so/will wake, read, write long letters/and wander restlessly here and there/along the avenues, as the leaves are drifting' (p. 18). That's what I'm doing at this point in the process of making an autoethnographic text – wandering restlessly here and there. It's uncomfortable but I'm in my element. It's undefined but purposeful … free, liberating.

Getting Stuck

A couple of months ago, on my way here, my writing and I were stuck. I wrote to get unstuck:

> It's strange how one thing leads to another. Serendipity? Or a subconscious awareness of what is floating around one's mind that leads to selecting certain elements from whatever external things engage one's attention at the time – and then to notice the coincidences between them?

> Towards the end of the third lockdown when it was permissible to meet in the garden, Karen, whom I hadn't seen for months, came over. We had that now-familiar conversation about having no news because of having done nothing of note. Had I been doing any writing, she asked? In fact, I hadn't. I had finished a major project some time previously and had moved through a sense of loss to a mounting yearning to be writing again

but without any idea of what. I was ill at ease. It was uncomfortable, this state of excited/anxious anticipation without any sense of even the beginnings of a resolution.

The next morning, online, I came across a video interview with Dick Cavett in which Paul Simon describes how, during the process of writing *Bridge over Troubled Water*, he became stuck. Cavett asks what made him stuck. He replies: 'Well, everywhere I went led me to where I didn't want to be so I was stuck'. I suppose I noted it because of the 'stuckness' *I* was feeling. Reading usually acts as a stimulus to writing for me, sometimes in an immediate way but more usually when the laying down of words, thoughts, phrases and ideas forms a sediment that can later be dipped into or from which something emerges like the thin wisp of vapour signalling the coming to life of a volcano beneath. Fire that may explode onto the surface or die back down to quietly smoulder for longer because the time isn't yet right.

As with my writing, my reading had recently come to a halt after a fairly long run – six books one after another, finishing with Laura Cumming's *On Chapel Sands*. No other book in the to-be-read pile was appealing to me then but in any case, I wanted to sit with Cumming's (and her mother's) story – and her telling of it through images – for a while longer. It was a bit like gorging greedily but then realising that, although you're not ready to leave the table, you need to stop, savour, digest. So I turned instead to my desktop folder containing articles I'd collected in passing, as of possible interest. Which brought me, via an article by anthropologist Kathleen Stewart (1988) on nostalgia, to a *New Yorker* article on Berlant's affect theory (Hsu, 2019). We like to imagine, Berlant suggested, that our life follows some kind of trajectory, like the plot of a novel, and that by recognizing its arc we might, in turn, become its author. But what we often feel instead is a sense of precariousness – a gut-level suspicion that hard work, thrift, and following the rules won't give us control over the story, much less guarantee a happy ending. For all that, we keep on hoping and that persuades us to keep on living.

The pandemic and its lockdowns disabused me of any lingering notions of a predictable route through life whose trajectory I could determine. But the Berlant article led me to an earlier interview with her (McCabe, 2011), shortly before the publication of *Cruel Optimism*. She described her stance at that time – a moment of 'economic crisis, austerity, and unemployment' – as one of 'depressive realism'. A stance that attempts to engage these constraints through the lens of 'affect, sensibility and consciousness' and thereby to open novel and refreshing ways of getting to know our present. It uses modes of engagement that demand we engage in the kind of political practice that constitutes a quest for practical forms of *getting un-stuck*. How can we fantasise a new reality, she asks? How can we overcome attachments to lives that 'don't work' and through doing so build a pathway to something new and better?

I am familiar with this discourse of imaginatively bringing alternative futures into being. Vidler (2000) for example, tells us that in the history of modern art and aesthetics, the fragment has a double signification. It acts as a reminder of a past that was once whole but is now fractured and broken; and through the effects of time and the ravages of nature, it has taken on the connotations of nostalgia and melancholy. As an incomplete piece of a potentially complete whole, he suggests, it points toward the possibility of harmony in the future, even a utopia, that it both represents and constructs.

Politically, we are certainly in desperate need of new stories about ourselves and how we might make more sustainable futures for all. Nevertheless, I always find that my first response to urgings to fantasise a new reality is to question whether those upon whom austerity and precarity have had the most serious impact might understandably find that their imaginative capacities have atrophied. Maybe they have to be allowed a period of mourning for a lost way of life (especially one that had never been realised), before being able to respond to Berlant's urging to 'overcome their attachment' to it. Maybe those of us who can find time to write and theorise about the power of stories (including autoethnographies) to create new worlds are in a privileged position. Such considerations aside, there it was again – this notion of getting un/stuck.

On Nostalgia

I had opened Stewart's polemic because I had been thinking about the concept of nostalgia for a long time. It's a concept that is usually denigrated for its association with a reactionary desire for a return to some mythical past, the mobilisation of which acts to exclude so much and so many. John Le Carré observed in a radio interview with James Naughtie (2019) that what really scared him about nostalgia was that it has become a political weapon: 'Politicians are creating nostalgia for an England that never existed, and selling it, as something we could return to'. The negative associations of an inherent conservatism within nostalgia isn't how I experience it (although I feel bound to note that one can hardly be unaware of the power of this version, what with Brexit, Black Lives Matter, statues being toppled, plundered museum artefacts being returned and all the cynical flag-waving our current leaders are surrounding themselves with in defence of a single, monolithic, ahistorical, and gendered narrative about who we are). Tannock (1995) suggests that nostalgia can be a progressive structure of feeling, while Boym (2001) argues that it is both released by and a reaction to changing conceptions and understandings of space and time. She identifies 'restorative' and 'reflective' components. The former attempts 'a transhistorical reconstruction of a lost home'. The latter works at 'the contradictions and ambivalences located within the passage of time'. It allows for a more flexible, challenging comprehension of the historical past. It is 'often deferring or resisting a return home' (p. XVIII), but also evoking a wistful response that 'cherishes shattered fragments of memory and temporalizes space' (p. 49). (For a literary discussion of these issues, see O'Brien, (2018).

So what am I reaching for through time and space?

I re-read Stewart. I'm unsure from the way she talks about Raleigh County, West Virginia, where the local economy of coal has collapsed bringing widespread unemployment, how she feels about the inhabitants who still live there. Living in the ruins and fragments of the old coal camps, she sees them as resisting the loss of a cultural home by continuously reinscribing places on a place whose meaning is emptying out. They are nostalgic, she suggests, not in the way that tourists are as they survey 'framed scenes from a maintained and exercised distance' but as alienated exiles, 'painfully holding on to closeness in a world that has already deserted them' (Stewart, 1988, p. 235). I think about Walkerdine's (2010) research on the people of post-industrial South Wales and the ways in which trauma can be psychically and socially transmitted not only between those who experienced it directly but across generations.

Stewart goes on to characterise the inhabitants of Raleigh as 'roaming from ruin to ruin' and quotes them in a vernacular: '"thangs have got down anymore" in these emptied out places from which they feel the younger ones ought to "git out and go"' (p. 235). It is a nostalgia, she asserts, of being inescapably haunted by the images they dwell in, feeling a responsibility to remember what happens, especially those things that try to erase someone: '"You cain't forget people and these thangs that have happened. If you forget, that's when you're really crazy"' (p. 235). For them, she continues, having a culture is a matter of people leaving their mark on the place and, in turn, 'the place and its history leaves marks on the people, even as bodily scars' (p. 235). Echoes of Gordon's (2008) writing about the 'hauntings' in Toni Morrison's (1987) *Beloved*, I think.

Stewart moves on to further descriptions – of the interiors of people's houses, whose rooms are apparently filled to overflowing with 'whatnots' and whose walls are covered with 'nostalgic pictures of the dead and souvenirs of lost moments'. Their yards are overflowing with 'junked, broken, or decaying objects' that they are constantly 'foolin with', as they dis-member and re-member things. Their continuity in life, she suggests, comes through continually piecing together what is constantly falling apart. 'Their "high art" is a *bricolage*' (p. 236, original emphasis). (Isn't this what we all do, I ask myself. Aren't all our lives bricolage, creating something from what's available to us?) Their continuing belief that things will get better is what constitutes a reactionary nostalgia, Stewart claims, built as it is on a faith in fictions – a faith that drives them to continuously dis-member and re-member what it is to be human in order that it can include them and their lives as they now know them.

Poet David Whyte (2019) offers another definition of nostalgia, not as a reactionary indulgence but as something telling us we are in the presence of 'imminent revelation' – about something already lived but not fully so, not granted sufficient importance and now wanting to be lived at a depth originally refused. As I read this, I can't decide whether it is the tone of consolation in his writing that, by way of contrast, makes me hear a patronising note in Stewart's anthropological quoting of others' vernacular speech. The contrast is also evident from the late Deborah Orr's (2020) reference to the phenomenon of lost identity in her autobiography. Referring to a plaque outlining the history of the 'Covenantors' Oak' under which John Knox's followers met to hold services in the seventeenth century – which appeared only after the Scottish town of Motherwell's decline as the centre of the steel industry – Orr observes that the heritage industry moves in when people don't know who they are any more and have to focus on who they were instead. Ambivalent as she was about everything that Motherwell represented for her, there is a note of compassion running through her accounts of the lives of those whose identity was so invested in the place in its glory days.

I find myself comparing Stewart's tone, too, to the compassion of Marit Kapla's (2021) best-selling paean to the ordinary people of *her* declining home village; Paul Batchelor's (2021) poems of 'oblivion' inspired by seventeenth-century laws that forced people to forget their histories; and Terry Eagleton (2021) on Benjamin's 'take' on oblivion, namely that there is a trade-off between past and present: the present can rescue the past from oblivion, while the dead can be summoned to the aid of the living. 'Time can be looped on itself', Eagleton comments, 'as in Proust's great narrative, to reveal a solidarity of the dispossessed across the centuries. It is the grandest narrative of all, though one that deflates the dream of inevitable progress for which most such tales are notorious'.

Reflecting on the notion of a 'solidarity of the dispossessed', I take a cup of tea with me into a sunnier part of the house. My eye travels to the bookcase. I get up, run my finger along the shelves, pick out Alan Garner's (1997) collection of essays *The Voice that Thunders*. Now there's a man who, in the re-telling of a lost rural working-class childhood, might be accused of nostalgia by some. In his essay *The Voice in the Shadow,* I read about Joshua Birtles, small farmer, who delivered eggs and vegetables to the boy Garner's house in his horse-drawn cart. Garner writes:

> He was huge in frame and spirit ... he was almost not credible, so completely was he the image of a pre-industrial, bucolic ideal that never was or could be, except in the sentimental minds of the urban middle classes. And he knew how he looked. 'You see', he said to me once, 'I'm just at the end, like, of one period, some way' (p. 159).

It would be a mistake, Garner contends, to think that because a man is content to keep to the old ways, his mind is not up to date: 'It is not that such individuals are living in the past, but that their intensity of life includes both past and present; and from that security they grasp the future' (p. 159).

I turn to *Achilles in Altjira* in which Garner talks about the English language, its Romance and Germanic roots and how he was taught, if only by default, to suppress, even to deride his primary native tongue. Standard Received English had been imposed on him; he had clung to it in order to be educated. But gain was bought with loss. What restored the loss was his family's sense of fusion with the land they had occupied for generations. And it was holding on to the violence that was done by one culture to the other and expressing it in the writing of his stories, without rendering the 'natives' of that land 'quaint', that saved him. He did it not by trying to represent dialect with what he refers to as a 'debased phonetic dialogue' that condescends but by trying to capture the cadence – what he calls 'the music of it all'. And he gives a beautiful example of how he does this, with a description of a line of men rhythmically moving in concert as they cut corn with scythes: 'I need Manchester Grammar School just as much as I need Alderley Edge. But I do need them both', Garner concludes (p. 57). Is this nostalgic? Whatever else it might be, it's storytelling at its finest and it makes me want to strain to hear the voice that thunders from my own lost working-class origins and to capture the persistent note of ambivalence it contains.

Where is my Alderley Edge? I don't come from a long line of folk living close to the Pennine shelf of East Cheshire for generations but rather, on my mother's side, from village folk whose Squirarchy condemned the degeneracy of the 'fallen'. Which included my maternal grandmother. The theme tune playing in the background of my childhood was *her* daughter's desperate need to escape from the stain of ascribed moral turpitude. The physical place of my childhood was the interior landscape of my father's shop. The people whose voices I listened to from a very early age belonged to customers and I listened with an ear being tutored by my mother to distinguish the 'respectable' from the 'common'. Well before grammar school, I was being set apart.

There is some indication in Garner's *Aback of Beyond* that the fact that he can claim such a powerful sense of continuity and belonging is due in no small part to his gender. He talks in this essay of the 'ferocious caste system' (p. 22) of the area. His grandfather was illegitimate, born of the union between members of opposing tribes. It was the mother who came from the 'superior' tribe and she was cast out by her own father, leaving the child's grandmother to bring him up as a 'grannyreardun'. The shame of his birth, we are told, affected the rest of his mother's life such that 'she never put her bonnet on again'; which is to say that she was made to feel the taint of her relationship with a man who came from 'the hovels of the unskilled families' (p. 22) so strongly that she never left the confines of the garden again until her death. She also, rather tellingly, disappears at this point from Garner's account, which goes on to follow the fortunes of his grandfather, who became a *skilled* (my emphasis) blacksmith.

Loss and Longing

Perhaps it's the *security* Garner identified in relation to Birtles that is key. What constitutes ontological security, at a personal, existential level (Giddens, 1991; Laing, 1960; May, 1977 [1950]; Tillich, 1952) and/or at state level? (See Gustafsson & Krickel-Choi (2020), for an interesting discussion of the distinction between the two.) What constitutes a sufficiently secure foundation from which to move on into the future without abandoning what we know from our own and others' histories? My own 'nostalgic practices' are naturally backward-looking. And there is certainly loss in the mix. And longing. But it is not a longing for a *return* to the past. Or a wish to stay there. What then? Maybe a desire to recapture *some* elements of what has been lost. Including perhaps something 'ill-defined because insufficiently experienced', as Whyte suggests. I refute the claim that 'You don't miss what you never had'. As does Mangan (2018) in her memoir of childhood reading, in which she observes of the vanished world of 'tiny, domestic non-adventures' she encountered in the 1928 Milly-Molly-Mandy stories: you can be nostalgic for a time you never knew. She offers both a political and personal analysis of their appeal. Politically, she sees them as vital balm for a wounded and shell-shocked nation: the little girl in the striped dress offered sanctuary, a quiet, idealised rural retreat from horror (p. 86). On a personal level, she sets her own childhood, growing up as the child of a stable marriage in a relatively deprived area of South London, in the context of a time and place when this made her unusual among her peers:

> It is possible that this awareness that my lovely life was the exception rather than the rule prompted me to try and shore it up with lovely safe stories about lovely safe families doing lovely safe things (p. 88).

Frank Cottrell-Boyce (2021), writing online about A.A. Milne, echoes these themes, pointing out that children's books of the 1920s are thronged with characters who never grow up. Christopher Robin is different, he suggests, because in the Hundred Acre Wood, *he* is the grown-up – dispensing wisdom and help, solving problems, putting things right. At the very end of childhood as he is, he is aware that it is soon going to end: 'That's why everything shimmers with its own transience'. In the dangerous world into which he is heading beyond the wood, (and, in the end, the real Christopher Robin was off to another war, Cottrell-Boyce reminds us), the best the writer can do is bring the good things to our attention:

> … to help us hold them in our hearts and memories, so that, when we need them, those little things – sorting out your books, picking a new bathroom, the honey and the humming – can be our stepping-stones through the bad times.

I think I'm engaged in much of my autoethnographic writing in a quest to re-trace a *sense* of something to its putative origins. But it would be a mistake to think that this impulse to search the past contains a desire to live there; rather it is an intensity of feeling that drives a search for something lost along the way, something that might be retrieved, brought into the clearer light of the present for proper examination. What does it look like? I won't necessarily know until I see it. And then perhaps I'll recognise its shape. At one time it might be a tailor-made tool for sloughing off what is no longer needed or fit for purpose. At another, it might be a dual-purpose walking stick. One that can offer support when the road gets rocky or be used to clear a path into the future when the way becomes obscured by undergrowth.

Memory Work

I have a memory that returns occasionally, sometimes when I'm exploring somewhere away from home, sometimes when gazing through the window at a new landscape as I pass through it on the train. It's more of an emotional memory than an image-based one, although in an attempt to grasp it I cast myself back into specific times and particular places.

I am a child and out alone. Age-wise, I imagine that I'm on my way to primary school. Except that in reality my route there involved going up to the *top* of our road to catch the bus that would take me halfway before I need to walk the rest of the way. But this journey does not contain some of the features I conjure up as I try to put concrete flesh on the emotional bones of this elusive memory. The features that appear as I see myself, in the state I half-remember, crystallise into a scene in which I'm looking over low walls into the front gardens of houses at the *bottom* of our road. One has a big, thrillingly exotic monkey-puzzle tree in it but it is another, further down, that detains me longer because of my delight in all the little paths, ponds, waterfalls and windmills, populated by a brotherhood of gnomes.

But that was the way I went to catch the bus to grammar school, by which age I think I'd probably lost the feeling I'm reaching for. It's one that involves, on the one hand, a lack of self-consciousness and on the other a hyper-consciousness, an experience of there being no barrier between me and the outside world, of which I am intensely, sensually aware. I think I'm happy. But that's probably retrojection since I don't think I was capable of this kind of self-reflexive analysis at the time. What I am aware of is a particular quality of air and sound and a sense of freedom. It must be summer because I'm not wearing a coat or a scarf or gloves. I'm just aware of being out alone in the world and at the same time not only safe within it but befriended by it. I've not yet learnt as a girl or woman to be vigilant when out alone.

While I was still straining to recapture the feeling, I came across a passage from Joyce's (1992) *A Portrait of the Artist as a Young Man* in which the character is described as 'unheeded, happy and near to the wild heart of life', feelings engendered not only by being 'young and wilful and wild-hearted' but by being 'alone amid a waste of wild air …' (p. 131). And that, like one of Mantel's scampering animals flushed from its covert, led me to Dylan Thomas's (1946, p. 68) poem *Fern Hill*. ('Now as I was young and easy under the apple boughs …'). Maybe it's a fraction of that that I'm reaching for through this 'memory work' (Kuhn, 2000).

As I struggle to articulate an experience that probably predates an ability to stand outside oneself and actively commit it to memory I am reminded of a passage in Frayn's (2011) *Spies* in which a boy is trying to work out the identity of an olfactory memory from childhood (a flowering privet, it transpires), which in turn provides a portal to a significant event in his life. By the time I got to grammar school I was already aware of class differences and of fitting or not fitting in, even if I wasn't able then to name this lack of ease. Perhaps it's that short pre-lapsarian period of childhood – or at least those moments in childhood of feeling 'unencumbered' in every way that I think were quite rare in mine – that are what I'm nostalgic for. Perhaps we all are.

Later, I read Dickinson and Erben (2016) on nostalgia. They cite Caillois (1998) on Durkheim's (1915) thesis of the sacred and profane, locating it in a context of the growth of secularization and rationalization. They observe that that process was also accompanied by 'a squeezing out of the playful and intuitive from adult life, relegating it to the separate room of child-hood and sealing its connecting door to adulthood' (p. 39). Attempting to break the seal of that connecting door may be what underlies the act of writing, as Ishiguro explains in relation to stories of his set in a Japan that he left at the age of five. He posits that he was driven by a need for preservation. As he came to realise that the Japan in his head might always have been an emotional construct put together by a child out of memory, imagination and speculation, he was re-building it in fiction, 'to make it safe, so that I could thereafter point to a book and say: "Yes, there's my Japan, inside there"'(Ishiguro, 2017).

The impetus to regain something lost is an experience C.S. Lewis (1952) discusses through the German concept of 'Sehnsucht' – an 'inconsolable longing' in the human heart for 'we know not what'. Lewis interprets it as an intimation of the divine, suggesting that the most probable explanation of his experiencing it is that he was 'made for another world' (Mangan, 2018, p. 225). Mangan, on the other hand, suggests that we can return to a place through books, citing her love as a ten-year old for Philippa Pearce's *Tom's Midnight Garden*, a story suffused with the pain and pleasure of yearn-ing. Her take on the divine, experienced when even an adult re-reading of that book enables her to step out of this world and all its inconsolable longings and to run wild in the gardens of the past, is that it's more to do with the power of the written word to transport us. Perhaps we're actually made for *reading*, she counters (p. 225, my emphasis). I'm with Mangan on this. With Rundell (2019) too, who suggests that there are times in life when children's fiction might be the only thing that will do (p. 10). But oh, to be able to *write* in a way that conjures old or new worlds for the curious to inhabit, not as science fiction but as the alchemy of imagination made at once concrete on the page and infinitely malleable in the spaces between writer, page and reader.

What am I trying to write my way into here? I'm still not sure, but at least I'm writing …

★★★★★★

And now, a thin wisp of vapour is rising and misshapen fragments are erupting. But as in Igoe's autoethnographic textile design-making practices, they are 'rag-ged and frayed, not smooth and sharp … they don't tessellate'. And like her, at this stage, 'I won't try to make them either' (2021, p. 10).

I return to Holdengräber. He cites Missac (1996) on Benjamin's musings about his collecting, in which he suggests that a stamp lives on even when 'mutilated' (franked). This 'stain' frees stamps from *use* and allows them to become part of a collection. It is a sign of 'erlosung'. Missac elaborates the triple meaning of that word: rescue, release (absolve), redeem. And it is a mutual relationship, Holdengräber explains:

> The collector takes upon himself the responsibility of being the historian, the genealogist, the archaeologist, each object is a microcosm, a concentrated essence of the whole. He is the interpreter of the fate of the object and is, for a time, its fate.
>
> *1992, p. 107*

Groping Ahead

Perhaps each of the fragments of a life that we select, rescue, release, redeem or preserve when making a storied self (a self who is a member not so much of a collection as the collective we call society) is also a microcosm, a concentrated essence of the whole. Of course, in remembering and assembling fragments that constitute the making of an autoethnographic text, I too am only an interpreter of an incomplete collection. As Stanley (1993) points out, Barthes' (1975) 'self who writes' (as opposed to the 'self who is') does not have unproblematic access to the past and thus the past has to be recovered in traces and hints, rather than appearing before us whole and entire. Further, for the 'self who is', time moves on outside the text, so that the 'self who writes' becomes part of the 'self who was' – 'a part of the past and its sets of multiple overlapping but not coterminous stages in the assemblage of the 'self who is' currently' (p. 48). When authors choose a re/membered fragment from their pasts, therefore, they are doing so to enable a *certain* telling of a *certain* story (Phipps, 2010). And I am only 'for a time' *its* fate.

Is this the question I've been tussling with: whether a re-enchantment of the present (through the past) is possible? If so, for me, it will come through writing. For Carson too. She writes:

> I don't know that we really think any thoughts, we think connections between thoughts. That's where the mind moves, that's what's new, and the thoughts themselves have probably been there in my head or lots of other people's heads for a long time. But the jumps between them are entirely at that moment. It's magical …. Not knowing what one is doing is no prohibition on doing it. We all grope ahead.
>
> *cited in Brockes (2006)*

Addendum

In the making of the kind of conventional academic article I became adept at, I'd have followed a kind of hand-me-down pro forma. I'd have mapped out at the outset the ground I was going to cover. Had an idea of my destination.

Composed an argument. Summarised 'findings'. Making an autoethnography, however, is for me striking out, sloughing off that straitjacket, writing 'in the buff', making connections, tracing and 'presencing' absences. It's wandering restlessly here and there. It's the honey and the humming. And the tea. With no definitive 'Conclusions' section. That convention is too finite when what we're engaged in is a process. As Steedman (2000) says, 'there is no – there cannot be an – End, for we are still in it, the great slow-moving Everything' (p. 1177).

When you get to the ('for a time') end of an autoethnographic text and look back to review, reflect, perhaps remould what you've crafted, there may still only be intimations of something 'shimmering with its own transience'. Or it may begin to take on a more solid shape in the form of new discoveries. Like what? I can't tell you. I'm still making them (out). In any case, I wouldn't want to spoil the surprise for readers who might be making their own, along the way. I wouldn't want to deny an opportunity to be 'vulnerable to delight', as Seamus Heaney's father found himself, in his grandson's unexpected but irresistible embrace, which came 'of a sudden, one-off', before the 'steady dawning of whatever *erat demonstrandum*' (Heaney, 2010, p. 8).

References

Barthes, R. (1975). An introduction to the structural analysis of narrative. *New Literary History*, *6*, 237–272.

Batchelor, P. (2021). *The acts of oblivion*. Manchester: Carcanet Press.

Berger, J. (2014). *And our faces, my heart, brief as photos*. London: Bloomsbury.

Boym, S. (2001). *The future of nostalgia*. New York, NY: Basic Books.

Brockes, E. (2006). Magical thinking. *The Guardian* (online), 30 December. Retrieved from https://www.theguardian.com/books/2006/dec/30/featuresreviews.guardianreview7

Caillois, R. (1998). *L'homme et le sacré*. Paris: Gallimard.

Chang, H. (2008). *Autoethnography as method*. Walnut Creek, CA: Left Coast Press.

Connor, S. (2011). *Paraphernalia: The curious lives of magical things*. London: Profile.

Cottrell-Boyce, F. (2021). AA Milne's pacifism and patriotism. *New Statesman*, 24 March. Retrieved from https://www.newstatesman.com/culture/2021/03/a-a-milne-pacificsm-patriotism-political-non-fiction-happy-half-hour

Deighton, J. (2017). *'These fragments I have shored against my ruins': Anne Carson's shattered poetics of grief in nox* (Unpublished PhD thesis). Dalhousie University, Halifax, NS.

Dickinson, H., & Erben, M. (2016). *Nostalgia and auto/biography*. Durham: BSA.

Durkheim, E. (1915). *The elementary forms of the religious life: A study in religious sociology*. London: G. Allen & Unwin.

Eagleton, T. (2021). The Marxist and the Messiah. *London Review of Books*, *43*(17), 9 September. Retrieved from https://www.lrb.co.uk/the-paper/v43/n17/terry-eagleton/the-marxist-and-the-messiah

Eliot, T. S. (1961). *Selected poems*. London: Faber and Faber.

Fisher, T. (2021). Paraphernalia and playing for design. In E. Igoe (Ed.), *Textile design: Theory in the making* (pp. 127–139). London: Bloomsbury Visual Arts.

Frayn, M. (2011). *Spies*. London: Faber & Faber.

Garner, A. (1997). *The voice that thunders*. London: The Harvill Press.

Giddens, A. (1991). *Modernity and self-identity: Self and society in the late modern age*. Palo Alto, CA: Stanford University Press.

Goode, J. (2007). Telling tales out of school: Connecting the prose and the passion in the learning and teaching of English. *Qualitative Inquiry, 13*(6), 808–820.

Goode, J. (2019). Exhuming the good that men do: The play of the mnemonic imagination in the making of an autoethnographic text. *Time & Society, 28*(4), 1645–1667.

Gordon, A. F. (2008). *Ghostly matters: Haunting and the sociological imagination*. Minneapolis, MN: University of Minnesota Press.

Gustafsson, K., & Krickel-Choi, N. C. (2020). Returning to the roots of ontological security: Insights from the existentialist anxiety literature. *European Journal of International Relations, 26*(3), 875–895.

Heaney, S. (2010). Album 5. In *Human chain*. London: Faber and Faber Ltd.

Holdengräber, P. (1992). Between the profane and the redemptive: The collector as possessor in Walter Benjamin's 'Passagen-Werk'. *History and Memory, 4*(2), 96–128.

Hsu, H. (2019). Affect theory and the new age of anxiety. *The New Yorker*, March 25.

Hughes, S. A., & Pennington, J. L. (2017). *Autoethnography: Process, product and possibility for critical social research*. Thousand Oaks, CA: Sage.

Igoe, E. (2021). Too much to tell. In E. Igoe (Ed.), *Textile design: Theory in the making* (pp. 9–19). London: Bloomsbury Visual Arts.

Ishiguro, K. (2017). *Nobel lecture*. Retrieved from https://www.nobelprize.org/uploads/2018/06/ishiguro-lecture_en-1.pdf

Joyce, J. (1992). *A portrait of the artist as a young man*. Hertfordshire: Wordsworth Editions Ltd.

Jung, C. G. (1962). *Symbols of transformation: An analysis of the prelude to a case of schizophrenia* (2nd ed.). New York: Harper & Brothers.

Kapla, M. (2021). *Osebol: Voices from a Swedish village* (trans. Peter Graves). London: Allen Lane.

Kuhn, A. (2000). A journey through memory. In S. Radstone (Ed.), *Memory and methodology* (pp. 179–196). Oxford: Berg.

Laing, R. D. (1960). *The divided self: An existential study in sanity and madness*. London: Penguin Books.

Lewis, C. S. (1952). *Mere Christianity*. London: Geoffrey Bles Ltd.

Mangan, L. (2018). *Bookworm: A memoir of childhood reading*. London: Square Peg.

Mantel, H. (1996). *An experiment in love*. London: Penguin.

May, R. (1977) [1950]. *The meaning of anxiety*. New York, NY: W.W. Norton.

McCabe, E. (2011). Depressive realism: An interview with Lauren Berlant. *Hypocrite Reader, Issue 5,* June. Retrieved from https://hypocritereader.com/5/depressive-realism

Meyer, M. (2012). Placing and tracing absence: A material culture of the immaterial. *Journal of Material Culture, 17*(1), 103–110.

Missac, P. (1996). *Walter Benjamin's passages*. Cambridge: MIT Press.

Morrison, T. (1987). *Beloved*. New York, NY: Alfred A. Knopf Inc.

Naughtie, J. (2019). John le Carré: 'Politicians love chaos – It gives them authority. *BBC Radio 4 Today Programme*. Retrieved from https://www.bbc.co.uk/news/entertainment-arts-50012504

O'Brien, P. (2018). 'Takes you back even if you were never there originally': Class, history, and nostalgia in Gordon Burn's *The North of England Home Service*. *Textual Practice, 32*(8), 1405–1423.

Orr, D. (2020). *Motherwell: A girlhood*. London: Weidenfeld & Nicolson.

Phipps, A. (2010). Ethnographers as language learners: From oblivion towards an echo. In P. Collins, & A. Gallinat (Eds.), *The ethnographic self as resource: Writing memory and experience into ethnography* (pp. 97–110). Oxford: Berghahn Books.

Piaget, J. (1926). *The child's conception of the world.* Savage, MD: Littlefield Adams.

Rilke, R. M. (2012). *Letters to a young poet.* Lancaster, TX: Snowball Publishing.

Rooney, S. (2021). *Beautiful world where are you.* London: Faber and Faber.

Rundell, K. (2019). *Why you should read children's books, even though you are so old and wise.* London: Bloomsbury Publishing.

Scott, S. (2018). A sociology of nothing: Understanding the unmarked. *Sociology, 52*(1), 3–19.

Stanley, L. (1993). On auto/biography in sociology. *Sociology, 27*(1), 41–52.

Steedman, C. (2000). Something she called a fever: Michelet, Derrida, and dust. *The American Historical Review, 106*(4), 1159–1180.

Stewart, K. (1988). Nostalgia – A polemic. *Cultural Anthropology, 3*(3), 227–241.

Tannock, S. (1995). Nostalgia critique. *Cultural Studies, 9*(3), 453–464.

Thomas, D. (1946). *Deaths and entrances.* London: JM Dent.

Tillich, P. (1952). *The courage to be.* New Haven, CT: Yale University Press.

Vidler, A. (2000). *Warped space: Art, architecture, and anxiety in modern culture.* Cambridge, MA: MIT Press.

Walkerdine, V. (2010). Communal beingness and affect: An exploration of trauma in an ex-industrial community. *Body & Society, 16*(1), 91–116.

Whyte, D. (2019). *Consolations: The solace, nourishment and underlying meaning of everyday words.* Edinburgh: Canongate.

2

WHEN THE SLAVE SHIPS CAME

Panya Banjoko

Introduction: Making Poems on Slavery – Giving Voice to Lions

Outside of the poetry collections I have published, I have written three poems yet unpublished or anthologised (until now) about the Transatlantic Slave Trade. The poems, *Brought and Sold* (1992), *When I Think About Slavery …* (2007), and *When the Slave Ships Came* (2022), took shape at significant phases in both my writing life spanning 30 years and as a heritage professional in Nottingham, traversing the last two decades. In addition, each poem was created 15 years apart, a fact of which I was unaware until contemplating this chapter. The temporal gap may be a testimony, as Fred D'Aguiar conjectures, to our need to have '[our] own versions of the past, to see the past in [our] own images, words' and that to write about slavery is in effect an effort to 'kill slavery off' (1996, p. 125). Perhaps this is the case, and maybe if I continue to voice the injustices, past and present, it might one day be truly acknowledged and hopefully eradicated lessening the daily struggle of being Black.

A central thought when making poems about slavery is a desire to reclaim hidden narratives and subjective history. If 'Lions have no historians' as African American activist and scholar W.E.B. Du Bois literalised in *The Superior Race* (1923, p. 5), I write to *give the lions a voice*. Nigerian anticolonial writer Chinua Achebe took up the same motif creatively in *The Art of Fiction* (1994), extending the analogy through a proverb: 'Until the lions have their historians, tales of the hunt shall always glorify the hunter'. Ben Okri (2018), in compiling *Rise Like Lions: Poetry for the Many*, explores the impact which political poems have on ideas, vision, protest, change and truth. In making my poems, I also use my voice to call for justice and change, and I attempt to insert my own story into history. This creative intervention is one way of contributing to the always–ongoing campaign

DOI: 10.4324/9781003309239-4

for racial justice, equality, and fairness, including within the heritage sector, an area I am particularly interested in as founder and keeper of Nottingham Black Archive (NBA) and through my long and knotted relationship with Nottingham Castle Museum and Gallery (NCMG). Even before NCMG's £30 million restoration project, and relaunch as the independent registered charity Nottingham Castle Trust in 2021, its position within the Black community was strained. Researcher and academic Richard Sandell in *Museums, Society, Inequality* (2002) drew attention to a display at NCMG 'dating from the 1970s' that '"insensitively contrasted, on one side of a gallery, ethnographic" objects and on the other the military collection of the Sherwood Foresters Regiment'. It was an 'overtly colonial interpretation' which 'angered many local communities and was eventually replaced with *The Circle of Life* exhibition in 1994' (2002, p. 9). The 'us' and 'them' message that Sandell identified in the curation and exhibition of history deepens the divide between the museum sector and the diverse communities it purports to serve.

I also drilled down into audience development initiatives at NCMG to examine the impact on the African Caribbean community's perceptions of the museum service in 2008. I assessed how far, if at all, audience development projects changed attitudes, shaped perceptions, or increased visitor figures. When asked about potential barriers that could prevent members of the Black community from visiting NCMG, several key differences emerged. For example, Front of House (FoH) staff perceived no barriers to engagement and asserted that they did not 'get involved in that side of the work' (Banjoko, 2008, p. 40). By contrast, members of the African and Caribbean community highlighted FoH staff, as epitomised in the following comment: 'If you have security guards [FoH] following you around, if you are confronted with this before you even get into the building, do you want to take the next step?' In sum, my findings confirmed that Black and ethnic minority visitors were more likely to experience a hostile reception and that this impeded their visitor experience and attitude towards museums.

Since the Castle's relaunch in 2021 it has continued to be troubled with issues around race and diversity. One case in point is the insidious treatment I received as one of their commissioned curators after my curation of the *Don't Blame the Blacks* exhibition at the Castle from 22 June to 22 August 2021. What should have been a moment of celebration for the people raised to prominence by the exhibition and for the wider Nottingham community ended in a campaign for racial justice. As founder of the NBA, I work to keep Black history in the present via my curation of the multiple local stories it holds. Yet, I find myself still challenging racial discrimination, an unfortunate and inevitable reality for Black British citizens in the UK. What I had called for on 17 August 2021 was for staff to provide support but instead attempts were made to trap me in the visitor centre and a senior staff member responded by calling me aggressive. Following my complaint on how the matter was handled, the Charity Commission on 14 January 2022 issued formal advice and guidance to the Trust, over 700 people signed a petition for the assigning of a new representative board after the failure of the

Trust to investigate the matter promptly and with diplomacy, and many members of Nottingham's community (Black and white) boycotted Nottingham Castle.

The issues I experienced are part of structural issues continuously highlighted by the few Black professionals in the museum sector. It is an issue that was acknowledged by the Arts Council in their Annual Diversity Report half a decade ago (Picheta, 2018). The Arts Council found that people from a Black, Asian, and minority ethnic background as well as disabled people continue to be underrepresented in museums and arts organisations. The Museum Association has also continued to highlight issues around diversity and inclusion and attempted to 'create dents' in the make-up of museums through its Diversify programme in 1998 (Shaw, 2013) and by highlighting that the heritage sector consists of a workforce and governing body dominated by the white middle class. People from minority-ethnic backgrounds are underrepresented at all levels and particularly in senior management. This underrepresentation has a wider impact: it discourages people from joining the profession, or aspiring to be in that profession. The unwillingness from governors and senior managers of museums to open their doors to others is a long-standing problem.

The 'experiencing' I want to enact, then, through writing and making poems on slavery is for the status quo to feel the viciousness of slavery, and for societies to act in rectifying the imbalance which is both historical and contemporary in creating disadvantage: racial profiling by the police, inadequate social provision, racial inequalities in health services, the Black attainment gap in education, and many other issues we contend with. Black women in particular experience additional layers of discrimination as highlighted in Kimberlé Crenshaw's work on 'intersectionality' showing that 'the intersection of racism and sexism factors into Black women's lives in ways that cannot be captured wholly by looking at the race or gender dimensions of those experiences separately' (1991, p. 1244). McKinsey and Company's research cited in Krivkovich et al. on 'Women in the Workplace' found that:

> Women who are 'Onlys' – meaning, they are often one of the only people of their race or gender in the room at work – have especially difficult day-to-day experiences. Onlys stand out … they tend to be more heavily scrutinized. Their successes and failures are … put under a microscope … they are more likely to encounter … behavior that reduce them to negative stereotypes.
>
> *(Krivkovich et al. 2018, para. 1)*

I write against these experiences, the incestuous and insular nature of the heritage sector, its unwillingness to move with the times, and to see the benefits of inclusion rather than perceived disadvantages. I also write to show that Black poets and heritage practitioners can make imaginative and material connections between the individual and the social; the self and culture; and the personal and the political. The Transatlantic Slave Trade legacy continues to grip the lives of Black people and it takes away so much of who we are, personally, professionally, and spiritually. Until the legacy of slavery is acknowledged – poor employment prospects, substandard education, police profiling, fragmented families – poems must continue to be written, and stories told (however painful).

Slave poems by Black writers take on multiple perspectives and whether published or unpublished, Black poets through the ages have grappled with the subject in varying forms and from multiple perspectives without resolution. I stand on the shoulders of writers such as Grace Nichols (1983, pp. 63–64) who approached the subject from the point of view of a woman about to give birth to a child conceived out of rape and hate in her poem *In My Name*: 'my tainted/ perfect child/my bastard fruit/my seedling'. Guyanese-born novelist, poet, and academic David Dabydeen (1986, pp. 28–30) explores the erotic energies of the colonial experience in 'Slave Song': 'Bu yu caan stop me cack floodin in de gold-mine'. Ghanaian poet and academic Kwame Dawes (2012, pp. 232–233) situates the impact of slavery now in a UK city. '*Bristol*' speaks to the inherited legacy of the Transatlantic Slave Trade: 'I leave the cold wet of Bristol. […] Spires and the ostentatious slave money'. Many more poets have examined slavery and coloni-alism, including Nottingham-born D.S. Marriott (2006, p. 8) who often features slave ships in his work and writes critically of how the long history of slavery and colonialism fuses in his poetry: 'we stepped off the boat the tide,/the long impe-rial gain,/extended to all colonies'. Contemporary poets draw on a long literary history in Claude McKay who wrote many sonnets and among them *Enslaved* (1922) (Poets.org, no date) is among the most personal: 'Enslaved and lynched, denied a human place'. There is no end to these poems.

There is no end to these poems because the Middle Passage, a journey forcibly undertaken by millions of enslaved Africans as victims of the British Empire, is contentious world history. It was difficult history long before African Caribbean people began to make their way across the seas in the hope of finding financial security and adventure as Commonwealth citizens in Britain. David Olusoga (2017) surfaced many stories in *Black and British, a Forgotten History*, including the story of Jonathan Strong in 1765, 'a minor, a child of around sixteen, who had been beaten almost to the point of death and then thrown into the gutter' by David Lisle, his owner (p. 113). When Lisle attempted to reclaim Strong after his miraculous recovery from near death it set off a chain of reactions which highlighted the vicious brutality inflicted on Black people and the lengths that the privileged and powerful will go to in order to maintain control and own-ership of their perceived 'property'. This is not a surprise. This attitude and sense of entitlement and privilege is embedded in the systems through which Black individuals are expected to perform to the best of our ability. It is also embedded in a system that refuses to acknowledge its past. In a summary of Black British writing in the 1980s, Lauretta Ngcobo recognised that, 'although we hold on to the shreds of that former heritage', there is a 'strong reluctance on the part of white society' to engage with such difficult history (1988, p. 17). Jeanette C. Espinoza echoes her in *Why Do Black People Always Want to Bring Up Slavery?* (2021) drawing attention to the complicated circumstances of Black people needing to speak out against enslavement and a knotted legacy of racial inequalities. Espinoza runs through a series of routine comments she has received when she does. Representative samples include:

> Slavery was hundreds of years ago. Why are Black people still talking about it? [Black people] just need to try harder and stop complaining; [Black people] make everything about race and slavery. They need to just get over it.
>
> *(2021, para. 1)*

But she points out:

> [W]hy would talking about an event that absolutely DID happen, that absolutely WAS documented ... and absolutely DOES have residual effects that have been studied and recorded, upset some White [supremacist] people so much?
>
> *(2021, para. 9)*

So, when I write about slavery and perform my poems, I am aware that the audience for such a poem is limited, and I am also aware of how white supremacists in an audience might feel, how they might react, and the real possibility that some listeners' fear of the subject may cause them to shut down their emotions. The subject may trigger Black people too, because it is not only white people who are apprehensive about slavery, as one historian, John David Smith identified clearly:

> For example, while many blacks stressed the importance of slavery to understanding the contemporary ... [race] 'problem' ... others urged [Black people] to deemphasize slavery – to look forward to a bright future, not backward to a sordid past.
>
> *(1980, p. 298)*

As I explicate my making process I start from where I am today on the brink of joining the world of academia as a researcher of Black history, as a community archivist making accessible the work of NBA, and as poet making creative interventions into difficult subjects. I start then from the present and work my way through to the past to a time when I first began to write and perform poetry and explore my cultural identity.

When the Slave Ships Came

When the Slave Ships Came was penned in 2021. It is unlike my earlier poems *Brought and Sold* and *When I think About Slavery ...*, in that it came about through the time made available to me undertaking a practice-based PhD at Nottingham Trent University. My PhD, *The Politics of Poetry in Nottingham: Nottingham Black Archive and African-Caribbean Writers and Networks in the 1950s and 1980s*, offers historicised insight into how political groups in Nottingham have mobilised for protest over contentious political issues and traces where and how poetry figures in this process. The key resource, NBA, is the archive I founded in 2009 as a result of a racially insular heritage sector in Nottingham. In this context, it felt logical to make a poem about slavery and to intervene as I created a collection. It is a continuing call for slavery's legacy of disenfranchisement to be recognised, and for reparations to be made. For me, this is the most radical of the three poems I have created to date, and it comes directly influenced and strengthened by my being the keeper of a Black archive. If *Brought and Sold* and *When I think About Slavery …* were written for performance and were written at a time before a Black archive existed, *When the Slave Ships Came* is made directly from my engagement with Black history as situated within NBA. It is also made specifically for the page and symbolises for me a letting go of the past. When Okri explores the impact political poems may have on developing ideas, protest, change and truth, he writes, 'poetry is often roused into being by the ways in which power throttles life and spirit' (2018, p. xiii). With time to study the archive and contemplate how my spirit had been 'throttled', I put *When the Slave Ships Came* onto the page. This act has taken away the need for me to revisit the feeling in the same way as I have done with the two previous poems. I am no longer bound by having to speak of the horrors of slavery, instead I transfer the feelings to those who may not otherwise come up against such history in this way.

In making *When the Slave Ships Came* (Figure 2.1), I studied again the atrocities meted out to Africans on that journey from Africa to the Caribbean and sculpted words generated from free writing into short phrases and sentences and then sorted

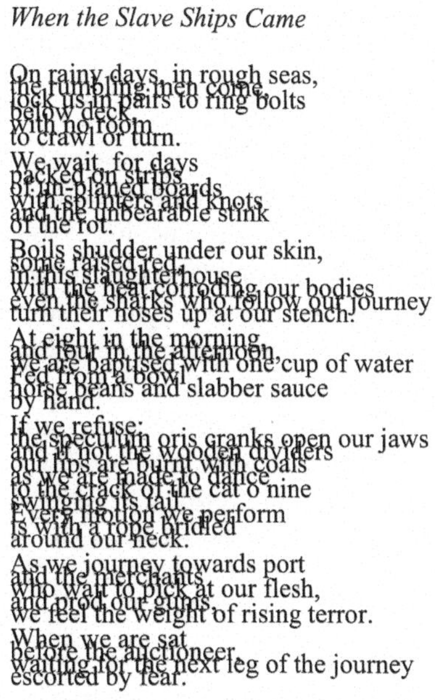

FIGURE 2.1 *When the Slave Ships Came.* Image by author

them into neat stanzas, but I realised the poem was too controlled, too orderly, too polite and had none of the rawness I was seeking to convey. Re-creation of the cramped conditions of a ship's hold, and the feeling of being confined in spaces with barely enough room to breathe, was what I wanted to achieve. This led to a period of revision which involved removing stanza breaks and end-stopped lines but, still, there was not enough turmoil. Slavery was brutal, raw, and gritty, yet the poem was neat and orderly. I wanted readers to experience physical difficulty, to be uncomfortable, to feel awkward, to be immersed. I decided that the only way I could replicate the cramped conditions and force readers into an immersive experience was to alter the layout of the text and so I set the line spacing at 0.4 point. At this setting, some text was obscured but not left completely unfathomable, and readers would need to struggle to read it as I struggle in this world as a Black woman because, as Ngcobo affirms, writing by Black women 'is seldom genteel since it springs from our experiences which in real life have none of the trimmings of gentility' (1988, p. 4). So, form not only dominated the content, but it also obscured it.

I also see the obscuring of text as my contemporary antebellum act and I draw inspiration from artist, academic, and critic Keith Piper who has examined how 'the American Slave Plantation has been redrawn as a site where complex codes of resistance, subversion, bluff, performance and collaboration can be seen to be played out' (2013, para. 2). This can happen, Piper argues, through the construction of a 'trickster' character that 'has appeared and reappeared as a subversive figure of myth and cultural discourse, both globally and throughout history ...' (2013, para. 1). So, what could be assumed as passive victimhood is silent subversion. Piper's analysis of the character Kizzy, the daughter of Kunta Kinte, a fictional African slave, as depicted in the 1977 film adaptation of Alex Haley's novel *Roots* (1976), illustrates how subversive acts are performed. Kizzy secretly spits into a cup of water and hands it to Missy Anne to drink. This surreptitious act of rebellion while limited in its impact to alter the circumstances of her status is a symbolic albeit small act of resistance. I am spitting into a cup of water in *When the Slave Ships Came*. My subversion is driven by the will to trick readers into wanting to decipher the poem, to force them to come 'face-to-face' with history and in doing so perhaps they are able to feel what it is like to struggle, to be at a disadvantage, to have limited information – and freedom. As Judith Schalansky (2020) explains: 'writing cannot bring anything back, but it can enable everything to be experienced' (2020, p. 25). The political act of making this work provided some personal relief because it enabled me to clear away the debris, detritus, dust, and some of the history that holds me hostage and to broaden the scope of who is responsible for dismantling racial inequalities.

When I Think About Slavery ...

Fifteen years prior to making *When the Slave Ships Came,* I crafted *When I think About Slavery* ... It was written when the beneficiaries of Empire paused for a moment to commemorate the bicentenary of the 1807 Act for the *Abolition of* the

Slave Trade in 2007. This moment, as the subsequent 'ending' of the Transatlantic Slave Trade was being venerated, prompted discussion about a formal apology and reparations for the horrors inflicted upon millions of Africans. To mark the moment, NCMG commissioned the making and accessioning of a 'Globe of Freedom' into its collection. I was commissioned as a freelance practitioner to fill the gap and to work with young people and a visual artist to realise the Globe. At this point, I was questioning my relationship with the NCMG and firming up my voice as a performance poet in Nottingham. I was also thinking about how my work as a freelance practitioner, although impactful in relation to audience development, was limited in terms of making structural changes, and I was beginning to think if the heritage sector would not tell our stories we would need to tell them ourselves. This was the point where my work towards the building of a Black archive was set in motion.

The commissioning of an object for the NCMG's collection underlined the fact that the Nottingham heritage sector needed to do more to connect to Black people. It highlighted that the museum (then and now) remains largely a monoculture. In 2007 there were no senior members of the museum's team from a global majority background in Nottingham. The same situation is true in 2022. I believed then, and I believe now, that to generate change required a step change beyond thinking only about the delivery of audience development initiatives, that the sector needed to implement diversity urgently in its staff, especially in terms of curators, senior managers, and governors. These thoughts were compounded by an experience at Westminster Abbey in the same year. I had been invited through my work at NCMG to attend a bicentenary commemoration service at Westminster Abbey on 7 March 2007. This was a high-profile prestigious and meticulously planned event. However, approximately 45 minutes into the service, an incident occurred which would attract national attention, and which would lead me to write *When I think About Slavery* ... The service was filled with the empire's 'great guardians' and David Smith (2007) an *Observer* reporter recounted for the *Guardian* what had happened. With many others, including me, Smith witnessed:

> [A] man [who] strode rapidly into the space in front of the altar ... The Queen, Prince Philip, Tony and Cherie Blair, John and Pauline Prescott, Gordon and Sarah Brown and the Archbishop of Canterbury watched in stunned disbelief. ... Toyin Agbetu of the African rights organisation Ligali, was only a dozen feet from all of them.
>
> *(2007, para. 3)*

Agbetu had been seated in the Poets' Corner when he decided to interrupt the service, and I was later to learn that Agbetu was not only a poet but also an activist. In Smith's report Agbetu revealed: 'I had always planned to make this demonstration ... The Queen has to say sorry. It was Elizabeth I ... She commanded John Hawkins to take his ship' (2007, para. 12).

Before Agbetu was ushered out by seven guards, he turned to face Prime Minister Tony Blair and I heard him say, 'why are the words sorry so hard to say?' When Agbetu left Westminster Abbey, the service continued as though he had never spoken out, but what changed for me was a resolve to amplify the question: 'why was it hard to say sorry?' Agbetu's words were the provocation to see differently and to raise my voice against the heritage sector. What I had witnessed troubled me, and I needed to record and document it through poetry. When I began to write the poem, the audience – managers, curators, and historians – were at the forefront of my mind as I crafted the words. I also had a clear picture of when and where it would be performed once completed – at the NCMG.

In the making of the poem, there was a period of sitting still with my thoughts, undertaking several free writes, and digging deep into the history of slavery while my thoughts melded with what was going on specifically in the context of Nottingham's heritage sector. I chose to write in the first person to give the poem a personal feel and used names of African people, 'Kofi' and 'Aminah' in the opening stanza to show that real people, with real lives, had their existences brutally disrupted. The narrative then began to move forward and take a shape of its own. I made links between empire gaining wealth and Black people losing their culture. And I employed techniques such as rhyme and rhetorical questions to make the poem memorable and to encourage the listener to think about the circumstances of slavery and its impact. It was a contemplative piece looking both at the past and at the present. A version of Agbetu's words became the penultimate and final lines reinforced with the use of rhyme. I performed the poem accompanied by my daughter who sang a refrain echoing the words, 'mama's boys gone, daddy's girl lost, and grandma dies of a broken heart'. It was performed only once at NCMG on the evening of the 'Globe of Freedom' being accessioned into the museum's collection in 2007.

> *When I Think About Slavery …*
> I think of Kofi, Aminah, Kwame and Kwabena.
> I think of mama's boy gone,
> Daddy's girl lost
> and Grandma dies of a broken heart.
>
> I think about barbaric treatment.
> Mutilated lives,
> devoured hope,
> denied the right to dignity,
> a nation crippled and the ripple flows through.
>
> I think about empire's wealth
> built and made,
> profits and gains from lives slain,
> a culture lost
> and the cry of a people made.

I think about frantic faces,
tired.
Those who journeyed
survived,
who strived and thrived to overcome despite.

I think of man's inhumanity to man.
Was that ever creation's plan?

I think about those in the now,
the do-gooders and the don't-ers.
The price paid for principles,
the lives lost for truth.

I think about remnants and fragments.
Refugees and asylum seekers
and the colonial purse keepers.

I think in this whole wide world
for all of us
there should be room,
how much more
will mother earth allow us to consume?

I think about it all
Freedom
Equality
Justice
Liberty
and pray that one day
words as simple as sorry
won't be so hard to say.

Brought and Sold

It is interesting that in the early stages of my creative development as a writer one of my first performance pieces was *Brought and Sold* made in 1992. It was made in the dub poem genre, penned specifically for sonic performance. Choosing dub poetry as a vehicle meshed with my cultural grounding. I was exposed to writers such as Jean 'Binta' Breeze and particularly her performance of 'Riddym Ravings *(the mad woman's poem)*' (1988, pp. 58–59). Her work resonated personally and aesthetically, and one of the things that drew me to her poem was its lyricism. She performed the abstract (and beautiful) ramblings of a homeless Black woman and her experience of Bellevue (a psychiatric hospital) with skill.

Breeze's work was new, adventurous, and refreshing, and she stood as a rare example of a Rastafarian woman speaking out on meaningful issues. Michael Bucknor argues that, through 'graphic configuration, aural structure, and spatial arrangement', Breeze 'recomposes the oral within the scribal' (1998, p. 303). She was a significant role model for me in this way because her delivery was slick, verbally dexterous, and I would try to emulate that when making *Brought and Sold*. Breeze had amplified the voice of Black women routinely ignored and I intended to do the same with a poem written from the perspective of an enslaved woman. The language was raw and unrefined, and there was mention of the poetic persona being raped and brutalised. I wanted to touch on the violence, like Dabydeen who acknowledged that when writing his poems on slavery, he found 'the language is uncomfortably raw … like a wound' and he had to 'shed' his 'protective sheath of abstracts and let the tongue move freely in blood again' (1986, p. 14). I wanted to personalise the trauma and juxtapose its narration with a memorable refrain written using a nursery-rhyme rhythm as Breeze had done to infuse a similarly unnerving quality in her work. *Brought and Sold* was never made to live on paper and I can find no traces of it in my poetry archive. I have only retained the first six stanzas in my memory the rest remains lost like the many souls who died in captivity. With its design as a spoken word piece the way I have recorded it here cannot testify to how it was received as a sonic performance. 'Nooooo!!!' was articulated as a prolonged howl and held until the sound faded into a whimper, as with 'Pleaseeee!!!':

Nooooo!!! she wailed
impaled by a foreign body.

Shackles and chains
Shake and make
A sound you hate.
Pleaseeee!!! She begged
Shuffled chained legs

A senseless rape
while others gaped
who's the primeval ape?
Have mercy,
Some compassion
… my submission?

Taken by force
And whipped like a horse
As a matter of course.
I want my mammy
My daddy …

This splitting of the poetic persona into a woman begging for mercy, and the narrator telling the tale is symbolic of how complicated it was for me negotiating a stance 30 years ago. There was a need to tell the story but there was also pain and anguish in the telling. The choice to create *Brought and Sold* using a distinct nursery-rhyme rhythm was to give the poem an unnerving quality. It also made it suitable for a sonic performance. I eventually stopped performing *Brought and Sold* in the early 2000s when one of my daughters, then aged 14, confided in me that the poem made her feel sad. It made me feel sad too.

Conclusion

The task of balancing conflicting emotions remains an internal battle between writing about this dreadful period in world history while at the same time wanting to bury it, especially when each poem requires that I delve further and further into the past to retrieve accounts and burrow into them. The processing and healing that should have taken place after centuries of brutality is yet to transpire and reparations yet to occur and each poem stands as a final act until another is born. My poems are an ongoing process of revision with no clear end in sight. Perhaps the distance between each of them is the need for recovery. The time and dedication given to each could be described as a 'life's work' and the seemingly never-ending task of campaigning for equality. While the opportunity to explicate aspects of my autoethnographic practice brings me up against some difficult history, it also provides an opportunity to highlight injustices. When D'Aguiar 'tried to imagine without success a last poem, a last play, a last novel, ... about slavery' (1996, p. 125), he did so in the context of imagining a final act, for now *When I Think About Slavery* is my final act.

References

Achebe, C. (1994). The art of fiction no 139. *The Paris Review*, (133). Retrieved from https://www.theparisreview.org/interviews/1720/the-art-of-fiction-no-139-chinua-achebe

Banjoko, P. (2008). *Attitudes and perceptions of the African Caribbean community*. Unpublished MA thesis. Leicester, UK: Leicester University.

Breeze, J. B. (1988). *Riddym ravings and other poems*. London: Race Today.

Bucknor, M. (1998). Body vibes: Spacing the performance. *Thamyris: Mythmaking from Past to Present*, 5(2), 301–322.

Crenshaw, K. (1991). Mapping the margins: Intersectionality, identity politics, and violence against women of color. *Stanford Law Review*, 43(6), 1241–1299.

D'Aguiar, F. (1996). The last essay about slavery. In S. Dunant, & R. Porter (Eds.), *The age of anxiety* (pp. 125–147). London: Virago.

Dabydeen, D. (1986). *Slave song* (2nd ed.). Oxford: Dangaroo Press.

Dawes, K. (2012). Bristol. In J. Kay, J. Procter, & G. Robinson (Eds.), *Out of bounds British Black and Asian poets* (pp. 232–233). Northumberland: Bloodaxe Books.

Du Bois, W. E. B. (1923). *The superior race*. Retrieved from http://blackfreedom.proquest.com/wp-content/uploads/2020/09/dubois31.pdf

Espinoza, J. C. (2021). Why do Black people always want to bring up slavery?' *An injustice!* Retrieved from https://aninjusticemag.com/why-do-black-people-always-want-to-bring-up-slavery-5bb9b33c0b1c

Haley, A. (1976). *Roots* (13th ed.). London: Picador.

Krivkovich, A. et al. (2018). *Women in the workplace.* Retrieved from www.mckinsey.com/featured-insights/gender-equality/women-in-the-workplace-2018

Marriott, D. S. (2006). *Incognegro.* Cambridge: Salt.

Ngcobo, L. (Ed.), (1988). *Let it be told: Black women writers in Britain* (2nd ed.). London: Virago Press.

Nichols, G. (1983). *I is a long memoried woman.* London: Karnak House.

Okri, B. (Ed.) (2018). *Rise like lions: Poetry for the many.* London: Hodder & Stoughton.

Olusoga, D. (2017). *Black and British: A forgotten history* (2nd ed.). London: Pan Books.

Picheta, R. (2018). *Diversity shortcomings.* Retrieved from https://www.museumsassociation.org/museums-journal/news/15012017-diversity-shortcomings-underlined-by-arts-council-england-report

Piper, K. (2013). Antebellum acts: trickster depictions and the American plantation. International Symposium Art Across the Black Diaspora: Visualising Slavery in America. Rothermere American Institute, University of Oxford, 29th May 2013. Retrieved from https://vimeo.com/67624323

Schalansky, J. (2020). *An inventory of losses* (2nd ed.). London: MacLehose Press.

Shaw, L. (2013). *Diversify reflections and recommendations: the final report on the MA's workforce diversity scheme.* Retrieved from https://ma-production.ams3.digitaloceanspaces.com/app/uploads/2020/08/18145034/19042013-diversify-final-report.pdf

Smith, J. D. (1980). A different view of slavery: Black historians attack the proslavery argument, 1890–1920. *The Journal of Negro History, 65*(4), 298–311.

Smith, D. (2007). You, the Queen, should be ashamed! *The Guardian,* 27 March. Retrieved from https://www.theguardian.com/uk/2007/mar/27/race.world1

SECTION II
Making a Drama Out of It

3

REFLECTIONS AND CONFESSIONS ON THE MAKING OF A PERFORMATIVE AUTOETHNOGRAPHY

University Performance Development Reviews and the Academic Self

Karen Lumsden

Introduction

This chapter provides an insight into the pendulum of self-reflection and critical inquiry in my attempts to deconstruct, process and make sense of my experiences of the neoliberal university in the UK. I discuss the making of a performative autoethnography of my experience of a Performance Development Review (PDR): a surveillance tool which is implemented by management in order to assess, observe and judge the performance of academic staff in relation to their research, teaching and impact activities. In education contexts, tools such as PDRs become 'part of the fabric of disciplinary power', and for the employee, 'there is always room for improvement' (Foucault, 1980; Tomkins, 2020, p. 62). As I go on to explain below, the PDR is also masculinist in its framings of those behaviours deemed to be evidence of success, and the ways in which these behaviours are constructed, performed and surfaced by the academic.

The autoethnographic performance of my PDR experience helps to illuminate this surveillance tool and its effects on the academic subject. By swimming beneath the surface, I am able to explore my personal experiences and everyday life as a female academic. The making of this autoethnographic performance provided analytical and critical insight into the managerialist mechanics of the university and how it impacted on my academic identity and emotional well-being in that I never felt 'good enough'. I was haunted by feelings of self-doubt, uncertainty and anxiety and felt that I did not belong. However, making the autoethnography functioned as a form of self-care was cathartic in helping me to process and make sense of the pressures and stresses of performance management

DOI: 10.4324/9781003309239-6

culture in academia and its impact on our personal life and academic identity. As Frandsen and Pelly note:

> By reading autoethnographies we witness power struggles and contextual complexity that can be best understood from a position of both 'being wrapped up in it' (experiencing it) as well as 'being outside of it' (reflecting upon it, writing about it, theorizing it).
>
> *2020, p. 252*

By fictionalising and exaggerating the below performative narrative, I can criticise, parody and resist a form of 'organisational confession'. Approaching the performance via the notion of 'tragic laughter' (Bussie, 2007; Classens, 2015) helps to subvert and survive the abuses of the academy and retain a sense of an autonomous self. The gendered implications and impacts of this process are also reflected on in relation to 'imposter syndrome' (see Lumsden, 2022). I argue that 'confessional writing' (Van Maanen, 1988) (on 'organisational confession') helps to explore and deconstruct power, reality and identities via personal experiences (Adams & Holman-Jones, 2011; Pinto, 2022) and also 'demystifies' the process and its effects (Sparkes, 2002). Ironically, today, being a 'good academic' means being able and willing to 'perform' a certain public identity and 'confess' allegiance to the tenets of the neoliberal university. 'Confessional writing' helps us to make sense of this process, its effects on self, and to reconcile our private self with the public academic self.

The chapter proceeds as follows: first, I present an overview of the PDR in UK academia, its relationship to audit culture and the neoliberal university, and the implications for academics. Then, I provide an overview of the value of performative autoethnography and the role of confessional writing in making the personal public, and unearthing hidden power relations, structures and inequalities, while providing critical analysis and space for activism and change. The chapter then proceeds to introduce the performative autoethnography of the PDR. The latter half of the chapter focuses on the making of the performative autoethnography – that is the backstage work involved in my attempts to process, write, present and reflect on this snapshot of academic life. This includes how the sharing of this confessional story via performance enabled me to engage in self-care while also mourning the loss of a stable academic identity and instead valuing an 'unsettled identity' (Grant, 2007). A pendulum analogy is adopted to describe a process of engagement and disengagement, with the author swinging back and forth via her identification with/in the academy and her re-positioning outside of the academy as critic and stranger. The chapter demonstrates that in addition to providing a space for critical and analytical inquiry, performative autoethnography acts as a 'tool of liberation' (Denzin, 2003) in assisting us to make our private troubles public via confessional writing.

Managerial Surveillance and Accountability: The PDR as 'Organisational Confession'

Utilised in the academy to ensure the accountability of employees and as part of audit culture (Shore, 2008) and new public management principles, the PDR is masculinist in its framings and understandings of behaviours and actions deemed to be evidence of success, and also in the way in which these are presented, framed, performed and surfaced by the academic in the neoliberal university. As a result of audit culture, 'academics are depersonalized, quantified, and constrained in their scholarship' (Sparkes, 2021, p. 1). Audit culture is evidenced through 'a suffocating array of metrics and technologies of governance' (Spooner, 2018, p. 895) such as the PDR. Gill (2015) argues that these trends reflect the rise of the 'quantified self' in the academy.

It has been argued that 'neoliberalism produces disciplined academic subjects who come to accept forms of assessment', such as the PDR, as 'the norm' (Berg, Gahman, & Nunn, 2014, p. 64). A competitive environment (Back, 2016) has been ushered in, in which academics are pitted against one another, and are either winners or losers, depending on how well they play the neoliberal academic game. The merit system and audit culture which define the game are based on, created by, and situated within, masculinist institutional structures and ideologies, and anything outside of this is therefore 'other', including the work of those who occupy feminine, raced, working-class and or disabled subject positions, and are therefore disadvantaged in this system (Bagihole & Goode, 2001; Berg et al., 2014; Gill, 2010). As Berg et al. (2014, p. 57) write:

> ... the academy is being dramatically transformed by processes of neoliberalisation, in which new forms of academic subjectivity are being produced via more hierarchical power relations that interlock with already-existing forms of exclusion including patriarchy, classism, ableism, heterosexism, and racism.

These performance measures and technologies are now increasingly aligned with monetary merit and reward mechanisms (i.e. pay rewards and salary increment increases), thus further exacerbating and reaffirming pre-existing inequalities. Self-promotion is central to the academic career and one has to be prepared to put one's self forward for performance awards and promotion (Bagihole & Goode, 2001).

The academic PDR is also based on quantifiable and positivist notions and ideologies associated with disciplines like engineering, natural sciences and business, placing scholars of arts, humanities and social sciences at a disadvantage (i.e. journal impact factors, citation scores, h-index, altmetrics, etc.). As Thornton argues:

> ... the ideal academic has become a 'technopreneur', a scientific researcher with business acumen who produces academic capitalism. This new ideal academic evinces a distinctly masculinist hue in contrast to the

less-than-ideal academic – the humanities or social science teacher with large classes, who is more likely to be both casualised and feminised.

2013, p. 127

The PDR consists of a manager (or senior staff member) taking on the role of the 'reviewer' (i.e. judge) and the (junior) academic performing as the 'object' of the audit culture gaze who must surface and make visible their activities, achievements, future plans and successes (whether real or imagined – i.e. it is the *performance of success* which is important, not always its attainment). The PDR can thus be viewed as a tool of self-disclosure and confession. For Foucault (1980), self-disclosure is interwoven with issues of power, especially when constituted as confession (see also Tomkins, 2020). He writes:

> One does not confess without the presence (or virtual presence) of a partner who is not simply the interlocutor but the authority who requires the confession, prescribes and appreciates it, and intervenes in order to judge, punish, forgive, console, and reconcile; a ritual in which the truth is corroborated by the obstacles and resistances it has had to surmount in order to be formulated; and finally, a ritual in which the expression alone, independently of its external consequences, produces intrinsic modifications in the person who articulates it: it exonerates, redeems and purifies him; it unburdens him of his wrongs, liberates him, and promises him salvation.
>
> *Foucault (1980, pp. 61–62)*

In education contexts, tools such as performance development reviews become 'part of the fabric of disciplinary power', and for the employee, 'there is always room for improvement' (Tomkins, 2020, p. 62). Thus, the PDR is but one strategy through which to monitor employees, hold them accountable, and effect a form of compliance from academic subjects: 'When we confess, we give ourselves over to institutions of authority …' (Tomkins, 2020, p. 61).

Self-disclosure is a mechanism through which the academic subjects themselves to 'disciplinary norms and expectations' and accepts and incorporates 'a self-moulding in their image' (Tomkins, 2020, p. 61). Academics are expected to make themselves and their work 'visible' – to make a 'spectacle' of themselves in the academy (Ball, 2015; Sparkes, 2021). A focus on the performance of success (and how well this is done – how we use 'university-speak') rather than the substance of our research, teaching and scholarly endeavours, has negative consequences for the academic worker, alienating them from their work and bringing to the fore the various disparities and inequalities in 'how' academics are rewarded and 'who' is rewarded for their efforts. This chapter highlights a paradox: the PDR is viewed as a 'compulsory' confession; however, this contrasts with the confessional writing in this chapter, which is also 'performative', but which is a form of resistance and is liberating.

Performative Autoethnography and Confessional Writing: Critique, Resistance, Parody

Autoethnographies of the neoliberal university and academic life are not new (see Andrew, 2019; Bottrell & Manathunga, 2019: Jubas & Seidel, 2016; Moriarty, 2019; Ruth et al., 2018; Sparkes, 2007, 2021; Warren, 2017; Zawadzki & Jensen, 2020). However, this is the first autoethnography which offers an enactment of the PDR. This critical and political autoethnographic performance (Denzin, 2003) challenges and unravels the masculinist culture of the PDR by peering and swimming beneath the surface (and under the rocks), to explore backstage experiences and everyday life as a female academic. Autoethnography is defined by Tami Spry (2001, p. 710) as 'a self-narrative that critiques the situatedness of self with others in social contexts. Performance autoethnography as Denzin argues, is a 'tool of liberation' and a 'way of being moral and political in the world' (2003, p. 258; Denzin, 2018). It is a confessional form of inquiry through which researchers can explore and deconstruct power, reality and identities via their own personal experiences (Adams & Holman-Jones, 2011; Pinto, 2022). As Sparkes (2002) notes, confessions can function as a means of 'demystification'. He sees confession as writings which 'draw on personal experience with the explicit intention of exploring methodological and ethical issues as encountered in the research process' (Sparkes, 2002, p. 59). As noted above, in this chapter, there is a contrast between two different forms of confession – the compulsory confession of making a spectacle of oneself for an external authority, and the confessional process of demystification and (self-driven) exploration and meaning-making via a performative autoethnography and reflections on its making.

As a form of 'self-revelatory performance', autoethnography encourages the researcher to 'explore themselves and their process to find a relationship with the audience before, during, and after the performance' (Emunah, 2015; Pinto, 2022, p. 46). The purpose is not always to tell a complete, finished, and polished story, or to conclude for the audience, but through the performance, to open the eyes of the audience to the personal experience, its wider significance, but also how through its effect on the audience, they themselves can infer the personal and cultural significance for themselves. Moreover, in their reflections on the process of writing and performing stories, Douglas and Carless (2013, p. 55) make the point that it is through these processes that it is 'sometimes ... possible to "make sense" of social phenomena in ways that would otherwise have proved elusive'. For researchers (such as arts-based researchers) who are 'coming to know' it is 'less about the "quality" of the product (whether it is considered "good" or not), and more about what the researcher/s come to see or understand through engaging in the creative process' (Douglas & Carless, 2013, p. 55).

I consider my performative autoethnography to contain various *layers of confession*. First, the PDR itself functions as a tool of self-disclosure and is an 'organisational confession', demonstrating to managers in universities the extent to which I, as an academic, am complying, constructing and performing an acceptable public 'academic self' – constantly achieving, striving and being 'excellent'. The second confessional layer involves the use of 'confessional writing' (Van Maanen, 1988) via a performative autoethnography to reflect on and process the impact of the PDR on my sense of self – both personally and professionally. In a sense, this chapter is a 'confession of a confession'. In his autoethnography of making a spectacle of himself in the audit culture of the academy, Sparkes (2021, p. 1) reflects that these stories can 'assist us to re-attune ourselves and resist the process of becoming artificial persons', as is demanded by university audit culture.

In the performance which follows, the audience are presented with two versions of the author and two responses to the reviewer's questions: one, from the performing-public-academic self, referred to as the 'Academic', and the other from the hidden-private-self, 'Karen'. There are also occasional 'stage-directions', such as addressing an audience directly. The PDR, although grounded in reality in terms of the general format that a PDR follows, the questions asked by reviewers, the responses from both academic and private selves, and related pieces of work often touched upon in the responses, also includes an element of fiction and exaggeration, in order to blur reality/fiction and parody and critique the 'boasting' expected in order to 'sell' and 'perform' our public academic selves, and the realities of the harm this creates for our hidden-private selves. In approaching the experience via a humorous lens, I draw on the notion of 'tragic laughter' (Classens, 2015) in order to subvert and survive the abuses of the academy. According to Bussie, this laughter highlights the existence of an '… autonomous self who not only exists but also makes choices independent of social authorities and thinks outside their ideological framework. Laughter is a form of free thought, which is in and of itself a negation of oppression' (2007, pp. 39–40). Therefore, as Sparkes (2021) argues, 'playful or tragic laughter as a strongly corporeal experience can serve an important function in resisting this process and refusing to become an artificial person in the audit culture' (p. 9).

The reflection which follows the scripted performance, regarding its making, demonstrates how the pendulum swings between these two selves, in order to make sense of the disjuncture between, and splitting of the two, and that confessional writing via this performative autoethnography can act as a form of catharsis and self-care in terms of reconciling these two selves and the separate 'worlds within me – the academic and the personal' (Bochner, 1997).

Confessional Layer 1: A Performative Autoethnography of the PDR[1]

REVIEWER: *So Karen, let's begin with a review of your feedback and objectives from the last PDR. What reflections do you have? What thoughts on the objectives set and your ability to achieve them? Challenges faced? Additional objectives not recorded in last year's review? Hmm?*

ACADEMIC: *Well – I've made considerable progress on the objectives listed in my last PDR. Journal articles have been submitted to LEADING INTERNATIONAL*

HIGH IMPACT JOURNALS *including Feminist Media Studies, Theoretical Criminology, British Journal of Criminology. Two accepted so far, of course! Co-authored a book chapter for a Gender & Violence collection with Routledge .... Application for a University Fellowship ACHIEVED! One of my PhD students completed this year, and another student's viva is scheduled for March. As for international reputation, one visit to ANU, Canberra, another coming up to the University of Southern Denmark ....*

KAREN: *At least he had the grace to flinch slightly when I mentioned publishing in 'Feminist Media Studies' ... I wonder if he's remembering that I gave a talk to students recently about autoethnography and writing from experience – I also better not mention that Leuven conference where I'm doing an autoethnographic performance of a PDR! That would be too critical! ... Of course, what he also won't remember is how I sweated blood to get that PhD student through – and how unsupportive HE was when I needed to discuss some of the difficulties the student was experiencing ... as usual he just zones out at any mention of teaching; and as for offering a colleague support – well that obviously uses up his own invaluable research time so he can't be doing with that.*

REVIEWER: *And in terms of your research achievements since the last PDR? Tell me about your publication strategy? And, you know – some evidence of the visibility and impact of your publications?*

ACADEMIC: *Well, of course I've targeted leading international peer-reviewed journals. Did I mention that already? Five publications in journals. And, as we both know, anything higher than an impact factor of 1 is high for a social science journal so my article in 'Mobilities' – at 1.569 is pretty damn good, hah ha! First ever application of Elias' 'process sociology' to the understanding of automobility/car culture too [self-satisfied smile]. All the others higher than '1' naturally [turns head away slightly and mumbles: 'apart from the practitioner policing journal but we'll move swiftly on from that]. As for the rest, well, I think you'll agree, it's pretty impressive: four book chapters, 17 presentations at various events, seminars, national and international conferences all BOOSTING my growing international reputation, and an edited collection. You remember the one: 'Reflexivity in Criminological Research'? Oh yes – very well received – [searches in pocket and brings out piece of paper and reads] ... "Here you go: 'This book stands out among the criminological research methods literature. It is emblematic of the current potentials to be found in criminological scholarship around the globe. It will be valuable and enjoyable reading for anyone who has ever conducted criminological research, and even more so for anyone currently in the field or planning to be so soon .... I cannot recommend this text enough'." [Pause for another self-satisfied smirk to audience].*

[Turns back to reviewer]. And by the next PDR I'll have finished my monograph on 'Reflexivity', I have published articles in leading international peer-reviewed Social Science journals and have attended five more conferences ... and so on. [Sits back to acknowledge own accomplishments].

KAREN: *Bloody hell – did I really do all that?! Actually, it is quite impressive. No wonder I'm absolutely knackered. But will anyone actually read it or CITE any of it?*

REVIEWER: *Hmmmm ... But what funding have you brought to the Department in the last 12 months?*

ACADEMIC: I've brought in over £900,000 these past 12 months including as Co-Investigator on a College of Policing grant awarded via the Higher Education Funding Council and also a contract awarded by a local police force.

KAREN: I won't mention the funding applications which were unsuccessful. We don't get any kudos for those or the work which goes into them. No one publishes reflexive accounts of their 'failed' research projects. Also, I better not mention that the nightmarish bureaucratic process of having to deal with the award of the police contract has taken up most of my time – ending up 6 months behind schedule. Like – the start date of the work being delayed by 6 months because of the delay in agreeing the contract, and the lengthy process to hire a Research Assistant. And then there was having to provide a statement to the Research Office in an email which outlined why this activity was 'research' and not 'enterprise'. Luckily they had a document which they had already prepared which outlined and defined what they constitute to be 'research activities'. That was demoralising.

REVIEWER: Could you summarise and reflect on your impact activities over the last 12 months?

ACADEMIC: Well, I SUCCESSFULLY collaborated with police forces in England and played a CRITICAL role IMPLEMENTING a partnership with them. We held their HIGHLY SUCCESSFUL launch event at the university. Development of this work was ACHIEVED via a research grant which focused on the co-production of research and evidence-based policing. The Research Assistant who I SUPERVISED spent seven months seconded to police forces in the region. As a result of this, FUTURE research and enterprise opportunities were developed for us and colleagues across the university. We have published on this work in LEADING journals. And the INFLUENCE of my work has been GLOBALLY RECOGNISED via the number of invitations I have had to talk about this work.

KAREN: Is this what they mean by impact activities? How can we really know and measure impact? What about harmful impact?! In any case, …. most of it happened by accident or happenstance. And I better not mention the stress of having to manage the expectations of police – who often want academics to do research for them without any funding.

REVIEWER: Now – can you reflect on your levels of collegiality across the Department, the School and the University?

ACADEMIC: REFLECTING on my levels of COLLEGIALITY, I would first say that I played a KEY/INSTRUMENTAL role for three years as Placement Director for the Department, building up the placement year from only one student in the first year to the numbers we have today – over a third of students going on a placement year. When I return from the University Fellowship year, I will take on the substantial leadership role of Programme Director for our degrees. Other CRITICAL roles held include the lead of the Policing Research Group and also the LEAD of a successful mini-centre for doctoral training, Policing for the Future, which has five PhD students funded. I managed two full time Research Associates on projects over the last 3 years and have published with PhD students who have gone on to SECURE academic careers at WORLD LEADING INSTITUTIONS.

KAREN: Not the collegiality question! …. When my unsuccessful Readership promotion application came back with minimal feedback, what they did acknowledge was my 'collegiality' – but we all know that counts for nothing. International high-flying *self-interested academic yes, collegiality and caring about students/colleagues, no. I wasn't allowed to submit that fellowship funding application because of the programme director role and resourcing. Disappointing … particularly given that they didn't tell me in advance, approved the application before I started writing it, and then didn't tell me it wasn't going to be approved until the day of institutional approval. I was really anxious that week, more than usual anyway ….*

REVIEWER: *Ok, thanks for that. So, given your performance over the last year and your plans for the next 12 months, what would you say your overall performance rating is? The categories are: Excellent, Very Good, Good, Satisfactory and Unsatisfactory. We both have to suggest a rating and then agree on it. But this is only suggested ratings to the Senior Management Team. Ultimately they have the final decision on ratings after having reviewed all of the PDRs.*

ACADEMIC: *[To be read very fast like a list]. Well … given the number of high quality journal articles I have published over the past year in high impact journals, the successful edited collection, the book chapters, the invitations, the international conferences and research visits, my international reputation and status, my leadership activities across the Department, School and University which demonstrate how INSTRUMENTAL I have been in ensuring our CONTINUING SUCCESS and GLOBAL REPUTATION, the over £900k in funding, and my future career and research projections for the next 12 months, GOING FORWARD, [Pause for dramatic taking of breath] I would have to say that my performance this year has been …. [triumphant] 'Excellent'!*

KAREN: *Excellent, – given what I have survived this past year, damn right excellent. (But also I <u>have</u> to say excellent, otherwise I am not the ideal self-promoting academic subject that they want us to be).*

REVIEWER: *Outcome agreed is 'excellent'. Of course, this is subject to the approval and discussion of the Senior Management Team. We can only give out so many 'excellent' awards ….*

KAREN: *[Rolls eyes, shakes head, sighs]. So – we're all still pitted against each other then! So much for collegiality!*

Confessional Layer 2: Reflections on Making a Performative Autoethnography

The above autoethnographic performance highlights points in time where the 'becoming-academic-self' was at the fore, highlights instances in which key actors in the teaching, research and service practices of academia reminded me of my status, and also where internally this was projected, anticipated or consciously (re)enacted by me. Echoes of imposter syndrome (Lumsden, 2022), as felt, experienced, and lived, can haunt us throughout our career, and remind us that academic identity is unstable, especially in the current neoliberal higher education climate, and involves a process of ever-becoming, reimagining and reinventing our 'selves'. We are haunted by what was, what is and what could be, for us as academics. As Gordon notes, haunting is 'the domain of turmoil and trouble, that moment (of however long duration) when things are not in their assigned places, when the cracks and rigging are exposed ... when disturbed feelings cannot be put away' (2008, p. xvi).

Moreover, in higher education, females are treated as '"less than" males, assumed administrators, infantilized for their views or commonly assumed to be students (thereby not being recognized as "real" academics) ...' and this '... has a personal impact on one's experience of the work environment' (Shipley, 2018, pp. 27–28). As the quest for 'excellence' and 'outstanding' performance, and a 'never quite good enough' performance culture continues at pace, privatised feelings of imposter syndrome will be further exacerbated (Lumsden, 2022).

This highlights the need for an ethics of care and collaboration, in order to repair our spoiled identities and contest the damages done by/via the managerialised and masculinsed neoliberal academy. Barbara Grant suggests one means of addressing the toxic and harmful structures and practices of the neoliberal academics is via the concept of 'a thousand tiny universities'. According to Grant, on the ground level, we can challenge these forces which are out of our control by taking perspectives from within our smaller 'tiny' worlds and effecting change wherever we can (Pfaendner, 2018). She also approaches the need to ascertain an academy identity from a 'mourning after' standpoint that values an unsettled identity (Grant, 2007). She argues that this gives us the 'possibility for a less defensive, even more productive, basis for relations with ourselves as academic developers and with the colleagues alongside whom we work' (Grant, 2007, p. 35). Les Back (2016, p. 114) calls for 'generosity' in academia, not just as a matter of 'being nice to others', but also as a 'survival strategy' or 'a prophylactic against the corrosive aspects of intellectual cruelty' which are part of the neoliberal university.

The above also highlights the discomfort experienced internally when faced with the expectation to perform success in response to audit culture, a behaviour which is increasingly evident in the performance of academic self via social media tweets and the need for public visibility. Alvesson (2013, p. 1) observes that in modern society the status quo is to be 'labeled in the most attractive and pretentious terms'. This involves crafting and creating an academic self-image which is a 'positive, well-polished, and status-enhancing image, even if it is somewhat superficial' (Sparkes, 2021, p. 2). To exist as an academic and become accepted in today's marketised and individualised academic culture means tweeting about work, productivity and academic successes. Billig (2013, p. 24) refers to a 'culture of boasting' in academia; a culture which I'd argue now pervades all aspects of the lives of academic workers. As Sparkes writes: '... even if successful, the psychosocial costs' of boasting 'are high as it can lead to inner conflicts and feelings of inauthenticity and low self-worth' (2021, p. 2).

Creating this autoethnographic performance meant reliving that discomfort, becoming familiar with it, and accepting it. It allowed me to step back and reflect upon instances of my own complicity in the system. For Sparkes, this 're-attuning' helps to connect our 'feelings to a wider landscape of scenarios, associations and experiences' (2021, p. 8). The making also helped to highlight the split between my personal self and academic self (see Bochner, 1997; Douglas & Carless, 2008). In his autoethnography of his father's death, Bochner refers to his academic and personal worlds and reflects on 'the large gulf that divided them' (1997, p. 418). According to Bochner: 'The sad truth is that the academic self frequently is cut off from the ordinary, experiential self. A life of theory can remove one from experience, make one feel unconnected' (1997, p. 422). As Lee (2007) notes, 'negotiating writing through confessions can be transformative'. Therefore, the making of this autoethnographic performance was cathartic in helping to make sense of an intrusive management surveillance tool and the discomfort it engendered in me. It is exposing and also reveals via confessional text an academic self which is fragile and vulnerable (see Lee, 2007). This autoethnography was performed on three occasions: at the European Congress of Qualitative Inquiry symposium in Leuven, Belgium in 2018, at the British Autoethnography Conference in Bristol, UK in 2019, and online to PhD students for an Autoethnography Symposium at Kings College London in 2021. Performing this autoethnography to academic audiences was experienced not only as nerve-wracking, anxiety-inducing, but also exciting, cathartic and liberating, in terms of what kind of reaction it would prompt from the audience and how this would also affect me. Sharing my story also provided a space for the collective discussion of the perils of academic life and the pressures we each face in all universities. Hence, each 'live' performance constituted a reinforcing – indeed, a successful 'remaking' – of an 'empowered', authentic self. And each subsequent performance became easier, as the experience was continually (re)processed, (re)made and reflected on.

Autoethnography, as noted, also functions as a form of resistance, including in this instance towards 'established conventions of academic life' (Frandsen & Pelly, 2020, p. 265; see also Ford & Harding, 2010; Raineri, 2013). We can try to resist through critique, parody and 'tragic laughter' (Bussie, 2007; Classens, 2015); however, resistance can also be difficult, 'as self-subjectification is an important part of normalizing power, in which the discursively carved out identity positions become internalized and self-regulated' (Frandsen & Pelly, 2020, p. 262). Therefore, autoethnography, performing this authentic artefact to an audience of peers, and reflecting on the process of making it, is one means through which we can try to resist the internalisation and self-regulation of an 'ideal' academic self and performing subject. Talking and writing about the actual performing of the performance (confessing, [reflecting] on the confession [performance] of the confession [PDR]) also provides an opportunity to step back and view the experience from afar, and reminds us of the value of autoethnography for making our private troubles public and surfacing the previously 'unsaid', so that we can avoid being 'haunted' by those experiences which may cause us pain and shame – in this case, the shame attached to not meeting the expectations set for us by the neoliberal academy. As Berlant notes, sometimes the thing which we desire is actually an 'obstacle to our flourishing' – which she refers to as 'cruel optimism' (2011, p. 1). The 'cruel optimism' of academia is that the goal posts are constantly shifting – we are playing a game in which we perform and continually try to attain/reach success. We can never win this game, or reach the finish line … To the university machine, we are imperfect academic subjects, constantly in need of more moulding, shaping and disciplining. If we refuse to accept the rules of the game, we can walk away: as university mangers would tell us, 'there are always plenty more at the factory gates'.

Conclusion

As we witness and live through the toxic changes which have occurred in higher education in the last few decades, we mourn what came before (whether real or imagined) and are forced to interpret and reinterpret what broken pieces of academia remain. However, as Grant notes, what is important is 'the interpretation of what remains—how remains are produced and animated, how they are read and sustained' (Eng & Kazanjian, 2003 cited in Grant, 2007, p. 36). This process is intertwined with feelings and experiences of imposter syndrome – both public and private, as our notions of our own academic identity and the process of becoming/unbecoming a ('good enough') academic must also be examined and understood within the process of 'mourning' which is felt in relation to the vast changes inflicted on universities in the UK and beyond (Lumsden, 2022).

Performative autoethnography is a form of confession. In this multi-layered chapter, it functioned as a means of confession on my experiences of the organisational discourses and tools of confession such as the PDR. Pendulum swings in my reflections between the performing public-academic self and the hidden-private self, illuminates the struggles in attempts to comply with the system, while also resisting and critiquing the neoliberal university and all it entails. The pendulum acts as a metaphor for the process of making, crafting, and reflecting on the experiences of the PDR and performing it via autoethnography. The performance, although grounded in reality, is also exaggerated and fictionalised, in order to parody the expectation of a 'boasting' (Billig, 2013, p. 24) and bragging academic performance which demonstrates to management that we are 'excellent' and 'world-leading' academics (whether they have enough 'excellent' awards to go round or not). Hence, the modern academic is always striving, but never meeting the expectations of, or quite reaching the goals set by the neoliberal university. 'Competitive individualism' is rife in the academy (Back, 2016), pitting us all against one another. Approaching the above autoethnographic performance via the notion of 'tragic laughter' (Bussie, 2007; Classens, 2015) helps to somewhat subvert and survive the violence enacted on academic subjects via organisational discourses of confession and disciplinary tools (Foucault, 1980). For me, the making of this performative autoethnography and enacting it in a 'live' performance as a way of making/reinforcing my authentic personal AND academic self was cathartic and functioned as a form of self-care. It helped bring to the fore my autonomous self, who was able to reflect, critique, parody and somewhat resist the constraints and expectations of the neoliberal university, instead of being eaten alive by audit culture through the PDR.

Note

1 This autoethnography was first performed as '"Performance Development Review" (PDR): An Autoethnographic Account of Proving One's Worth in the Academy' at the Wimmin Swimmin: Breasting the Waves in Shark-Infested Academic Waters Symposium at the European Congress of Qualitative Inquiry in Leuven, Belgium in 2018. A version of the performance is included in my chapter on experiences of imposter syndrome in the academy (Lumsden, 2022).

References

Adams, T., & Holman-Jones, S. (2011). Telling stories: Reflexivity, queer theory, and autoethnography. *Cultural Studies-Critical Methodologies, 11*(2), 108–116.

Alvesson, M. (2013). *The triumph of emptiness: Consumption, higher education, & work organisation.* Oxford: Oxford University Press.

Andrew, M. (2019). Double negative: When the neoliberal meets the toxic. In D. Bottell, & C. Manathunga (Eds.), *Resisting neoliberalism in higher education: Volume 1. Seeing through the cracks* (pp. 59–81). Basingstoke: Palgrave Macmillan.

Back, L. (2016). *Academic diary: Or why higher education still matters.* London: Goldsmiths Press.

Bagihole, B., & Goode, J. (2001). The contradiction of the myth of individual merit, and the reality of a patriarchal support system in academic careers: A feminist investigation. *European Journal of Women's Studies, 8*(2), 161–180.

Ball, S. (2015). Accounting for a sociological life: Influences and experiences on the road from welfarism to neoliberalism. *British Journal of Sociology of Education, 3*, 817–831.

Berg, L. D., Gahman, L., & Nunn, N. (2014). Neoliberalism, masculinities and academic knowledge production: Towards a theory of 'academic masculinities. In A. Gorman-Murray, & P. Hopkins (Eds.), *Masculinities and place* (pp. 57–76). Aldershot: Ashgate.

Berlant, L. (2011). *Cruel optimism.* Durham: Duke University Press.

Billig, M. (2013). *Learn to write badly: How to succeed in the social sciences.* Cambridge: Cambridge University Press.

Bochner, A. (1997). It's about time: Narrative and the divided self. *Qualitative Inquiry, 3*(4), 418–438.

Bottrell, D., & Manathunga, C. (2019). Shedding light on the cracks in neoliberal universities. In D. Bottell, & C. Manathunga (Eds.), *Resisting neoliberalism in higher education: Vol. 1. Seeing through the cracks* (pp. 1–35). Basingstoke: Palgrave Macmillan.

Bussie, J. (2007). *The laughter of the oppressed.* London: Bloomsbury.

Classens, L. (2015). Tragic laughter: Laughter as resistance in the book of job. *Interpretation: A Journal of Bible and Theology, 69*, 143–155.

Denzin, N. K. (2003). Performing [auto] ethnography politically. *The Review of Education, Pedagogy & Cultural Studies, 25*(3), 257–278.

Denzin, N. K. (2018). *Performance autoethnography: Critical pedagogy and the politics of culture.* London: Routledge.

Douglas, K., & Carless, D. (2008). Nurturing a performative self. *Forum: Qualitative Social Research, 9*(2), Art.23. https://www.qualitative-research.net/index.php/fqs/article/view/387

Douglas, K., & Carless, D. (2013). An invitation to performative research. *Methodological Innovations Online, 8*(1), 53–64.

Emunah, R. (2015). Self-revelatory performance: A form of drama therapy and theater. *Drama Therapy Review, 1*(1), 71–85.

Ford, J., & Harding, N. (2010). Get back into that kitchen, woman: Management conferences and the making of the female professional worker. *Gender, Work and Organization, 17*, 503–520.

Foucault, M. (1980). *Power/knowledge: Selected interviews and other writings 1972-1977*. New York: Pantheon.

Frandsen, S., & Pelly, D. M. (2020). Organizational resistance and autoethnography. In A. F. Herrmann (Ed.), *The Routledge international handbook of organizational autoethnography* (pp. 252–268). London: Routledge.

Gill, R. (2010). Breaking the silence: The hidden injuries of the neoliberal university. In R. Ryan-Flood, & R. Gill (Eds.), *Secrecy and silence in the research process: Feminist reflections* (pp. 228–244). Abingdon: Routledge.

Gill, R. (2015). *The quantified self of academia*. Paper presented at Public Engagement and the Politics of Evidence, July 23–25, University of Regina, Saskatchewan.

Gordon, A. F. (2008). *Ghostly matters: Hauntings and the sociological imagination*. Minneapolis: University of Minnesota Press.

Grant, B. M. (2007). The mourning after: Academic development in a time of doubt. *International Journal for Academic Development, 12*(1), 35–43.

Jubas, K., & Seidel, J. (2016). Knitting as metaphor for work: An institutional autoethnography to surface tensions of visibility and invisibility in the neoliberal academy. *Journal of Contemporary Ethnography, 45*, 60–84.

Lee, K. V. (2007). Confessing takes courage. *Forum: Qualitative Social Research, 8*(1), Art.6. https://www.qualitative-research.net/index.php/fqs/article/download/212/467?inline=1

Lumsden, K. (2022). Becoming and unbecoming an academic: A performative autoethnography of struggles against imposter syndrome from early to mid-career in the neoliberal university. In M. Addison, M. Breeze, & Y. Taylor (Eds.), *The Palgrave handbook of imposter syndrome in higher education* (pp. 577–592). Basingstoke: Palgrave Macmillan.

Moriarty, J. (2019). *Autoethnographies from the neoliberal academy: Rewilding, writing and resistance in higher education*. London: Routledge.

Pfaendner, B. (2018). *A thousand tiny universities – My impression From HERDSA*. 24 July 2018. Retrieved from https://teche.mq.edu.au/2018/07/a-thousand-tiny-universities-my-impressions-from-herdsa/

Pinto, R. M. (2022). Auto-ethnographic playwriting and performance for self-healing and advocacy. In E. Huss, & E. Bos (Eds.), *Social work research using arts-based methods*. Bristol: Policy Press.

Raineri, N. (2013). The PhD program: Between conformity and reflexivity. *Journal of Organizational Ethnography, 2*, 37–56.

Ruth, D., Wilson, S., Alakavuklar, O., & Dickson, A. (2018). Anxious academics: Talking back to the audit culture through collegial, critical and creative autoethnography. *Culture and Organization, 24*, 154–170.

Shipley, H. (2018). Failure to launch? Feminist endeavours as a partial academic. In Y. Taylor, & K. Lahad (Eds.), *Feeling academic in the neoliberal university* (pp. 17–32). Basingstoke: Palgrave Macmillan.

Shore, C. (2008). Audit culture and illiberal governance: Universities and the politics of accountability. *Anthropological Theory, 8*, 278–298.

Sparkes, A. (2002). *Telling tales in sport and physical activity.* Champaign, IL: Human Kinetics.

Sparkes, A. (2007). Embodiment, academics, and the audit culture: A story seeking consideration. *Qualitative Research, 7,* 519–548.

Sparkes, A. (2021). Making a spectacle of oneself in the academy using the h-index: From becoming an artificial person to laughing at absurdities. *Qualitative Inquiry,* Online First. https://doi.org/10.1177/10778004211003519

Spooner, M. (2018). Qualitative research and global audit culture: The politics of productivity, accountability, and possibility. In N. Denzin, & Y. Lincoln (Eds.), *The Sage handbook of qualitative research* (5th ed., pp. 894–914). London: Sage.

Spry, T. (2001). Performing autoethnography: An embodied methodological praxis. *Qualitative Inquiry, 7*(6), 706–732.

Thornton, M. (2013). The mirage of merit. *Australian Feminist Studies, 28*(76), 127–143.

Tomkins, L. (2020). Autoethnography through the prism of Foucault's care of the self. In A. F. Herrmann (ed.), *The Routledge international handbook of organizational autoethnography.* London: Routledge. https://www.routledgehandbooks.com/doi/10.4324/9780429056987-5

Van Maanen, J. (1988). *Tales of the field.* Chicago: University of Chicago Press.

Warren, S. (2017). Struggling for visibility in higher education: Caught between neoliberalism 'out there' and 'in here' – An autoethnographic account. *Journal of Education Policy, 32,* 127–140.

Zawadzki, M., & Jensen, T. (2020). Bullying and the neoliberal university: A co-authored autoethnography. *Management Learning, 51,* 398–413.

4

MI AMIGO GIOVANNI

A Digital Engagement of Friendship, Community and Queer Love Through a Zoom Performance

Edgar Rodríguez-Dorans and David Méndez Díaz

Introduction: 'Mi Amigo Giovanni'

Mi amigo Giovanni is a theatre play that follows the friendship between Edgar and Julio (fictionalised in the play as Elliot and Giovanni), the co-founders of the community group Arkadium Teatro & Danza.[1] Galvanised by the death of his friend Julio, Edgar wrote this tribute play as a way to continue his relationship with him and relive memories of the company they founded. The theatre play became a digital autoethnography (Atay, 2020) which was crafted in response to the death of Julio, and as an attempt to preserve the living memory of the deceased. The play engages with death as articulated by Lykke (2022): '… death as vibrant; death not in opposition to life, but existing in a flat continuum intertwined with it; death as an articulation of the vitality and vibrancy characterizing all matter' (p. 8). Created through 'documents of life' (Plummer, 2001) and conversations between friends, family, and strangers, *Mi Amigo Giovanni* narrates how Edgar and Julio met as teenagers and traces their relationship throughout university, their professional beginnings, their love relationships, and their relationships with their family and friends.

This chapter presents a duoethnography (Norris & Sawyer, 2012) which reflects on the experience of writing, rehearsing, and staging the online performance. In Norris and Sawyer's (2012) words, duoethnography 'is a collaborative research methodology in which two or more researchers of difference juxtapose their life histories to provide multiple understandings of the world' (p. 9). In this collaborative endeavour, the playwright/director – Edgar – and one of the leading actors in the performance – David – use a dual voice to reflect on and explore their experience of bringing *Mi amigo Giovanni* to the digital stage via Zoom. The chapter discusses how this performance was created at the intersection of death, community, and gayness, and traces this process over a three-year period

DOI: 10.4324/9781003309239-7

(from 2019 to 2022). The writing in this duoethnography, consisting of separately recorded accounts and later, joint entries by the authors, reveals crucial aspects of the process of crafting this performance (how drama was used as a tool to make sense of and communicate experience), and demonstrates the potentialities of digital performance to transform notions of community, friendship, and mourning and reveals a dimension of collective embodiment in the group performance.

2019

September, London

Edgar: I am at Heathrow airport, waiting for a connecting flight to Mexico City. I am travelling to see *mi amigo Julio* at the hospital. I try to speak with him, but his phone is now in the possession of his fiancé. I have been informed that my friend's health has deteriorated.

Over the next ten hours, I am on the plane, hoping to see my friend and come out of this situation together, as we have done previously when we experienced struggles. During the flight, I am out of contact. When I arrive in Mexico, and I can use my mobile again, the news I receive is that my friend has passed away.

During the following 48 hours, which cover the wake and the funeral, I see people I have not seen in years, with whom I used to perform on stage. I never imagined we would be meeting under these circumstances.

September, Mexico City

David: I have just graduated from the National School of Theatre Arts. I feel ready, prepared, and trained for the professional world of theatre! However, I soon realise the theatre elite in Mexico is small. You need to know producers, actors, and directors in order to access stable job opportunities, even in the institutional sphere. Despite this, I am fortunate to participate in creative processes that give me new tools and signal new artistic paths.

October – December, Mexico City and Edinburgh

Edgar: A couple of months have passed since Julio's death, and people gradually stop mentioning him in their conversations. I talk about him with people who knew him, and for a moment, we conjure his memory. He is there through our talk. The conversation then moves on to a different topic. I sense that people do not mention him unless I do. I notice subtle cues of conversation and behaviour through which people want to comfort me and come to a conclusion.

I travel back to the UK and continue with my life while struggling to accept he is dead. I engage in a series of activities to reconnect with his memory: seeing our pictures on my phone, reading his texts, listening to his voice messages stored on WhatsApp, playing the videos I have of him, and listening to the songs we used to like. Knowing that he is not an embodied presence anymore, I am aware of how these virtual mediums '… re-order the forms in which our lives are assembled, displayed and stored' (Plummer, 2001, p. 98). One day, a friend who is also mourning tells me he sends messages to Julio via his Facebook profile, which makes him feel like Julio reads them. Listening to this friend makes me realise that Julio and I used those digital spaces as avenues to develop and experience our friendship, and there is no reason I cannot keep using them.

I purchase books about bereavement, death, and dying. I seek movies and documentaries concerning the topic of death because I want to understand what to do with this grief. As much as it hurts thinking about his death, hurting is the only thing that helps me. I read authors who seem to be in the same position I am: trying to stay with the stories of those who have died. Among these books, Paxton (2018) uses the concept of 'continued bonds with the deceased', which I embrace, as it acknowledges that the symbolic presence of the dead stays in our psyche. The memories and the lived experiences remain with the living, even when the deceased have long departed; the relationship is ongoing, dynamic, does not cease, and never will. I find unexpected relief in the fact that I do not have to let him go.

Thus, I continue living, and I carry his memory with me. I want to write a story about us and our queer love. I start talking about this with my mother and a couple of friends. They seem enthusiastic. *'It will be a way of bringing the theatre group together again'* − I think. *'We will need to start rehearsals, preparing choreographies, I will have to travel to Mexico more frequently, I'll need an assistant director and assistant choreographer, I'll need to get a venue, not to mention the writing task'.* I realise that coordinating this production while I am living across the Atlantic will be a complicated project.

2020

March, Edinburgh

Edgar: I am following the news of a new virus.
  It sounds serious.
  An ominous pandemic brings new focus.
  I try to remain connected with my mother in Mexico.
  The grieving does not go away.

April, Mexico City

David: The Covid-19 health emergency arrives in Mexico.
  In just a few months, technology allows us to continue with artistic endeavours and create from our homes. I see institutional calls to create short videos, TikToks, and Instagram reels to tell stories of day-to-day life during Covid-19. An opportunity to re-signify reality through a cell phone camera.

May, Edinburgh

Edgar: A friend in Mexico suggests we use Facebook Live to gather and dance like we used to. I am sceptical about how the physical sharing of space and dancing together could translate into a virtual experience, but, still, I give it a try. I announce to friends that we will be doing Saturday dancing sessions via Zoom. The dance sessions start, and some people from the theatre group connect from Mexico, Canada, Germany, and the UK. In the upcoming weeks, I reunite with people I have not seen since we shared the stage years ago. Some newcomers join the group too. The togetherness I experience convinces me that the theatrical endeavours I dream of are possible.

Our remote dancing sessions mirror the distance between Edgar and Julio. This digital engagement has the symbolic function of showing me that my migration story prepared me for the Covid-19 pandemic. When people comment they have not seen their families in months, I reflect, along with other immigrants, that this was the reality for us even before the pandemic. When people comment they are fed up with online connections and cannot wait to see people in the real world, we reflect on how for us immigrants, those are our regular ways of connecting with our loved ones. As Cuban (2017) explains: 'When emphasizing the power of the technology, intimacy is re-developed although changed' (p. 13). Living in a different country from our friends and families has allowed us to use technologies to put the notion of 'place' on hold and establish digital ways of relating to one another. Since I migrated to the UK, virtual contact is the regular way of connecting, while in-person presence is a luxury. Being attuned to virtual ways of being makes me realise that, while the pandemic is scary, I am not longing for in-person presence more than I usually am. While academic discourses have contested the perceived divide between the 'virtual' and 'real' worlds, I hear people in everyday conversations repeat that they want to meet 'in real life' – meaning in person. Instead, I reflect on how, for me, the digital world is part of the so-called real world, and the meaningful interactions I have over digital platforms are real too. As Atay (2020) writes:

> … we encounter multiple cyberspaces and stories within them every day, all the time. Within these spaces, we form and cultivate communities, belonging to some and not others, and we continuously enter into and exit from a number of communities. In these spaces, we also think about who we are, make sense of our identities, and represent ourselves on social network sites, dating and hook-up applications, and our web pages.
>
> *p. 269*

Like Atay (2020), I reflect on how my digital world is interwoven into my everyday life and realise I can make the most of it. I call the Facebook Live group and propose creating an online theatre project. People respond with surprise. We have not staged a play together for six years. However, I tell them that we are gathering to create what I feel is a 'living memorial' for Julio. Most people accept the invitation. Some decline the invitation as their life circumstances mean that they are not able to engage with the project but ask to be invited to watch the performance when it is ready.

December, Edinburgh

Edgar: While the theatre play would be performed by the members of Arkadium, I am aware that no one in the existing group is in a position to play the main characters. Therefore, I post a casting call in various online forums:

> Community theatre company is looking for two actors who wish to participate in a play with LGBTQ+ content to play the characters of Giovanni and Elliot, two college students who meet throughout their university studies. The play portrays their romance and friendship.

> The production involves acting, dancing, and singing, and will be carried out via Zoom. Interested people must have a computer, webcam, and a reliable internet connection. Ability to tap dance is desirable.

Several actors contact me to audition. As part of the casting process, I ask applicants to send me their CVs and a brief statement expressing the reason for their interest in this project. An overt statement about their stance on an LGBTQIA+ project and community theatre work are two of the main elements that I consider when reviewing applications.

December, Mexico City

David: I come across a casting call posted in a Facebook group. The pandemic is ongoing and I am trying to understand how this world crisis is affecting me. I am so frustrated with myself, holding many negative thoughts such as: '*How am I supposed to be an actor if I cannot work?*'

Amidst this, when I see the casting call to apply for the role of Elliot, one of the lead roles in *Mi amigo Giovanni,* the only thing I think is: '*I'm going to apply even if I don't know how to tap dance*'. I am interested because it is an LGBTQIA+ project. I have become tired of not feeling represented by the characters I play in fiction. I'm a gay man, and I need to know the stories of my community. I need those stories to tell us we are not alone and we are stronger together. As Tony Adams (2011) writes: '... these representations can inform (live) social interaction—providing strategies for persons—all persons—to better navigate same-sex attraction as lived; art can imitate life, but life can also imitate art' (p. 166).

I want to perform LGBTQIA+ characters that represent me and explore so many gay stories that are yet to be told. Ken Plummer (2022) remarks that '... many of the stories told today are not happy ones. They do not suggest that the changing world has brought contentment and joy to all' (p. xix). Perhaps the story I want to tell is *my* life story: as a gay son, gay lover, gay student, *everything* with all my gayness, of which I'm proud.

I apply to the casting with a slight hope of returning to in-person theatre. However, it does not seem likely as the casting takes place online. A creative process of acting via Zoom? At the time, I do not realise the impact this will have on me and my vocation as an actor. 'A creative process of acting via Zoom?' – I wonder how this idea fits with my acting training.

2021

January: e-Casting, Various Geographical Locations

Edgar: Elliot is the character name I use for myself in the script, a performative device to distance myself from the text, write it more freely, and protect myself from the potential psychological cost of addressing the topic of death.

Giovanni is the character name I use to refer to my friend Julio in the play. The rest of the characters are based on real people too. The use of character names is important for two reasons. First, it allows us to widen the actor's creative range, as directing and providing notes to the actors can be centred on the performance of the fiction, rather than trying to imitate the person the characters are based on. Second, character names aim to protect mourners from the potential harm of being repeatedly exposed to grief. The use of character names differs from the use of pseudonyms, as we are not seeking anonymity, but a creative distance that allows us to engage with the fiction. For some members of the theatre group, the death of Julio was traumatic and, while the play as a memorial aims to facilitate community mourning, those who were closest to the circumstances of the death acknowledged we needed some distance from the event. As Yeboah (2020) writes:

> For the narrators who have opened up their wounds to a room full of strangers, grief does not end when the curtains fall. There is no 'new' life awaiting them. The life of trauma is long and its effects not easily resolved.
>
> *p. 147*

As the person devising the play, I considered the potential harm to the performers when acting or witnessing difficult scenes concerning loss, discrimination, and homophobia. Actors can take elements from the people whose lives inform the characters, but, ultimately, I reminded the actors that we were dealing with fictionalised narratives.

Edgar: I select ten actors who applied to the casting and offer them an audition. I invite four theatre group members to accompany me in the selection process. It is vital for us to make a collaborative decision about which actors should represent the characters. Having people accompany me in this task feels like an act of 'witnessing', in which those who met Julio would vouch for the suitability of the actor to portray a dramatised version of him. My need to invite others to witness this process seeks to create a production that pursues a continuous caring collaboration as exemplified in Charon's work, *Narrative Medicine*, which aims to honour stories of illness. She writes:

> Whether that representation is in visual art, a fictional text, or the spoken words of a patient in the office, the one who absorbs and *confirms* the representation must have the capacities to witness and give meaning to the situation as depicted. Only then can its receiver be moved to act on behalf of its creator.
>
> *2006, p. 113, original emphasis*

Thus, the actors auditioning for the roles are asked about the meanings they give to the scene they acted. As the project belongs to all of us in the theatre company, this has to be a community decision rather than an individual one.

David: Community theatre online? The casting has specific indications. A subtle question resonates in my head and leads me to confront myself, to be honest, and not respond with romantic ideas of what theatre should be. *'What does theatre mean for you?'* I respond:

> My name is David. I am 25 years old. I am an actor who graduated from the National School of Theatre Arts. I am interested in generating theatre to develop our profession. Above all, I want to get involved in paid theatre that is created, performed and represented by our LGBTQIA+ community, where entertainment is part of the creation and the represented life is universal for the public in some way, whether such theatre is audio-visual or face-to-face because as Eugenio Barba said: 'even in hell, there will be theatre'.

Edgar: I read David's statement, and I feel stimulated by his thought process.

David: In addition to familiarising myself with the text for the scene I would perform at the audition – which would become one of my favourite scenes between Elliot and Giovanni – I also have to prepare a movement sequence with a song by Thalía, which I have not heard before. This is enriching for me because it opens up a panorama of expanding musical references.

Edgar: Choosing the song for the audition is easy. I have listened to *Gracias a Dios* (Juan Gabriel, 1995) by Thalía, hundreds of times, as I dedicated it to Julio when we were lovers. Seeing the song being performed helps me with the mourning. It was as if Julio and I were together in a parallel reality.

David: Once my audition is done, the next day, an email with the subject 'Audition outcome' arrives:

> Hi David,
>
> I am writing to offer you the role of Elliot in the project. We liked your energy and performance during your audition. All who were present at the meeting agreed that you made us feel an intimate connection with your

co-star, and that was vital for the project. We also think that your choreography was one of your strengths. You did a great job, and we liked your professionalism.

And that's it. I'm in this new narrative!

February to May: Multiple Geographical Locations

David: During my training as an actor I witnessed – and was educated through – 'pedagogical violence' (Matusov & Sullivan, 2019). There was a narrative transmitted from some teachers to students on the notion of being willing to make any kind of sacrifice – even if it is painful or likely to cause psychological issues – for the sake of theatre. '*You have to give your life to the theatre*'. Repeatedly slapping each other for the sake of realism in a scene, making us undress unjustifiably, being exposed to our peers, and feeling intimidated were practices I was subjected to. And I complied because I believed that these practices would help me become a better actor. Is it possible to instead 'create' through loving and caring for each other? The process of staging *Mi amigo Giovanni* suggests that it is. I experienced a creative light that I have never seen: more than 15 people gathered online, being there without being there in a traditional in-person way, to create a mosaic of intimate spaces unifying fiction through text, gesture, body, sign, and symbolic moments. I had not learnt to make theatre in that way.

Still, it is hard to replace established ideas and make way for a new creative, social, and technical construction of my pandemic self. A performance via Zoom places me out of my comfort zone. Everything happens from my house and my anxiety grows because this virtual process is entirely new. My computer is my only confidant: it feels like a dystopian future when I talk to my screen and there are no physical eyes in front of me, just pixels and a screen light that ruins my eyesight. I could call this facet of my life: adaptability and resilience through my digital self.

Throughout rehearsals (which took place during lockdown), I optimised the time spent completing my day-to-day activities. I set an alarm to allow 30 minutes of preparation before connecting to Zoom and being confronted with the different Zoom screen 'boxes' (or 'windows') which my companions all inhabit. All I do is move around my house from room to room to arrive on time; a different dynamic than it would have been in person. The idea of connecting to rehearse and give a performance fills me with excitement and nervousness: turning my camera and microphone on for everything in my personal space to be seen and heard – intentionally or unintentionally. Amidst the sounds which I cannot control are street merchants selling their products, car alarms, conversations, shouts, and laughter. It should be noted that for a few months during the staging I am residing at my boyfriend's house in Guadalajara. So, I am using my boyfriend's personal space – a blue atmosphere different from my warm green room. This does not directly affect Elliot's world, but it affects my world as an actor. Elliot exists inside of this virtual fiction, but I-David-actor have to adapt my boyfriend's room into a noise-free area for an hour and a half of Zoom rehearsals and warm up my body in silence because I do not want his family to hear my warm-up screams. I need a private moment to prepare and get all of my equipment ready: ring light, mobile phone, and laptop, as there are moments in the play which require me to change devices. As Atay (2020) articulates, these '… media technologies continuously disembody and reembody our experiences' (p. 271).

Edgar: As the rehearsals continue, I notice the actors' creative exploration, which has to do not only with their acting but also with the technologies they use. Their performance does not rely on the body alone as it would in a face-to-face rehearsal. Their digital selves are mediated by the use of tripods, ring lights, and other devices which give them the opportunity to construct their digital selves in a way which individually suits them. Some members of the cast abandon their laptops and move completely to their mobile phones. They explain that their phones give them the mobility they need for different choreographies to portray the angle they need for each scene.

April – Multiple Geographical Locations

Edgar: Music, embodied memory, and collectivity play a significant role in crafting this digital autoethnography – crafted as a theatre play, performed via Zoom. Creating a play about a person who is absent in the embodied sense due to death posed the persistent question of how we could evoke his presence. One night, the song *Love Generation* (Harden et al., 2005) plays on YouTube, and it vividly reminds me of Julio, as he choreographed it for one of our previous shows. As I listen to the music, the feelings of connectedness to my friend are immediate: his smile, his dancing body, and his energy are vivid in my mind. I feel this choreography needs to be part of *Mi amigo Giovanni*. However, the choreography becomes one of the most elusive 'documents' to gather because *Love Generation* was presented in a production for which there is no video recording or photographs available. Extracting the choreography involves putting together music, collective memory, and bodily movements to recollect the intentions of the dance and recover movement sequences. We transform ourselves – the community – into research instruments and sources of 'embodied knowledge' (Spry, 2016). While rehearsing this choreography, the song transports me to a time in history when Julio created joy in us via his moves. Just like he spread love years ago, the movements generate an incomparable feeling of relationality within me, as if I was able to experience like him, to feel like him, *to be him* for a few minutes.

Since Julio's death, I had the dreadful feeling that we could no longer create memories, that I would continue living without being able to share the beauty and the difficulties of this world with him. One day I hear the song *Infinite Things* (Faith, Coffee Jr., & Wimberly, 2020), and it brings me to tears as the ethereal feel of the music and every lyric, one after the other, speak the things I want to say to Julio – *'I'm sorry that the world just ain't good enough for you'*, *'you deserve so much better'*, and *'Didn't know I needed saving, till I held you in my arms'* (Faith et al., 2020). The song and the choreography accompanying it disrupt the idea that my relationship with Julio had ended and became stagnant due to his death. He is here, and he is not here (Lykke, 2022). Suddenly, the concept of 'continued bonds with the deceased' (Paxton, 2018) makes embodied sense. While I had acknowledged and embraced the theory, it is this song which establishes it in my body and emotions. I am creating new memories with Julio and the group. The virtual rehearsals mirror the distance that death places between the living and the deceased. We are psychologically present without being physically present. We reframe the longing for physical presence and reengage with each other in digital modality.

David: For the theatre group, music became our meeting point. There was a song we were supposed to dance to, but Edgar changed it to *Infinite Things*. When I heard about the change, something happened inside me: suddenly, everything in the story made sense. I connected the text with the character in a different way. That song means so much to me because I used to listen to Paloma Faith with my boyfriend Diego. It was our musical refuge. When I dance to *Infinite Things*, I think of him, and it seems many people in the theatre group connected with this song too in their own ways.

Edgar: The choreography of *Infinite Things* facilitated a digital experience which looked both inwards and outwards: it made me feel alone and accompanied, exposed and unseen as the movement sequence required dancers to pose in dramatic ways, looking away from the camera, then straight into the lens, then give their back to the audience and return for a close-up, look at the horizon, and then directly into the eyes of others.

David: My attempts to put into words something that is felt seemed limited. The myriad of emotions that emerged from the music in convergence with our dance seemed close to being at one with the group and with the music, not in a traditional way of seeing synchronicity in the ensemble, but togetherness in a dance canon: the melody and the dance began sequentially instead of synchronously. The delayed transmission in Zoom created an unintentional staggered response which shaped our relationship; we responded to the music first and then witnessed when and how the music might reach others.

This process highlights the different temporalities which existed within the same performance. For example, the music was mediated by digital formats: Edgar and I commented on how we have listened to part of the soundtrack of this play under different circumstances. I listened to *Love Generation* (Harden et al., 2005) while in primary school, and Edgar while in university, but neither of us listened to the live version. We did not listen to Bob Sinclair in concert – never as an in-person experience. This is a testament to the ubiquitousness of digital forms of existence and the inseparable nature of virtual and organic lives (Waugh, 2017). Still, when the whole ensemble gathered to dance, it felt like all of our individualities converged in the performance.

Edgar: At this point in the process of staging the play, it became clear to me that this is not only a personal story anymore. We were doing a project which emerged at the crossroads of digital (Atay, 2020) and performative (Spry, 2016) autoethnography, mediated by the digitalised relationship imposed by geography, death, pandemics, the digital era we live in, and our bodies as the medium of inquiry.

Stacy Holman Jones (2016) writes that theory is a story told in a particular academic language that sets the framework for specific happenings to occur. She explains that theory provides the settings for what is possible and what is not. Our rendition of *Mi amigo Giovanni* as a homage to Julio was made possible by autoethnography because, even though I did not plan from the outset that this play would be a digital autoethnography, the process shows that it is a story that speaks about the realities of many young gay men who encounter others like them and create love as they go (Rodríguez-Dorans, 2020). There is potential for autoethnography everywhere, in every person and every life story, but it takes theory to realise the epistemic power that lies in each personal story. For gay people, when we realise how hegemonic discourses on normative sexuality have impacted our lives, the potentiality of being protagonists of our own stories is realised (Plummer, 1995). Julio and I selected and sometimes created our own theatre plays, however, during the 20 years of our theatre group, we never dared to use our personal stories as the source of our productions. We did not recognise that *our* stories could be told or would be interesting to read/watch. The fact that I studied autoethnography a few years ago made this research possible. Had I not come across this scholarly approach which recognises that access to knowledge creation is often denied to marginalised groups, perhaps I would not even recognise the value in my own experience. Perhaps I would be doing research *about* others instead of *with* others. Perhaps I would not even recognise the academic value of the play, the community that created it, the dialogue with David, and the potential of what has gone from being a digital performance to become a duoethnography where we recognise our bodies as a site of research (Norris & Sawyer, 2012).

July and August: Multiple Geographical Locations

David and Edgar: The group presents an excerpt from the play at the International Conference of Autoethnography (2021), which takes place online. We perform in Spanish with English subtitles. We show Elliot and Giovanni's friendship, love, and queer brotherhood to a global audience. We discuss how the performance was crafted from memories and conversations with friends, family, and strangers and 'documents of life' (Plummer, 2001), such as photographs and videos, and, importantly, choreographies.

This is the first of a series of online performances which we present to different audiences globally. We have to psych ourselves up twice as much during performances. There is an exorbitant psychological expense for the performers.

We wonder why we end up so tired after a virtual performance, if our bodies are not subjected to the demanding rigour of a 10 × 20 m stage. One answer to this could lie in the concept of 'Zoom fatigue', for which Bailenson (2021) identifies cognitive load, reduced mobility, eye gaze at a close distance, and the constant mirror effect of the camera on the user. The reduced mobility and the eye gaze at a close distance make sense in this context, as we are moving within a limited space, and we always come back to focus on the camera. Our stages are our personal spaces, our cameras and our little framed faces.

The August premiere at the Edinburgh Fringe Festival (Rodríguez-Dorans, 2021a,b) is especially exhausting and meaningful as we organise it to take place on Julio's birthday. It is our ceremony of love: a live memorial that reclaims some of the epistemic power that social institutions throughout history have taken away from gay men as our stories had not been visible. Here we are presenting this gay story of love. We are reclaiming that power through our performance and togetherness.

2022

April: Mexico City and Manchester – Ongoing Conversations and Conclusions

David and Edgar: Coming together to write this chapter has made us reflect on the potential of digital performance. We want to make sense of the experience of staging the play and what brought us together. We talk – on a Zoom call – about writing this chapter and discuss how to put our experiences of crafting this duoethnography. We listen to each other and take notes. Google Docs – another digital space – allows us to draft together. We reflect on how love, life, death, music, and tech connected us. We talk about mirrors and seeing each other reflected in the play.

David: What we see in others reveals information about who we are. This mirror – the Zoom interface, the text, the performance – where we see different qualities and personal aspects of ourselves reflected in each other reveals something I did not know I needed: a community. *Mi amigo Giovanni* was a moment in my life that showed me a new way for a creative online process. We were far away from each other, connected through wires, screens, hardware and software, but we still *felt* each other through the text, choreographies, gossip, laughs, and experiences shared at every rehearsal. I was a newcomer to the Arkadium theatre company, but I felt welcome to dive into everyone's stories and lives. So many mirrors – little virtual squares – I could see myself reflected in.

In this chapter, we have traced the process of the creation and performance of the duoethnography over a three-year period. This makes me think of then, now, and the ongoing, and how I am growing as an actor with Elliot. I think of reality and fiction as two levels of reflection which help me to enhance my understanding of what I see of the other in myself. To act, you need to be yourself and act with what you have. So, I know that Elliot is a loving, empathetic, fun, and passionate character. I could see things in myself that I found in Elliot. I knew this character was not a creation of the imagination but was based on someone real. However, I wanted to imprint my essence onto the character. I began to build from my experience and creativity while still being faithful to the story of Elliot/Edgar. I identified with Elliot through his love for dance and the first love that became the love of his/my life. I saw myself in Elliot/Edgar through all those hopes and desires of being a gay man. I emphasise that because in this macho, conservative society I live in, led by an obsolete patriarchal system, it can be difficult for us – gay men – to be the protagonists of our own stories.

Edgar: I have been gay since I was a child, and I want to write about how important it is to congregate with other gay and queer people to talk about our experiences. Throughout these 30+ years of queerness, I have met several queer others, and it has been phenomenal to realise the power that emerges from our togetherness, a 'protective relationality' (Rodríguez-Dorans, 2021a,b) reflected right here in the text that we have created – remotely – when acknowledging the importance of our own stories and the embeddedness of our lives in digital ways of relating.

May: Manchester and Mexico City

David: Writing this chapter has been a collaborative endeavour, not only between the named authors, but also between the members of the theatre group. The post-production writing helped us to make sense of the experience of staging *Mi amigo Giovanni*, a digital performance crafted through text, conversations, documents, and the body. This duoethnography has seen our personal stories overlap (Norris & Sawyer, 2012) to reflect on the play as a temporal artefact that transcended its ephemeral nature and its personal significance. The performance was performed live for a five-show run but it is long-lasting, as it was recorded in video and in our bodies through choreographies that embodied knowledge of the possibilities and limitations of digital connections.

Edgar: The death of Julio provoked affective ripples around him and mobilised a series of events, some of which have been documented in this duoethnography. Crafting this chapter allowed us to observe the theoretical, technical, performative, relational, and affective dimensions that interweave when making a 'dramatic' autoethnography. I experienced the death of my friend deeply and intensely – subjectively. This motivated me to write what became a community theatre play. This was only made possible through the dancing, through the protective relationality symbolised by the togetherness of our bodies. The physicality of our bodies was bridged by the technologies that allowed us to talk, see each other, dance, write, and experience together. The realisation of this endeavour's epistemological value was made possible through the work of artists, researchers, scholars, people who have highlighted the potential of personal stories to speak about broader social issues. Writing about that process of this autoethnographic performance and the subsequent duoethnography involves synthesising those dimensions and might tempt us to present a neat narrative of what has been a complex series of events surrounding my friend's death. This autoethnography is ongoing, as is our friendship that keeps on giving.

The potentiality of *Vibrant Death* as conceptualised by Lykke (2022), highlighted earlier in this chapter, challenges the idea of death as inert, motionless, absent and proposes a death that is active, moving, and present. A death that vibrates, generates, and continues giving. As a testament of this love for Julio, a new group of people connected. Julio created 'Giovanni' through me, because he impacted my life in ways I am still discovering. Julio is not alive, yet he is very much alive within me and those he touched. As David said to the theatre group: *'I never met him, but I'll never forget him'*.

Note

1 We used pseudonyms for dramatic purposes, to allow actors to engage with the fiction. However, we did not pursue anonymity. We believe that, for the play to be performed creatively, we needed artistic licence to immerse ourselves in the story from a safe distance. The name of the group is not a pseudonym and the people fictionalised in the story could be easily identified. We believe it is important for the group and those involved to remain cognisable. As Wolcott (1973) has pointed out, removing all identifying details would 'risk removing those very aspects that make it vital, unique, believable, and at times painfully personal' (p. 4).

References

Adams, T. E. (2011). *Narrating the closet: An autoethnography of Same-sex attraction*. Walnut Creek, CA: Left Coast Press.

Atay, A. (2020). What is cyber or digital autoethnography. *International Review of Qualitative Research, 13*(3), 267–279.

Bailenson, J. N. (2021). Nonverbal overload: A theoretical argument for the causes of Zoom fatigue. *Technology, Mind, and Behavior, 2*(1), https://doi.org/10.1037/tmb0000030

Charon, R. (2006). *Narrative medicine: Honoring the stories of illness*. New York: Oxford University Press.

Cuban, S. (2017). *Transnational family communication: Immigrants and ICTs*. New York: Palgrave Macmillan.

Faith, P., Coffee, C. Jr.,, & Wimberly, P. (2020). Infinite things [song]. On *infinite things*. Sony Music UK.

Gabriel, J. (1995). Gracias a Dios [song]. On *En éxtasis*. EMI Latin.

Harden, D., Le Friant, C., Pine, G., Woodhouse, J., Schreiner, J. G., & Wisniak, A. (2005). Love generation [song]. On *western dream*. Yellow Productions, Defected.

Holman Jones, S. (2016). Living bodies of thought: The 'critical' in critical autoethnography. *Qualitative Inquiry, 22*(4), 228–237.

International Conference of Autoethnography (Producer). (2021, August 4). *'My friend Giovanni': An autoethnography of shared mourning through queer community performance*. [Conference presentation]. Retrieved from https://www.youtube.com/watch?v=VBd4ceEGQvk&t=1197s

Lykke, N. (2022). *Vibrant death: A posthuman phenomenology of mourning.* London: Bloomsbury Academic.

Matusov, E., & Sullivan, P. (2019). Pedagogical violence. *Integrative Physiological and Behavioral Science, 54,* 438–464.

Norris, J. L., & Sawyer, R. (2012). *Duoethnography: Dialogic methods for social, health and educational research.* Walnut Creek California: Left Coast Press.

Paxton, B. (2018). *At home with grief: Continued bonds with the deceased.* New York: Routledge.

Plummer, K. (1995). *Telling sexual stories: Power, change and social worlds.* London: Routledge.

Plummer, K. (2001). *Documents of life 2: An invitation to a critical humanism.* London: Sage.

Plummer, K. (2022). Foreword: Transforming everyday gay life. In E. Rodríguez-Dorans, & E. Holmes (Eds.), *The everyday lives of gay men: Autoethnographies of the ordinary* (1st ed., pp. xii–xx). London: Routledge.

Rodríguez-Dorans, E. (2020). With our clipped wings: A research-based performance on gay men's identities devised through narrative portraiture. *Text and Performance Quarterly, 40*(2), 190–209.

Rodríguez-Dorans, E. (2021a) *Mi amigo Giovanni* [Video]. YouTube. Retrieved from https://www.youtube.com/watch?v=rd2Fm4Qo6z8&t=5837s

Rodríguez-Dorans, E. (2021b). Testing proximity and intimacy: An everyday reappropriation of private and public space. In E. Rodríguez-Dorans, & E. Holmes (Eds.), *The everyday lives of gay men: Autoethnographies of the ordinary.* London: Routledge.

Spry, T. (2016). *Body, Paper, Stage: Writing and Performing Autoethnography.* Walnut Creek: Taylor and Francis.

Waugh, M. (2017). My laptop is an extension of my memory and self: Post-internet identity, virtual intimacy and digital queering in online popular music. *Popular Music, 36*(2), 233–251.

Wolcott, H. (1973). *The man in the principal's office.* New York: Holt, Rinehart &Winston.

Yeboah, O. N. (2020). I know how it is when nobody sees you': Oral History performance methods for staging trauma. *Text and Performance Quarterly, 40*(2), 131–151.

SECTION III
Crafting Selves

5

THINKING WITH OUR HANDS WHILE BECOMING AUTOETHNOGRAPHERS

Rommy Anabalón Schaaf and Javiera Sandoval Limarí

Introduction

In this chapter, we discuss the creation of an audio-visual piece called *Through the Shadow of Our Mothers: Becoming Autoethnographers in Three Acts* that allowed us to reflect on our autoethnographic practices and on the different ways of thinking that were unlocked in our work by creating with our hands. To this end, we discuss the video clip we created and the three artefacts we produced for this video, which we called: *The Blanket*, *The Portrait*, and *Our Trees*. We describe the process of analysing our relationship with our mothers and how we connected our autoethnographic work with a feminist decolonial lens, in order to understand our positionality as Latinx artists and researchers.

When faced with the opportunity of presenting our work and our processes of becoming autoethnographers, we decided to create a video for the 2021 International Symposium on Autoethnography and Narrative (ISAN). In this video, we wanted to explore how our mothers became our shadows, constantly haunting us (Rhee, 2021) and how through the process of creating artefacts we (re)connect with them to understand ourselves and our research. This helped us not only to heal ourselves by talking with and about our mothers, but also, to engage with our academic work from a feminist decolonial perspective (Espinosa Miñoso, 2012; Lugones, 2010) which led us to understand analysis as an act of power and, following Curiel (2014), the need to examine ourselves in order to analyse others.

This chapter unfolds as follows: firstly, we describe the video, its origins, and our rationale for making it. Secondly, Javiera describes the process of crocheting *The Blanket* and what it meant for her in terms of thinking about her mother and the relationship this has with her research. Thirdly, Rommy explains how she started to draw, the complex relationship with her mother throughout her life,

DOI: 10.4324/9781003309239-9

and how she felt when she decided to draw her portrait for the video. Next, in the third act, we explain, through a dialogue, the process of thinking with our hands and how decolonial feminism became interwoven in our reflections and our research; reflections that happen around the image of *Our Trees*, an embroidered tree in the case of Javiera, and a drawing of a tree in the case of Rommy. Finally, we offer some comments on the process of creating the video and its aftermath.

The Video

The ISAN 2021 acceptance meant we needed to create a video the audience would look at before the actual presentation. Creating videos, recording our voices or images, was something that the virtuality of the world during a pandemic invited us all to do, as many activities, such as conferences and academic events were moved online. We thought about different ways of presenting ourselves and our work. We decided not to record ourselves talking, mainly because we felt embarrassed. Instead, we chose to invite the audience to our private sphere of creation, as we wanted to share three artefacts that we were making in order to think about ourselves and our research. The artefacts were created at different times, between 2019 and 2020: while Javiera's piece, *The Blanket*, was in the making since 2019, Rommy's piece, *The Portrait*, was motivated by the opportunity the ISAN presentation offered us and was created at the end of 2020. *The Trees*, the third artefact, was also created specifically for this symposium presentation, in 2020.

By the time we assembled the video we were living together, having many conversations about our research journeys and our artistic practices. Our house was full of art, with music, drawings, and crocheting/sewing happening every day. There was something in the process of creating artefacts with our hands that interested us. At the same time, we were both analysing our fieldwork data, as we were both doctoral students returning from months of data production and collection in Chile. The analysis was not very successful at the time, as we were rambling around various categories, codes, and nodes, which would not allow us to talk about our fieldwork experience with all the nuances it contained. We were reading about autoethnography, as it made sense to us to try to understand the data collected in fieldwork together with our own experiences as researchers. However, the possibility of talking about this at ISAN opened the door to connect our artistic practices with our personal reflections. We were both in the process of understanding how our mothers' ghosts were present in our research, and how their shadows were influencing our approach to analysing the data collected during fieldwork. We decided to look more closely at what was happening to us when we were crocheting/sewing and drawing, reflecting on the different insights about our data these creative acts were helping to unlock; how we were thinking about the stories of our fieldwork while we were creating art with our hands.

Each of the acts in the video was an invitation to think about our mothers, their shadows and ourselves, and how these conversations were informing the way we were making sense of the fieldwork data, by understanding and unveiling the lenses we were using to analyse it. In order to record our personal moments of creation, we had to be very aware of what our hands were doing, and the particularities of the time and space created to think with them. These moments were intimate, painful sometimes, mysterious at other times. We engaged in a dialogue with the shadows of our mothers through the artistic creation, dialogue that unfolded a different understanding of our data and of ourselves as researchers. By examining ourselves (Curiel, 2014), we acknowledged embodied experiences as a fundamental part of knowledge production and our journey of becoming autoethnographers.

Act 1: *The Blanket,* by Javiera

I started crocheting *The Blanket* (see Figure 5.1), because I felt empty. I was numbed after the passing of my mother, Maite. I was also speechless, as it was too sad to face the fact that I was living on a different continent for the last years of her life. *Tú decidiste irte, to leave her. For what? What has this country done for you? Besides taking the last days, months, years with her. Besides silencing your voice and replacing it with a whisper. Además de hacerte ver amarilla y pequeña y amarga.*

FIGURE 5.1 A fraction of *The Blanket.* Photograph by author

These ideas kept reverberating in my head. I needed to do something with my hands to calm my mind.

I chose crochet because she taught me how to do it when I was a young girl looking for media to express myself: discovering and expanding my hands' capabilities. I chose bright colours because they reminded me of the colours of the Andean textiles. I chose a circular pattern because it made me feel part of something infinite. I chose squares because I could start and finish one in one sitting. I chose weaving because I needed to create for myself a moment of time and a space to be fully present, to heal and recover.

My hands were moving back and forth, looping yarn, feeling its softness, passing it through. The repetitive movements of my hands created this space and time to reflect, to grieve, and to analyse. At that time, I was working on my PhD and had just returned from five months of fieldwork with a Haitian community in Santiago, Chile. In my original plans, I was going to spend all those months with mom as well, but she passed away weeks earlier. In the daytime, I was transcribing interviews, reading my notes, and playing with codes. In the evenings, I was weaving, moving my hands, with my body still, thinking about my mother, her disease, the last years, my youth with her, our craft. In the space and time that crocheting created, I started to find common threads between my fieldwork and my grief. I started to think about voice; how I felt silenced by my mourning; how Haitian children and families felt silenced as their language was not accepted in the school and other institutions in Chile; and how silence grew in my mother's mouth as Alzheimer's disease advanced. I was literally and symbolically weaving these different parts of my world and my research, finding new connections.

I was becoming an autoethnographer as I was embracing my mourning and interweaving it with my research, resisting the compartmentalisation of parts of myself, that is, the grieving daughter and the PhD student (Bochner, 1997; Hanauer, 2021). My hands were creating something from scratch, moving restlessly, allowing me to think differently, with my whole body. Honouring *The Blanket* as an art piece and the hands crocheting as a thinking process is a way to resist hegemonic Western ways of doing research, specifically, of doing analysis (Aguilar, 2017). I resist by acknowledging the space and time that the crocheting hands created, by thinking myself as part of a woven fabric, and by telling the stories of silence, of the mother who lost her tongue, and the children who lost their mother tongue. Through this practice, I also heal, acknowledging that there is space for healing in academia (Bochner & Ellis, 2016). *The Blanket* as an artefact, the video, and the reflective writings about this process created a continuous dialogue with the ghost of my mother and ways to remember her.

Visually, the first act of the video was an invitation to observe different moments in which the crocheting took place. Some of these moments were outside, in parks and in the woods, and some of them were inside, in my room and living room. I also played with sequences in the video, to recreate the feeling of repetition, as a key factor of the weaving practice. I invited the audience into my

FIGURE 5.2 Maite in her workshop. Photograph by author

intimacy, showing my hands as they crocheted and as I felt the softness of the yarn, my feet as I covered my body with the wool piece, which was becoming a blanket, to show the warmth it provided. Also, I shared with the audience a picture of my mother in her workshop (see Figure 5.2), where she was also creating with her hands. Sharing the intimate space where *The Blanket* was created was a way for me to show my vulnerability, as it was by connecting with the grieving vulnerable side of myself that I found a way to understand the data produced during fieldwork. The crocheting hands, the thinking hands, opened a space in which I could reflect on my story and the fieldwork stories in creative ways, making new connections that were not visible when analysing in a more conventional way. *The Blanket*, then, became method, a piece that is research and art.

Act 2: *The Portrait,* by Rommy

Reading, writing, and drawing are some of the things children learn to do at an early age. I enjoyed drawing, especially portraits, as a kid, but I stopped doing it when I entered university. I had to focus and put a great deal of effort in, in order to learn to read and write in a foreign language (English) and to use a register which was unknown to me, the academic one. I resumed drawing 20 years later in London when my PhD supervisor asked me to present a report of my first fieldwork trip (from March to July 2019) in Santiago, Chile. How could I present the data I had collected without spending days writing a report? I guess he felt my concern, and he asked me to draw a mind map: 'those with drawings and things that you like to do'. This sounded like a clever idea, but instead of a mind map,

I drew the portraits of the people I had interacted with so I could *observe* them more clearly. This was the first time I included drawings in my research process.

While in London, I had regular meetings with Javiera to discuss our research. It was a way to help each other think and make progress. We talked about our personal stories, our lives in Santiago, where we were born, our friends and our families. I knew her mother had passed away after a lengthy illness. This brought back memories about my own mother. I had stopped talking to her when I came to the United Kingdom to start my PhD four years previously, but she was still with me, sometimes haunting me, like a shadow. I imagined that, someday, I could draw a portrait of my mother to help me understand her, to make amends, but I was not ready yet.

When Javiera and I discussed the idea of presenting at ISAN 2021, and she told me about her blanket, I immediately thought about drawing the portrait of my mother (see Figure 5.3). It represented an opportunity for me to face

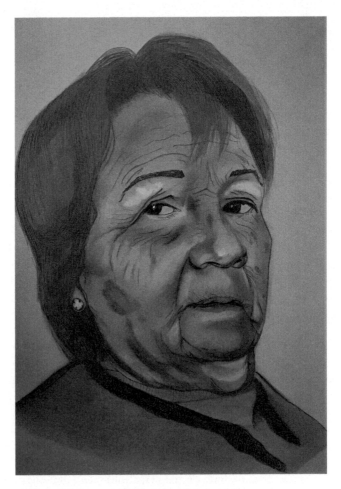

FIGURE 5.3 My mother's portrait. Photograph by author

her shadow. I spent around six hours drawing her portrait from a small, recent picture I had asked my brother to send me and recorded my hands while doing it. With every line on the paper, I reflected on some aspects of her personality and what I knew about her life story. She is, up to this day, when she is close to turning 80 years old, a difficult person to deal with; polite but not very friendly. She does not have friends or family to rely on and little by little her four children, including myself, stopped having any type of relationship with her. It was mentally damaging for all of us.

I usually start a portrait by drawing a silhouette of the face and then move on to the details of the eyes. My mum has hooded, droopy eyes. I always thought this was a sign of sadness, perhaps due to a life marked by poverty, the abandonment of her parents, and the impossibility of being a child because she had to act like an adult to take care of herself. I am the last of the four children, the only girl, and she raised me to become a 'good' woman and to do the things she could not do: to study, to be independent, and to see the world. My two eldest brothers had already left home when I was a kid and the one who was a year older than me used to spend his time helping my father, a car mechanic, in the car repair shop. I grew up listening to my mother's stories of frustration. How we had to live day-to-day. Of how bad and violent my father was. How miserable her life had been. And all of this while helping her with the dishes, removing debris from lentils, mending socks, ironing the blankets, polishing the old furniture, mopping, waxing and polishing the floor, hand washing clothes and listening to enforcing injunctions: 'dress like a lady', 'sit like a lady', 'eat like a lady', 'talk like a lady', 'a lady doesn't swear', 'a lady doesn't smoke', especially when I dared to do any of the things that my brothers used to do. She obliged me to take extra-curricular sewing and embroidery classes, cooking and drawing lessons at school but, at the same time, she always insisted that I had to study hard to one day have a professional career and not have to depend on a man.

As I was drawing her big nose, I thought about how strict, rigorous, and controlling she was. She was enormously proud of her (poor) German ancestors which meant she developed a sense of superiority over other people around her, because they had either darker skin or because they were poor. And she did not allow me to play or chat with kids who did not meet her standards. As a result, I was a very lonely girl. I think she did it, again, because she wanted me to follow a particular path in life, the one she wanted for herself. She did not have the chance to study. In fact, she left school when she was around 12 years old and started working as a maid. Only a couple of years later, she started a relationship with my father looking for the love and stability she never had and ended up pregnant with their eldest child when she was only 17. It was the early 1960s and she married him because it was the only way her own Catholic mother would accept her with a child.

Her face is now full of wrinkles and sunspots. The same sunspots that I am developing now in my early 40s. Her ears are small and she has never stopped wearing those gold and pearl earrings. They were for her a sign of femininity in the same way she considered certain clothes, ways of speaking and behaving, ways of *being*, to be. She bought me the same pair of earrings for my 15th birthday. I never wore them. I hated them because they represented a specific image of womanhood to which I did not want to align myself, I did not want to become her.

When I finally finished drawing her portrait, I spent some minutes looking at it. I wondered if I had been too harsh on her. She wanted to live vicariously through me, and I tried to resist, but I cannot blame her now. What were her choices? However, it is interesting for me that, considering my mother's story, I decided to take care of others. I became a teacher, and I consider myself to be a very loving person, something my mother was not. I treat all my students with love and respect, and I try to infuse this way of being in future teachers and colleagues even when I am aware that these traits are part of the emotional labour that women have been historically required to perform and which has become commodified in the job market, to the point that not only women can capitalise on them, but also men.

I watched the video of my hands drawing the portrait several times, not partly because I needed to reduce it to a couple of minutes to insert it into our presentation for ISAN, but also because I found the process fascinating. It was a meta-reflection, a reflection about the process of reflection while drawing, equivalent perhaps to the process of making sense of how others make sense of the world.

Act 3: *Our Trees*

In the video, we wanted to talk about our positionalities as artists and researchers, beyond the specificities of *The Blanket* and *The Portrait*. To this end, we decided to create two trees. This was motivated by the metaphor of a tree and a forest when thinking about the researcher and the researched (see for example Heller, Pietikäinen, & Pujolar, 2018). In line with our crafts, Javiera's tree (see Figure 5.4) was made using a freestyle sewing machine foot, which allowed her to move the fabric freely to create a design on it, with one continuous line. Rommy drew a tree with her face on the trunk, surrounded by other trees (see Figure 5.5).

What follows is a conversation that was motivated by the question of what the creation of the trees allowed us to see, how we connected our work with a feminist decolonial approach, and how we became Latinx researchers/artists in the process of thinking with our hands:

JAVIERA: When I think about my tree, I think about my fieldwork and all the contradictory feelings I had when starting to analyse those experiences. When was your fieldwork?

ROMMY: From March to July 2019.

JAVIERA: Mine too …. I spent all those months in and out of a school and visiting families in an impoverished community in Santiago. The school was in a *población* …. How would you explain a *población*, Rommy?

FIGURE 5.4 Javiera's tree. Photograph by author

ROMMY: Poor urban neighbourhoods?

JAVIERA: It resonated in me what Curiel (2013) critiques about doing research in modern/colonial terms, trying to explain to the Global North the experiences of racialised and subaltern communities. In a way, that is what I was doing.

ROMMY: In a way … however that is where the reflective task starts. To analyse these experiences is to exercise power, as we were deciding how these lived experiences would be told and with which lens they would be understood, and I think that in the unveiling of that lens is where the decolonial feminist

FIGURE 5.5 Rommy's tree. Photograph by author

framework connects with our use of autoethnography. It's kind of similar to what Curiel (2014) proposes about *doing ethnographies of ourselves*, to understand where we are standing in the interweaving of power, how we are producing knowledge by reproducing our privileges.

JAVIERA: Maybe by showing our vulnerability, as Behar (1996) proposes, we can start unveiling the lens, and that is what we did with *The Blanket* and *The Portrait*. But also, we had to decide how we were going to write about the communities where we did our research and the people who helped us. I remember that while I was analysing the fieldwork data, I was writing about going to a church, to a Haitian evangelical service. Every attempt looked like a caricature of an exotic culture because I was trying to explain them, the exotic racialised 'other'. I thought about Miner (1956) and his description of the Nacirema, presenting Americans as an exotic culture. I was trying to explain to a Western audience the daily faith of a racialised community from the Global South. I desisted and instead I decided to reflect and write about myself in the service, how I embraced being in a religious celebration, joining the joy of the parishioners and how I decided to talk to my mother in the service, as it was in her funeral the last time I went to a church. In the writing I described our conversations and how I felt connection and support from a community that welcomed me, the other, in their sacred practice. I think that moment was the first time that I really connected my mom's shadow with my research. How was it for you Rommy? How has your mom helped you to unveil your analytic lens?

ROMMY: For me, every line on the paper allowed me to reflect on my mother's life story. How she grew up, what she experienced as a woman in different socio-historical conditions, how she learnt to become a woman and how she taught me to be a woman. It was kind of zooming out and going beyond the relationship we had through the years. I hadn't thought about this before, I mean, the way our mothers played a role in the experience of 'being women'. These reflections helped me to consider my own position as a researcher and the lenses I used to interpret my participants' actions and the relationship we built together. My participants, female teachers, had been my students, then they became my colleagues and many of them became my friends. We all shared low socio-economic backgrounds and we were upgraded, at least nominally, by society, as we became university teachers. We are women who seem to have 'made it' because we invested in the promise of education but who still navigate uncertainty, a permanent feeling of crisis and violence in different forms, like my mother and their mothers before us. For me, this was also important because it implied a healing process: I understood my mother, forgave her, and let her go. So yes, that is the portrait. What about the tree that you sewed? What do you think it allowed you to reflect upon?

JAVIERA: To sew my tree was an exercise of finding order in chaos, as although when you look at it, it gives the impression of being a mess of different lines and stitches, it is just one continuous line. And that is how I felt: one continuous history and not a fragmented self. Autoethnography and the feminist decolonial framework allowed me to see myself with all my parts, and to acknowledge and honour all my sides. During the reflections that I had while creating my tree, I saw myself as artist and researcher, as both practices informed one another, in the same spirit that my history informed the social practices I was analysing. At the same time, the feminist decolonial framework and the work of Segato (2013) allowed me to see myself as Latinx in my *mestizaje*, with the many contradictions the concept has. However, as a concept that allowed me to position myself in the interweaving of power, with a story that ties me to my landscapes, in the Global South.

ROMMY: Well, it is similar to my case: my tree is about reflecting on the connections with my participants, the experiences we share and the experiences that are different for us. I decided to draw a tree which does not stand by itself; it is part of a forest. My face comes out of the trunk so that I can show how I am looking from my position as a woman, my experience as a female researcher, the lives of others represented by the other trees in the forest. As you said, it made me think about power, I mean, I was not even thinking about that when I was drawing, but once I had done it and looked at it, I thought about my position in the centre of the drawing, looking at some trees and turning my back to others. Our knowledge is always limited, and we cannot just assume that ways we think about the world, or the way we inhabit the world, are universal. As Curiel (2014) says, for example, postcolonial feminisms do not help us to account for the particularities of Latin American women. Another important aspect for me was to acknowledge the fact that I am doing research from the North about the South, even when I am positioning myself as a Latinx woman, I am still operating under the logics of the coloniality of knowledge (Lander, 2000) and that again, it is an act of power.

The trees in this third act are a metaphor of our positioning. They were part of an exercise to reflect upon it, to discuss how we stand as women, researchers from the South in the North, Latinxs and artists from a decolonial feminist perspective that allows us to look into ourselves first, to then tell stories of racialised, gendered, and classed bodies.

Final Thoughts

In this chapter, we wanted to reflect on the thought process that our hands unlocked when creating 'art in conversation' with and about our mothers; how the art pieces allowed us to do autoethnography; how through the video we shared our intimate spaces with the audiences, as another layer of our autoethnographic becoming; and how our making of autoethnography meant positioning ourselves as Latinx artists and researchers via a feminist decolonial perspective.

The knowledge we produced with our hands, whether crocheting, sewing, or drawing, created a time and a space to reflect. During these reflections, we reached conclusions that were not visible when engaging with our ethnographic data via a more traditional analytic perspective. It was through thinking, while our hands were moving, that we connected our stories and the ghosts/shadows of our mothers, with our academic work. We understand this thinking with our hands as ways of *becoming autoethnographers* through a feminist decolonial lens. We examined ourselves and our stories not only to understand the social, but also to understand our positionality in the interweaving of power. We reflected on the tensions of researching with gendered, racialised, and impoverished communities from the Global South and interpreting them, explaining them, and (re)presenting them in the Global North. By doing that, and by acknowledging the role of the shadows of our mothers, we attempted to unveil the lens used to analyse the data produced in fieldwork, as a way of challenging the power imbalance that occurs in academic research.

References

Aguilar, V. (2017). Entretejiéndonos por la vida en resistencia y rebeldía. In C. Walsh (Ed.), *Pedagogías decoloniales. prácticas insurgentes de resistir, (re)existir y (re)vivir. Tomo II.* Quito: Ediciones Abya-Yala.

Behar, R. (1996). *The vulnerable observer: Anthropology that breaks your heart.* Boston: Beacon Press.

Bochner, A. P. (1997). It's about time: Narrative and the divided self. *Qualitative Inquiry, 3*(4), 418–438.

Bochner, A. P., & Ellis, C. (2016). *Evocative autoethnography: Writing lives and telling stories.* New York: Routledge.

Curiel, O. (2013). *La Nación Heterosexual.* Bogotá: Brecha Lésbica y en la frontera.

Curiel, O. (2014). Construyendo metodologías feministas desde el feminismo decolonial. In I. Mendia Azkue et al. (Eds.), *Otras formas de (re)conocer. Reflexiones herramientas y aplicaciones desde la investigación feminista.* Bilbao: UPV/EHU.

Espinosa Miñoso, Y. (2012). De por qué es necesario un feminismo descolonial: diferenciación, dominación co-constitutiva de la modernidad occidental y el fin de la política de identidad. *Solar, 12*(1), 141–171.

Hanauer, D. I. (2021). Mourning writing: A poetic autoethnography on the passing of my father. *Qualitative Inquiry, 27*(1), 37–44.

Heller, M., Pietikäinen, S., & Pujolar, J. (2018). *Critical sociolinguistic research methods: Studying language issues that matter.* New York: Routledge.

Lander, E. (2000). Ciencias sociales: saberes coloniales y eurocéntricos. In E. Lander (Ed.), *La colonialidad del saber: eurocentrismo y ciencias sociales. Perspectivas latinoamericanas* (pp. 11–40). Buenos Aires: CLACSO.

Lugones, M. (2010). Toward a decolonial feminism. *Hypatia, 25*(4), 742–759.

Miner, H. (1956). Body ritual among the Nacirema. *American Anthropologist, 58*(3), 503–507.

Rhee, J. (2021). *Decolonial feminist research: Haunting, rememory and mothers.* New York: Routledge.

Segato, R. (2013). *La crítica de la colonialidad en ocho ensayos y una antropología por demanda.* Ciudad Autónoma de Buenos Aires: Prometeo Libros.

6

PUTTING OURSELVES IN THE PICTURE

An Autoethnographic Approach to Photography Criticism

Simon Denison

Introduction

It is a commonplace of contemporary thought that all work of critical interpretation is influenced by historical and cultural context and by the researcher's
perspective; that researchers are *present* in the interpretations they produce. In
autoethnography, the idea that our personal commitments, values, beliefs and life
experiences necessarily colour how we make sense of the world is fundamental to
how research is conceived (Bochner & Ellis, 2016). Many disciplines, especially
in the social sciences, take account of the presence of the researcher and have
incorporated the practice of reflexivity – a turning back on oneself, a conscious
self-awareness – as an essential component of research to provide a degree of
transparency about the context of origin, limitations and partiality of any given
interpretation (Dean, 2017).

The reflexivity inherent in autoethnography, however, is not equally well
established in all fields of critical interpretation. Writing as a teacher of critical
studies in arts-based UK higher education and a practising photography critic, I
have become increasingly aware of the dearth of reflexivity within photography
criticism – my own included. There are exceptions, of course, including a few
well-known examples (of which more below). I look out for them, collect them.
But generally, it seems to me, reflexivity plays a small role in this field. It is rarely
practised or discussed. I find this absence intriguing and provocative.

This chapter describes the experimental approach I have taken in making
research forays into this somewhat uncharted terrain. In order to include more
reflexivity within my own writing in a systematic way, I have developed a
self-reflexive analytic protocol which details the steps to follow when I engage
reflexively with images. The protocol is 'self-reflexive' because it addresses the
autobiographical factors that underpin meaning–making, such as emotions,

DOI: 10.4324/9781003309239-10

memories and values; seeking to uncover what Pels has described as the 'much-neglected … psychobiography of knowledge' (2000, p. 21). The protocol is discussed below, along with some of the ancillary methods I use as I work through the steps of the process. The chapter closes with an account of my self-reflexive reading of one particular photograph, to give an indication of how the process works and the effect the protocol can have on interpretation.

Why does it matter? Why should we want more self-reflexivity in photography criticism? Besides the general rationale of providing transparency about the basis of the critic's judgements, my interest is in exploring how 'putting one's self in the picture' can open up new ways of thinking about photographs and ourselves. The process discussed in this chapter was designed with that end in mind. Drawing from a long history of learning theory that addresses the effect of critical self-reflection on 'transforming' our understanding of the world (for example Brookfield, 2017; Dewey, 1910; Mezirow, 1991), I see self-reflexivity as a process capable of delivering enriched or extended interpretations of pictures, and insights into our habitual thinking processes and our emotional responses to artworks. For me, self-reflexivity is not a descriptive but an exploratory and critical process. By roving around our tacit landscapes of memory, values and emotions, and reflecting on the various influences that may lie behind our responses to photographs, self-reflexivity provides a way of releasing insights that might otherwise remain buried and making connections that might otherwise remain unmade. It can reveal to us aspects of our presuppositions and values – our unconscious or conscious biases and commitments – which, on reflection, we might prefer to distance ourselves from or modify. Self-reflexivity can thus potentially lead to fresh ways of thinking about pictures, ourselves and our relation to the world.

A practical consequence of engaging in the self-reflexive process outlined here is that we critics might start to produce a more authentic type of critical writing, one that manifestly springs from the writer's unique pattern of life experiences and responses to those experiences. Self-reflexivity is a slow process: it forces us to take our time, stop and think, and consider what we really think and feel, and why. It serves to prevent us from slipping immediately into the dominant patterns of thinking of our disciplinary culture or peer group and instead forces us to seek out the ways in which our responses to photographs are – as they must be – at the final reckoning uniquely our own.

Reflexivity and Photography Criticism

The claim that reflexivity is rarely practised in photography criticism may at first glance seem surprising. After all, it has long been understood that critics produce interpretations in terms of their own culturally situated perspective. For several decades, scholars have recognised that the meanings of images are not fixed and singular, capable of disclosure as objective truths, but are multiple and unstable, dependent on the viewer's prior knowledge, expectations and value perspective, and the contexts in which the work is seen (Clarke, 1997; Sturken & Cartwright, 2001; Wells, 2009). An image may be coded by image makers with an intended meaning and implicit ideological/value position, but a critic is expected to engage actively with its intended messaging as a critical 'reader' (Barthes, 1977b; Hall, 1993). And this is something that photography writers undoubtedly do, often with great panache and incisive critical insight.

Responding from one's own critical perspective, however, is not the same as being reflexive, which requires the additional step of self-examination and explicit disclosure of the assumptions and values that underlie our position (Dean, 2017). It seems evident that reflexivity in this sense is rarely found in writing about photography. As a critic, I am aware that reflexivity is neither requested nor expected by editors, and until recently it has played as small a role in my own writing as in the writing of others. In the theoretical literature of photography and visual culture, reflexivity is rarely discussed as a critical methodology. When the word 'reflexivity' appears, it typically refers not to critical practice, but to a form of *creative* practice in which a medium such as photography is used to comment on itself, either as a modernist or postmodernist trope (see for example the glossary of terms in Sturken & Cartwright, 2001, p. 364).

There are exceptions: reflexive writing does exist in photography, even if the term 'reflexivity' is not used. The best known example is perhaps Barthes' last book *Camera Lucida* (1982), a celebrated text in which photography theory is developed on the basis of a narrative of personal loss. Spence's pioneering photography-based autoethnography, *Putting Myself in the Picture* (1986), serves as a reference point for the title of this chapter. Other examples exist where writers have taken an autobiographical approach to writing about photography (for example Campt, 2012; Chandler, 2007). However, these appear to be rarities.

Rose's highly respected textbook *Visual Methodologies* (2012) is unusual in visual culture writing in strongly advocating the use of reflexivity in what she calls a 'critical visual methodology'. However, she notes that reflexivity is rarely used in critical writing in practice. Elsewhere, she claims that critics tend to keep themselves 'invisible', preferring a 'distanced analytical stand' to the recognition that they are 'essentially entangled in what they are studying' (2011, p. 547). The consequence is that:

> … [v]isual culture critics tend to write as if their judgement was self-evident, the only one possible, as if their account of a visual work is a process of description or revelation rather than construction. It isn't, of course, as I'm sure if directly asked they would readily admit ….
>
> *2011, p. 551*

Rose thus describes what I have observed myself: in spite of understanding in theory that meaning is perspective-dependent, photography writers in practice tend to adopt an illusory posture of critical detachment.

So why do critics not write reflexively? Why is reflexivity not demanded by editors? A large part of it, I suspect, comes down to the desire among photography/art writers for their work to be taken seriously, in an intellectual environment in which research based on personal narratives still 'has a hard time being accepted as legitimate inside the academy' (Brookfield, 2017, p. 69). Moreover, reflexivity risks undermining 'the "authority effect" in critical writing', as Miller observed over thirty years ago (1991, p. 7), by explicitly disclosing the partiality, the flaws, the very humanness of the researcher. For many critics, it must seem like a risk not worth taking.

Professional writers also recognise that self-focused writing can often appear both uninformed and uninformative, as well as naive, tedious and ridiculous. Williams, for example, in her guide to writing about art, describes 'virgin art-writing' as over-personal and anecdotal, using the artwork merely as a prompt for heady descriptions of personal feelings and reminiscence: 'The novice instantly forgets about the art, and lets memory take him … somewhere else …' (2014, p. 44). Critics have rightly been reluctant to fall into those sorts of traps. However, the risk of producing feeble, self-focused writing has long been recognised within the reflexivity literature. Several writers have stressed the importance of avoiding narcissism by keeping primarily focused on the research materials rather than oneself, and using self-referencing at a minimal level, only where elucidation is required (Finlay, 2002; Pels, 2000). In autoethnographic terms, this would equate to taking the 'analytic' approach of marshalling personal evidence not merely for its own intrinsic interest but also in the service of a larger argument about society and culture (Anderson, 2006). By exercising strict discipline over self-disclosure, the researcher allows reflexivity to work its magic. My own approach to using reflexivity in photography criticism pays close attention to these warnings, as will be discussed below.

A Self-Reflexive Analytic Protocol

My approach centres around a self-reflexive analytic protocol that lays out a series of steps to go through while thinking about a photograph or body of work in preparation for writing a critical review. The protocol serves a number of purposes: to direct the critic's attention towards particular 'sites' of reflexivity that seem useful for revealing the basis of our thinking; to provide a before-and-after framework to allow any interpretive changes arising from reflexivity to be detected; and to help focus the critic's mind on the photograph rather than themselves to minimise the risk of self-indulgence. All these matters will be discussed below.

The protocol serves as a vehicle for guided self-examination to help us notice and then reflect on the impulses, preferences, beliefs, values and commitments that may underpin our response to the photograph under review. The protocol does not in itself produce the finished piece of critical writing. To avoid self-indulgence, any writing for publication would use reflections generated by the protocol selectively, to give an indication only of the review's epistemological point of origin.

The protocol consists of eight steps, which can be summarised as follows, with thinking prompts:

1. Basic facts and context
    What are the basic facts about the photograph (who, what, where, when) and its context of production?
2. Intended meaning
    What do you take to be the photographer's intention, or intended meaning? (This might be deduced from context or visual rhetoric.)
3. Initial critical reading, without explicit reflexivity
    How do you read the photograph's connotations, its implicit values? Do you find yourself 'with' the image or 'against' it?
4. Reflexive analysis I: emotional response
    What is your emotional, visceral reaction to the photograph? How does it affect you?
5. Reflexive analysis II: memory and life history
    What events or experiences from your past, either distant or recent, help explain your critical and emotional response to the photograph?
6. Reflexive analysis III: worldview
    Which of your personal commitments, values and beliefs help explain your critical and emotional response to the photograph? On reflection, are you comfortable with this worldview or do you detect any tensions?
7. Reflexive analysis IV: emotional context of the viewing moment
    What are your general circumstances right now? How are you feeling, and how might that be influencing your response?
8. General reflections
    Following reflexive self-analysis, do you see the photograph, yourself or your relation to the world any differently?

The first three steps correspond to a 'standard' process of critical interpretation in photography, as I have long practised it. Step 1 provides an essential factual basis for analysis, ensuring that the critic understands, as far as possible, what an image *is*, in terms of its origin and function, and what it is *of*, among other matters, before any interpretation begins. Step 2 recognises that most images are intentional objects, made with an explicit or implicit intention by an image maker. At this stage, the critic reads the 'rhetoric' of the image, how it seeks to address us persuasively, by means of visual language and connotations, from a particular ideological point of view (Barthes, 1977a; Burgin, 1982). Step 3 provides a critical response to the image's rhetoric and its implicit values/ideology, from the critic's perspective but without explicit reflexivity. At this stage, the critic's response can take one of three forms. It can be a 'preferred' reading, which accepts and admires the image's rhetorical position and aesthetic effect;

an 'oppositional' reading which rejects the image's implicit messaging; or a 'negotiated' reading which lies somewhere between the two extremes (Hall, 1993). Mainstream critical writing typically stops at this point.

Starting with a standard critical reading in this way provides a control against which the impact of subsequent critical self-reflection can be gauged. At the end of the process, Step 8 calls for reflection and rethinking. Thus, a before-and-after measure is built into the design, as a way of teasing out any shifts of understanding that may have occurred. The first three steps were also designed to prevent an overly subjective response. By requiring the researcher to focus closely on the image and respond critically to it before engaging in self-reflection, the protocol averts the risk of using the image simply as a prompt to write about our feelings and memories. Users of the protocol are guided, in subsequent reflexive steps (Steps 4–7), to reflect on the personal reasons for why they had responded initially as they did, returning again to the image, and a possible rethinking, at the end (Step 8). The protocol thus helps ensure that reflexivity is used as it is *meant* to be used in interpretive research: to provide a metacognitive account, as Dean has written, of 'the means by which [researchers] arrive at a particular "reading" of data' (2017, p. 111).

Moving on to the reflexive steps: Step 4 draws attention to the researcher's emotional response to the image. Emotional responses were largely marginalised from mainstream critical analysis following the 'cultural turn' of the 1980s (Brown & Phu, 2014). Disclosure of feelings, like other forms of personal reminiscence, came to be seen as a sign of naivety; and over recent years, critics have tended to keep their feelings out of print. Neglect of emotion has not been confined, either, to art criticism: even within reflexive research in social science, according to Holmes (2010), the significance of emotion has generally been underplayed. However, scholars are increasingly recognising the influence of feelings on interpretation. '[F]eeling intervenes in the relationship between photographic signifier and signified', as Smith has written (2014, p. 31). Thinking, in other words, is embodied, driven by values which are sustained by personal experiences and feelings. At the same time, emotions are themselves cognitive and evaluative. Emotions are *about* something, as Sayer (2005) has observed. They are often 'influenced by past experiences' and serve as commentaries on the present. 'By taking them seriously we might be able to appreciate hitherto unnoticed things and assess what they tell us is happening to us' (Sayer, 2005, p. 37). The focus on emotional response at this point in the protocol is intended to generate a set of leads or pathways that can give us access to the tacit underpinnings of our thinking in the steps that follow.

The next two steps address worldview and its grounding in personal experience. The uncovering of a researcher's worldview or perspective lies at the heart of any self-reflexive project; and the protocol draws attention separately to memories (Step 5) and values/beliefs (Step 6) to explore the distinction between what we think we believe in and care about (values/beliefs), and memories/past experiences that may lie at the root of how we think and feel but may not have been consciously processed. Sometimes tensions are revealed between Steps 5 and 6 which can open up a space for critical self-adjustment. The linking of worldview to past life experiences draws from the work of a number of scholars. Bourdieu (1984, 1993), in his concept of 'habitus', has argued that upbringing, social positioning and life experiences produce a set of lasting dispositions that influence how we act and think. Sayer (2005), building on Bourdieu, emphasises our capacity to actively construct and *reconstruct* our worldview by taking a self-critical approach to our dispositions through the process of life-long 'internal conversations', which can lead us to diverge from the dominant views and interests of our social group. Sayer's account echoes Bakhtin's (1981 [1934]) idea that personal worldview or 'voice' evolves over a lifetime of continuous, dialectical engagement through 'inner monologue' with the changing conditions of our existence and the received ideas of culture. Following these writers, the protocol was designed on the assumption that the worldview that frames our interpretation of a photograph is not only constructed in response to the conditions of our life but can also be reconstructed following an act of critical self-reflection.

Step 7 focuses on the emotional context of the viewing moment. Context is a commonplace of mainstream critical practice within visual culture. Contexts as varied as historical, technological, social and cultural are reviewed as a matter of course, both at the macro level (for example, the cultural norms and expectations within which a work can be understood) and the local (such as where an image is seen, or juxtapositions between an image and associated texts or other images). However, just as emotional responses are generally downplayed in criticism, so too is the subsidiary category of the viewer's emotional or psychic context at the moment of the viewing encounter. A number of scholars working in contemporary affect theory, however, have suggested that our responses to the world are produced within a complex, ever-changing assemblage of subtle, fleeting factors, what Deleuze and Guattari (1987, p. 304ff) call the 'haecceity' of the moment (see also Gregg & Seigworth, 2010). The protocol was designed to tap into this 'haecceity' by considering the influence of such factors as mood, health, desires, anxieties, mental preoccupations and the ambient conditions (such as weather, time of day, whether one is alone or in company and so forth) at the moment of viewing the photograph. Matters such as these are rarely mentioned in mainstream criticism. By addressing them, the protocol allows us to explore the nature and extent of such subtle, transient influences on how we think.

Step 8 asks for general reflections, as a prompt for teasing out any rethinking that might have been brought about by the reflexive process. If the intention of introducing reflexivity in criticism is to engender forms of authentic rethinking of images – as well as of oneself and one's relation to the world – this step was included to focus the researcher's attention on bringing it to fruition.

This, then, is the protocol I use in my self-reflexive approach to photography criticism. How do I actually go about using it? My practice draws a little from the autoethnographic method proposed by Chang (2016), involving self-observation and self-reflection: observing what I see, what my responses are, and in what contextual circumstances, and reflecting on each element of the process. The key point is that I take my time; I engage in a slow form of research, moving patiently through the steps, devoting enough time to allow the retrieval of tacit knowledge, and any rethinking of my responses that might follow. It sometimes takes me the best part of a day to work through the protocol, and I always find it productive to revisit an image or body of work two or three times, leaving gaps of a week or longer – the longer the better – between readings.

To record my observations and reflections, I use an adapted form of the 'double-entry book-keeping' method of reflective note-taking described by Moon (2006), which allows reflections to be recorded in an iterative process over time. I find it helpful to use the tabular format of a spreadsheet to record my reflections, because it enables multiple cycles of reflection on the same image to be recorded within a structure that is visually clear (see Figure 6.1). The steps of the protocol are listed in the columns, and each cycle of reflections is recorded in the rows, with later reflections recorded directly underneath earlier reflections at any given step of the process. As each data-entry box within a spreadsheet is infinitely expandable, there is no limit to how much can be written at any point while maintaining the integrity of the tabular structure. In the second or

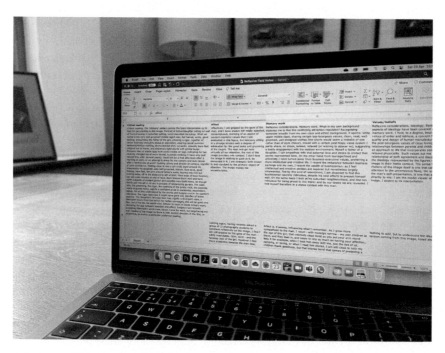

FIGURE 6.1 Using a spreadsheet to note reflexive responses to an image over time, following the steps of the self-reflexive analytic protocol in the columns, and with return visits to the image recorded in different rows. Photograph by author

any subsequent cycle of reflections, I find that I am often reflecting not only on the image but also on my previous reflections. Sometimes in a later reflection, I counter an earlier reflection or modify it, but normally there is something new to add: a new insight, a new observation. What seems clear from undertaking this process is that interpretations are never fixed and complete after one encounter. The longer and more frequently I look, the more I see.

Self-Reflexive Criticism in Practice

How, then, does the protocol work in practice? Let me give, as an example, an account of my self-reflexive analysis of a photograph that I have known and admired for years: the American photographer Joel Sternfeld's (2003 [1987]) 'Canyon Country, California, June 1983', from his book *American Prospects*.[1] It is a picture that I thought I knew well and have lectured about; one on which my interpretation seemed relatively set (or so I thought). Self-reflexive analysis, however, brought me to a different view.

The photograph is an outdoor portrait of what appear to be a white, middle-class father and daughter sitting on a low breeze-block wall in front of their home. The setting is suburban, at the edge of a town. The wide street on which they live snakes off into the distance behind them, with open hill-country visible beyond. The father is middle-aged, perhaps in his early 40s. He is well-groomed, with immaculately combed blond hair, in a cleanly laundered short-sleeved shirt and shorts, and with bare feet. He is good-looking, with a sportsman's physique, and he is smoking a cigar, signifier of a chief-executive persona – or of someone who aspires to that identity. He looks directly at the camera with calm self-assurance. Sitting next to him on the wall, to the left of the picture, is (presumably) his daughter aged around ten. She is blonde, also well-groomed and with bare feet. He has his arm around her, and she leans into him. She, however, does not look at the camera but looks off-frame to the left with an air of distraction.

As I have thought about this picture over the years, without explicit self-reflexivity, I have read it as belonging to a tradition of critically observant American road-trip photography – the original of the genre being Walker Evans's (2012 [1938]) *American Photographs* of 1938, to which Sternfeld's book undoubtedly pays homage in its title. What critics have come to expect from the genre is a set of observations of the strange within the familiar, examples of oddness, and small contradictory glitches that work to undermine the smooth surface of contemporary culture. This picture has long seemed to me to conform to that tradition.

The calm look, the grooming, the cigar, the clutching of the pretty child, the home location, all appear to signify a confident pride in identity, possession, status. And yet the glitch here, the loose thread that threatens to unravel the entire tapestry of the man's assurance – something we can see about him but he cannot – is that his shorts are obscenely tight, revealing a grotesque 'moose knuckle' genital bulge, turning him from an admirable-looking figure into a laughing stock.

At the same time, his daughter's faraway look carries a hint of foreboding. One can imagine the back-story: the photographer asks if he can take a picture. He, aware of his good fortune, good looks and beautiful family, says: sure, do you want to include my daughter in the picture? But she does not participate in his strategy of self-presentation, suggesting she cannot be fully controlled; and one day she will be gone, out of his life, his worldview. Moreover, his cigar appears to have gone out; a metaphor, perhaps, for impotence and failure. And he seems not to have noticed.

Thus, we can see of this confident man, who seems to stand as a metonym for the American business class, even for our late-capitalist system itself, that his position is vulnerable. Confidence appears as a form of wishful thinking, hiding common human frailty and foolishness underneath. The image reminds me of much of the work of the American portrait photographer Diane Arbus, from the generation preceding Sternfeld, who aimed to reveal in her pictures what she called 'the gap between intention and effect' (Phillips, 2003, p. 57), the gap between how people wish to present themselves and how they actually appear to others. I suspect, in my initial pre-reflexive reading, that Sternfeld saw all this, or something like this, and included the picture in his book accordingly. The image appears to interpellate me to think this way. Its visual rhetoric is dry, sardonic, wryly amused. I imagine I am giving a preferred reading to the image. I assent to what I believe I am being shown.

As I engage in reflexive self-analysis, however, and attempt to unpick the basis for my reactions, my thinking not only becomes clearer to me but I also start to question myself, and my interpretation begins to shift. Why have I always been so ready to find this man secretly ridiculous, so delighted by my observation that 'his cigar has gone out'?

Thinking about my feelings, I note that my reaction is more than simply oppositional. I feel a tension between attraction and repulsion. As I look at this figure, I recognise someone broadly from my own class and ethnic background. I too was born into a white (Anglo-Scottish) middle-class family with business people on both sides of the tree. I am attracted to the good looks and grooming of this couple, and I share some of their late-bourgeois, post-hippy values: clean, neat, well ordered, yet with shoes and socks thrown off in the summer, a certain relaxed physicality, and a close and loving, tactile relationship between parent and child. And yet, drawing on a different reflexive strand, working with memory, thinking about the worldview that I have constructed over a lifetime, I recognise that since teenagerhood and university I have distanced myself from corporate values, preferring to self-identify with a more creative and intellectual life. In my career, I have worked as a writer and magazine editor within the field of archaeology, an art photographer, photography critic, academic and teacher. Many of the people I knew and liked at school or university chose corporate careers, either in business or the professions. Like most self-identifying intellectuals, I regard the path I have chosen as somehow more interesting and valuable; and yet, in my various lines of work, I have never earned much, and

I resent the vast gap between business earnings and my own. So I begin to see that my interpretation of this picture has been influenced by the identity struggle of my life. My wanting to find Sternfeld's businessman ridiculous arises out of a mix of snobbery and resentment. But recognising him as someone I might easily have once known and loved, I start to feel less quick to ridicule, and my sense of empathy with him as a complete human starts to grow.

This evolution of my thinking continues as I think about the daughter. I myself am the father of a dearly loved son and daughter, both of them older than the girl in the picture; one has recently left home as a young adult, the other is nearing the same point. Like many parents, I worry about this wrenching change in our lives. During the period I was thinking reflexively about the image, I discussed it with a group of my students. To my astonishment, none of them picked up on the capitalist and social-identity discourses that the picture had put into play for me. Rather, every one of them identified with the child, seeing her as the victim of a harsh and controlling parental relationship. Some spoke of the man's 'forceful grip'. This struck me as a misperception, an unfair accusation. I see a loving relationship, a gentleness in the way he is holding her. She is leaning in. I remember holding my own children this way when they were younger. The result of this conversation was a rush of empathy for the male figure *as a father*, which made me realise how much I now, in my mid-50s, self-identify as a father rather than as the teenager and young man I once was. Now, instead of a kind of *schadenfreude* that this businessman's daughter will soon leave him, I start to feel sympathy, even pity. A whole new set of discourses around parenting and the pathos inherent in the parent–child relationship opens up for me. I even start to sympathise with him for his wardrobe failure, realising that we are all prone to accidentally making fools of ourselves. It could happen to any of us.

Reflecting on the overall impact of engaging in reflexive interpretation, the process seems to have greatly opened up my appreciation of this image as a richly affective and complex, ambiguous visual text. I now feel I have a much better understanding of my own thinking processes, and of some of the background triggers that led to my initial interpretation. I do not entirely reject my original reading. I still see the image as evoking the shallowness of capitalist self-confidence and the tensions that can exist within forms of self-presentation, but that reading has been extended and complicated. Reflexivity has brought me closer to the image: I feel I know it better and care for it more. My sense of the potential meanings to be drawn from it has been enlarged. Reflexivity has helped me to see something of the limitations of my original reading, and of my thinking about my place in the world and about other people. It has helped me recognise the prejudice and snobbery that were guiding my feelings towards a category of people and underpinned my initial reading. This is not an entirely comfortable realisation for me to make about myself, but it is one I am happy to accept and move forward from. It seems to offer the chance of a form of growth in a small way.

Conclusion

The self-reflexive critical approach outlined here is offered as a step towards a new autoethnographic type of cultural criticism in which writers are more overtly present in their writing than has been customary for many years. In this chapter, I have focused on photography, my specialist field, but the rationale and potential benefits of reflexivity are equally applicable, I believe, to all fields of cultural criticism, including books, music, films and all forms of visual culture.

Self-reflexivity seems to provide a mechanism for us to understand a little better how our interpretations and emotional responses are necessarily inflected by our experiences and the narratives we have constructed about ourselves and the world over the course of our lives. My experiments with self-reflexive criticism suggest that it allows us not only to uncover some of the background to our own patterns of thinking and feeling, but also to make new connections, experience fresh insights, develop enriched or even changed ways of thinking about the cultural forms we encounter and about ourselves. Most writers, I imagine, academic or otherwise, hope to have an effect on their readers: to inform, interest, engage and provoke a response. With self-reflexivity, if we use it with caution and self-control, I believe we have the chance to produce forms of writing that are not only more transparent, authentic and enriched, but potentially also more resonant too for our readers, as we reveal ourselves not as detached critical voices but as flesh-and-blood living people whose tastes, interpretations and judgements draw from a lifetime of wrestling with the struggle and puzzle and joy of being alive.

Note

1 The image can easily be found online by typing the title into any search engine. See for example: https://www.moma.org/collection/works/54273

References

Anderson, L. (2006). Analytic autoethnography. *Journal of Contemporary Ethnography*, *35*(4), 373–395.

Bakhtin, M. (1981 [1934]). *The dialogic imagination*. Austin: University of Texas Press.

Barthes, R. (1977a [1964]). The rhetoric of the image. In *Image, music, text*. London: Harper Collins.

Barthes, R. (1977b [1968]). The death of the author. In *Image, music, text*. London: Harper Collins.

Barthes, R. (1982). *Camera lucida*. London: Jonathan Cape.

Bochner, A., & Ellis, C. (2016). *Evocative autoethnography*. Abingdon: Routledge.

Bourdieu, P. (1984). *Distinction*. London: Routledge and Kegan Paul.

Bourdieu, P. (1993). *Sociology in question*. London: Sage.

Brookfield, S. (2017). *Becoming a critically reflective teacher* (2nd ed.). San Francisco: Jossey-Bass.

Brown, E., & Phu, T. (Eds.). (2014). *Feeling photography*. Durham: Duke University Press.

Burgin, V. (Ed.). (1982). *Thinking photography*. Basingstoke: Macmillan.

Campt, T. (2012). *Image matters*. Durham and London: Duke University Press.

Chandler, D. (2007). The landscape of disappointment. In M. Power (Ed.), *26 different endings*. Brighton: Photoworks.

Chang, H. (2016). *Autoethnography as method*. Abingdon: Routledge.

Clarke, G. (1997). *The photograph*. Oxford: Oxford University Press.

Dean, J. (2017). *Doing reflexivity*. Bristol: Policy Press.

Deleuze, G., & Guattari, F. (1987). *A thousand plateaus*. London: Bloomsbury.

Dewey, J. (1910). *How we think*. Boston: DC Heath.

Evans, W. (2012 [1938]). *American photographs* (75th anniversary ed.). New York: Museum of Modern Art.

Finlay, L. (2002). Outing' the researcher: The provenance, process and practice of reflexivity. *Qualitative Health Research*, *12*(4), 531–545.

Gregg, M., & Seigworth, G. (Eds.). (2010). *The affect theory reader*. Durham: Duke University Press.

Hall, S. (1993 [1980]). Encoding/decoding. In S. During (Ed.), *The cultural studies reader*. Abingdon: Routledge.

Holmes, M. (2010). The emotionalization of reflexivity. *Sociology*, *44*(1), 139–154.

Mezirow, J. (1991). *Transformative dimensions of adult learning*. San Francisco: Jossey-Bass.

Miller, N. (1991). *Getting personal*. New York: Routledge.

Moon, J. (2006). *Learning journals* (2nd ed.). Abingdon: Routledge.

Pels, D. (2000). Reflexivity, one step up. *Theory, Culture and Society*, *17*(3), 1–25.

Phillips, S. (2003). The question of belief. In D. Arbus (Ed.), *Diane Arbus revelations*. New York: Random House.

Rose, G. (2011). The question of method: Practice, reflexivity and critique in visual culture studies. In I. Heywood, & B. Sandywell (Eds.), *The handbook of visual culture*. London: Bloomsbury.

Rose, G. (2012). *Visual methodologies* (3rd ed.). London: Sage.

Sayer, A. (2005). *The moral significance of class*. Cambridge: Cambridge University Press.

Smith, S. M. (2014). Photography between desire and grief. In E. Brown, & T. Phu (Eds.), *Feeling photography*. Durham: Duke University Press.

Spence, J. (1986). *Putting myself in the picture*. London: Camden Press.

Sternfeld, J. (2003 [1987]). *American prospects*. New York: DAP.

Sturken, M., & Cartwright, L. (2001). *Practices of looking*. Oxford: Oxford University Press.

Wells, L. (Ed.). (2009). *Photography: A critical introduction* (4th ed.). Abingdon: Routledge.

Williams, G. (2014). *How to write about contemporary art*. London: Thames & Hudson.

7

DIGITAL AUTOETHNOGRAPHY

An Approach to Facilitate Reflective Practice in the Making and Performing of Visual Art

Joanna Neil

Introduction

Between October 2013 and June 2015, I experimented with digital autoethnography to observe, record and re-observe my own practice as a visual artist. Digital autoethnography has been described as:

> ...distinguishable from traditional autoethnography because the cultures analyzed are not primarily physical; they are digital...the work of digital autoethnography is situated within and concerned about digital spaces and the lived experiences, interactions, and meaning-making within and beside these contexts.
>
> *Dunn and Myers (2020, p. 43)*

I used tools such as a voice recorder, Go-Pro headcam, and private and public digital platforms. My identity as a researcher, teacher and artist is inextricably linked. A key question in this experiment, therefore, was how digital tools and platforms might help me develop reflexivity in relation to my artistic and teaching practice. Pink et al. (2016, p. 13) suggest that the 'ways that digital ethnographers might reflexively engage with their worlds is concerned with asking ourselves precisely those questions about how we produce knowledge', and in my case, how I make my art/artistic performances and develop my teaching practice. This chapter briefly describes two stages of this experiment with digital autoethnographic practice, entitled 'Digital Autoethnography: Interview with Self' (Neil, 2017) and 'Interview with Self Part II' (Neil, 2016), before presenting 'Interview with Self Part III' – reflections on the usefulness of digital technologies in both artistic autoethnographic making processes and the development of professional arts teaching practice.

DOI: 10.4324/9781003309239-11

Self-observation via digital technologies is a challenging territory. The ubiquity of the digital in a society which increasingly captures and shares 24/7 conjures images of narcissism, indulgence, confidence and knowing. The current abundance of documented selves on social media features the selfie as self-obsession rather than self-observation, the constructed self, the self as product and as an outward-facing projection of the self (Murray, 2015). For me, despite similar accusations of narcissism and self-indulgence (see Coffey, 1999; Delamont, 2009), autoethnography enables an encounter with a version of the self that proved both challenging and illuminating. It is a methodology that encourages experimentation and reflexivity and embraces uncertainty, in contrast to that familiar pouting selfie that represents a version of how the subject wants the world to see them. That image, it seems to me, is a constructed self, the self as product, a projection of the self 'outwards'. Digital autoethnography offered me an opportunity to look inwards. It was a way to make the familiar unfamiliar, a deconstruction rather than a construction of the self and, in this context, a way to understand and develop my creative practice in relation to art and teaching. The risk in doing this was that it might present a version of the self that is uncomfortable or unflattering to share – not the self at its 'best'. It is a risk that is magnified if the research is *about* one's self but not just *for* one's self. I wanted to use this research not only to gain insight into the experience of making visual arts but also to support my students with their own practices. Alongside McNiff (2013), I was asking:

> How do researchers minimize one-sided self-absorption when personal, often intimate, art making is a core element of research? Might standards of usefulness to others assure practical outcomes and complement the subjective aspects of artistic knowing?
>
> *p. 4*

In addition, I was asking: how can digital technologies empower students with their own reflective practices and transitions from students to practitioners?

Interview with Self Part I: 12 Questions November/December 2016

After using a digital voice recorder, Go-Pro headcam, blog and private platform to record myself starting a new body of work (drawing, experimenting with materials, reflecting and planning), the 12 questions I asked of myself were:

1. *You recorded different aspects of your making. Why did you start to do this?*
2. *How important was it to use digital technologies?*
3. *Why did you use these particular technologies rather than others?*
4. *What did you hope to find out?*
5. *What was it like to record yourself in this way?*
6. *What did you find out about your practice?*

7. *What did you find out about yourself?*
8. *How has observing yourself in this way helped you?*
9. *Has your work changed?*
10. *Is there anything else that has changed?*
11. *Will you continue to use these approaches in the future?*
12. *How important was sharing the recordings?*

I realised, when I started to look at various personal statements that I had made about my practice to accompany personal profiles and applications for artistic opportunities, that I had lost connection with these statements. They had simply been 'carried forward' without reflecting on the work itself.[1] Such statements about one's practice are often decisive and assured and this is what students see.[2] Even when we are allowed into the process by an artist, it is often the technical side of making their work or a narrative of how their ideas developed that are disclosed, not always how they reflect on their work, what making the work feels like, or how they make sense of what they are doing both in the making and over time. I wanted to understand more about what was experienced throughout the making process and that led to the idea of recording as much reflection as possible, engaged in while actually experiencing making a work. *What does reflection look like? How can it be captured? Why is it often absent from students' work in a critical or dialogic form? What might I learn from recording what I do and think? What might be revealed? What might surprise me or change my relationship with my work?*

The technologies were an extension of a blog I had been using to document my work and occasionally reflect on my research. I wanted the blog to continue as a way to have an audience. I had also been using Evernote[3] as a private space for documenting thoughts, ideas and links to interesting sources. Now, the use of audio recording on my phone also became important as a way of getting incidental thoughts down before I forgot them. I could listen back at various points to something that captured how I had been feeling at the time, through the pauses and intonation in my voice. Later, digital technologies like the Go-Pro camera acted as a third eye, allowing me to see again what I had already seen, and to see things I had not noticed at first. I was not sure if these technologies would reveal anything but having them recording me enabled me to focus on the making, rather than 'thinking about what I was thinking about or doing'. For me, the process of writing slows down thoughts, whereas speaking allows thoughts to flow, or to be expressed in a different way. Video recordings animated and presented the work in a different way again: static imagery came to life, enabling me to see and reframe them from different perspectives. The technology therefore provided a different dimension to view the work, a virtual space – and when hosted on the blog, a virtual space within a virtual space.

I initially used technology that was easily available and familiar to me, offering a private space where the raw information could go before I decided what to share, once I had mentally, and sometimes physically, processed the content (see also MacLaren, Georgiadou, Bradford, & Taylor, 2017). The Go-pro headcam was a fairly clumsy third eye, but with it fixed on my forehead, it did allow me to record what I was seeing fairly accurately. The video camera was a simple one which enabled me to record the experience of making from multiple angles, some from points of view I would not be able to experience on my own. It was important that what I was doing was not about the technology itself, but what the technology could facilitate more effectively.

I considered other technologies, designed to collect data, record and be responsive, and those designed for more covert activities like surveillance and spying. I tried out Google Glass and researched other eyeglass technologies as a potentially more accurate way to observe and capture experiences, even though the public image of this type of wearable technology was not always positive.[4] Might they be a way to engage students in observing and recording their own reflections? Practicalities, cost and current stage of development militated against their use, however. What was important to me at that time was that I could pick them up and use them straight away, although I retain an interest in surveillance equipment as a way to observe and record myself without being in control of when this is happening. It would extend an experiment I conducted during my art degree where someone took random photographs of me as I stumbled around a blacked-out room. The images showed me unaware of being documented at that moment. I wondered whether surveillance technology might be a means of producing a conscious-free selfie? Figure 7.1 is a good metaphor for what I was doing here with autoethnography: capturing moments of stumbling in the dark.

In recording and re-seeing my process, I hoped to understand something of my habits and approaches to making work, not only the different phases of my making process. I wanted to surface my thinking and feeling at different points in order to reconsider how they related to decisions about the work I made and to my teaching practices. I also hoped through this to make *better* work; work which had more depth, especially since, having explored possibilities relating to more commercial outcomes, I felt that I had lost my way. Teaching had started to distance me from my practice. Being a teacher and artist had made my identity difficult to grasp. I hoped to re-experience something of what it is like to be a student again through feeling completely exposed.

It all felt very experimental. In some ways, in fact, it felt exactly like making a piece of artwork. I felt uncomfortable at first, even awkward. I was reminded of what it feels like to play and pretend. Pretending or playing at being a researcher, questioning the validity of the research, being uncertain about what it might mean, whether the research might be useful. Because I couldn't predict what I was going to find out, I didn't feel particularly confident. Initially, I also felt quite self-conscious when recording my voice and my making. But it was also interesting to have this heightened awareness of myself and of the work *while it was being made*. I felt more connected to what I was doing. As I got more used to the recording equipment and techniques, I was able to immerse myself in the practice more easily without over-thinking, or simultaneously considering whether/how what I was doing 'worked' as a methodology.

FIGURE 7.1 Stumbling in the dark. Photograph by author

Afterwards, I wondered why it was important to me that the films were edited. I think I felt embarrassed at being visible when I was not ready – even though this lack of awareness and what it might reveal was exactly what I was seeking! Nevertheless, I did edit them to foreground *the making as a process* and in this way they became crafted artefacts: editing together several films taken from different viewpoints at the same time became a way to document and reflect on the making. They also became quite interesting short films in themselves. Often the view was a 'disembodied' one: parts of hands or arms, the sound of my voice, movement of a body I couldn't see, me looking through other filters like glass cabinets or a side view. They showed concentration, me half squinting at a drawing or object or up close to the drawing, my body poised for drawing, not smiling, but not 'not-smiling'.

Previously I would have made a statement about how I like to use banal objects in my work to elevate them or find their beauty somehow. But viewing the film, I did not know why certain things drew me to draw them. I found myself constructing narratives using imagery in relation to objects, revealing an aspect of wanting to tell stories and calling on symbolism to explain my attraction to certain shapes, forms or details. I found myself drawing on earlier childhood experiences of looking at images, to explain this experience. The account this gave me was factual but the narrative applied to it was a form of sense-making – a constructed and applied narrative.

The Go-Pro captured the movements of my body. A painstaking process of using film-editing software to slow down the footage to a tenth of a second enabled me to measure, in time, this co-ordination of eye, hand and memory.

Although not as accurate as using eye-glass technology, this observation enabled me to think in more depth about what is memorised and the co-ordination of body and mind (my hand was often left making marks as my head moved away), so that I discovered something out about the physicality of my making. Seeing a moving image of a drawing being created makes the 'static' product (a 2D drawing on a 2D piece of paper) animated: the lines, shapes and forms move, become movement, and emerge from movement. I felt a sense of securing what my practice was as I progressed, partly because I started to understand how my work was actually about sense-making and storytelling. I saw that there is also sometimes humour in what I do. I discovered too that while always present in my work in an autobiographical sense, I was also quite hidden or removed. I thought I had always been making work that revealed something about myself, but it had in fact been quite subtle – anything really revealing or personally absent, something created through a sort of passive engagement rather than any conscious attempt to remove myself from the work. I discovered that I think a lot, and that this sometimes gets in the way of making – I become too self-conscious even while sometimes becoming lost in making the work. In the recordings, I seem confident, even though I was feeling unsure and confused at times.

Some of the more repetitive processes like tracing drawings with the sewing machine – essentially the same image with each one taking on its own identity – allowed me to go into a more meditative state that I value. Only through recording the making and re-watching the footage did I see the connection between what I create and how I create it. Repetition and iteration are important not only in the themes, techniques and processes involved, but also for the physical and mental states of my body and mind. Having a better understanding of my physical self in the work made me want to include myself more physically in future pieces: for the work to become more *performative* in the future. In addition, I realised that I like writing and that the writing was not just a form of sense-making but, at times, a form of creative expression, a poetry of sorts. Theatre and poetry have always been interests of mine, but now I felt that they had been suppressed from a practice that had only been touching the surface. Reflecting on the making process became more than just thinking about what I had done and where I might go next; it became a dialogic way for me to interpret and reorder my making process – and my 'self'.

Looking at the making, myself, and pieces of work with different media, provided different ways to view and experience them. Drawings became a different sort of image when they were photographed, and they changed again when on a blog, where they might sit next to text or moving imagery. Now, a piece of work looked at in one context or setting was affected by the forms it was presented with. This helped to distance me from the immediacy of making and helped to make what I was doing unfamiliar. Unfamiliarity also came through seeing bits of me I wasn't used to seeing: what my face was doing when I was drawing, or what the materials I was using look like as they made contact with surfaces: the textures, absorbency, sound they made, the flow and relationship between my movement, the material and the mark. A heightened sense of awareness of these processes was created.

At the time none of this seemed to be making much difference to my approach to the subject matter or process as a whole, but I was challenged by how the methodology began to influence, or perhaps inspire, things that I *might* do. The video recordings, in some cases, became more than stand-alone pieces of work: they became vehicles to reflect with on an ongoing basis. The research gave me an approach to my work which enabled me to let go of certain habits. Paradoxically, while being more *aware* of what I was doing, I allowed myself to do things without *over-thinking* them. I became aware of what was familiar but also more willing to step outside of that. Sometimes there was a conflict. Sometimes I felt that the technology was interfering with or even contaminating the work I was making. My work was changing because of the new ways I was looking at it and this felt like a process of unpicking and understanding. I became interested in what was being created (apart from a material artefact); that is, the making of the work became its own reflexive methodology. The digital therefore brought something new to my practice and my methodology: it enabled me to slow down my making process, to quite literally slow movements down. This slowing down gave me a sense of connecting with my work, with the process, and with myself in new ways.

A lasting impact was that I gained a stronger connection to the way I worked, with the materials I used, and how I wanted to become more part of my work physically. The work I made later explored using the spoken word (scripted), and making-as-performance. This was a huge departure for me, a revisiting of my interests in theatre and poetry. The idea that my practice had been interfered with, or contaminated, now seemed ridiculous to me and made me think about how much control I used to want over my work. So letting go made me feel closer to my practice which, in turn, changed how I perceived myself as an artist, researcher and teacher. I became more present in my work. I felt empowered by my identities as artist, educator and researcher rather than compromised, particularly the dual identity of teacher and artist. I think this had stemmed from a perception that you can't be serious about making artwork unless you are earning a main living from it. Now I did not think being an artist had much to do with that; rather, it became about how you situate yourself and make sense of the different roles or identities you might have. How I might write about my practice also changed. I was less concerned with pinning it down or defining exactly what it was about. It continued to be an emerging thing. I still wanted to feel surprised by what I do. If and when I became too comfortable with what I was doing, I would attempt to make the familiar unfamiliar again.

I had also wanted to enable students to adopt the same approach but changes to my teaching went beyond that. The practice of recording spoken descriptions of things I wanted to draw before drawing them became an idea for a series of workshops in which participants used this technique to explore drawing as a verbally reflective activity. Having recorded tutorials with students, and then shared them with the students, my approach to tutorials and providing feedback also changed. The tutorials became more like conversations where the student speaks more than me. In fact, tutorials started to feel more like informal interviews where I was asking questions as a way to develop feedback rather than giving a critique or directive. Developing this use of digital autoethnography as part of my practice had triggered something, sending me on a different trajectory which I wanted to explore for a while. I accepted that it *is* a changing practice and became open to change.

In terms of the potential for using these approaches with others, I could see mileage in unpicking art and design pedagogy (see Barrett & Bolt, 2007), and in looking at other contexts for these approaches – for example, the tutorial as recorded interview or feedback as a podcast or film. Blogs would continue to be important since they had been a great vehicle for exploring different methods of reflecting. However, I wanted to be aware of the dangers in any ingrained approaches students may have with using social media, of the fact that sharing work on Facebook and responding to 'likes' can become quite passive and potentially directive, and that blogs can also become static repositories rather than environments for deep or dialogic reflection.

Although I had not started the research with a fully formed idea of what I was doing and why, sharing was vital to me as a way of developing a sense of other or audience. Even pretending that there was someone else reading, watching or listening seemed to give the process a greater purpose. I was observing and making for someone else. The emergent nature of the work was supported by talking at conferences, lectures to students and, of course, discussing ideas with colleagues, friends and supervisors. Initially, I thought of my sharing, particularly at conferences and on the blog, as selfish, that it was more for me and my benefit than for others, especially when the information was fragmented and possibly quite confusing and I was sharing as a way to make sense of something. As outlined, the visual recording had only ever showed parts of me, bits of arms, hands, feet, eyes squinting. They were unflattering but probably showed a confidence not felt rather than a vulnerability. The most difficult content to share was the sound recordings because my uncertainty and vulnerability was exposed the most with these. There was so much to think about!

Interview with Self Part II

For the 'Feminist Writings' symposium in Helsinki, I reflected on the fact that my earlier use of digital technologies had heightened awareness of my own physicality and now sought to develop 'the performative' in my practice further. In doing so, I hoped to find a space where practice and research were inseparable, as well as to find alternatives to the traditional conventions of presenting and displaying work and gaining academic acceptance.

'Interview with Self Part II' was a live performance that responded to spoken excerpts from the above questions and my answers to them, as well as incorporating visuals of experimental artworks that were made afterwards.

The performance not only was part pre-recorded and scripted but also had scope to extend the above reflections, constituting a live dialogic conversation with the audience. I was interested in what new forms of practice might emerge through performance. How might a physical audience as a supplement to technology and an imagined audience facilitate in-depth reflection on practice, in a space where reflection itself becomes the practice? In other words, where the barriers between making, performance and reflection are collapsed?

Prompted by the emotional and conceptual connections I made to imagery at the start of the research and the heightened self-awareness and physical presence I had found in the digital recordings in Part I, the experimental artworks I had been working on were a series of self-portraits. A photograph of a deep-sea diver from a childhood encyclopaedia resonated; I too was submerged and immersed in the process of research, exploring new territory but often feeling vulnerable and exposed. Ideas around being submerged in water, helplessness, sinking, buoyancy, and imagined selves led to photo shoots of 'performances in the home'. Exploring internal self-images and making them visible became an ongoing tableau and included a series of images as an empowered trapeze artist (see Figure 7.2).

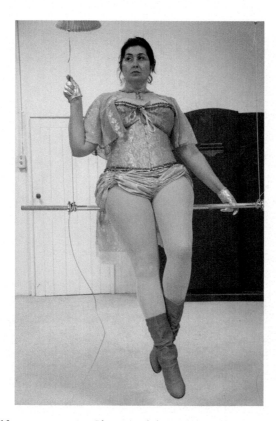

FIGURE 7.2 Self as trapeze artist. Photograph by author

The Performance

After a brief formal introduction to the context of the work, I identified the start of the 15-minute performance by wearing my trapeze artist cape. Sitting against a projected compilation of experimental work, I listened to and read aloud excerpts from my responses to the 12 questions (see Figure 7.3) in a dialogic exchange.

After the recorded and live reading of the questions I asked, 'So what does reflection look like?', and replied 'It looks like this'. I was referring to the experience of having seen excerpts of work projected, speaking and listening not only to my pre-recorded reflection but also to the narrative I was about to read which reflected on the work that had recently emerged. The presentation/performance space gave me a new context to construct a scripted narrative which delved deeper into thoughts that had surfaced from the questions and elaborated on some of the work seen in the performance. It was not only descriptive but also developed into creative writing in places where I was finding different words to express the work, its meaning and relationship to me:

> I thought my previous work had been about me at different times. Sort of autobiographical, childhood memories, experiences of having children,

FIGURE 7.3 Screenshot of performance: interview with Self Part II. Photograph by author

creating work that had a narrative, some fictional. But I came to realise that what I thought I was saying or revealing about myself was heavily veiled. The research meant I was not just seeing aspects of my physical making with fresh eyes but was experiencing a new understanding and analysis of my practice.

Me lying on the bed in this work is not just about being stripped bare, vulnerable and exposed (although a useful visual metaphor for how I feel now). There have been times at my most vulnerable when I have felt that there has been nothing to protect me, nothing left. Just a body. Feeling weighted down and not able to offer resistance to the feeling of being blown about by the wind or submerged and tossed about beneath the water. I am heavy and weightless in my resistance, stumbling and falling.

Feeling immovable, gripped with a paralysing fear and sadness, the bed is the first place for comfort. But when the mind and body refuse to move, it takes me hostage. I felt mute and only a shade of myself. Muted. The bedcovers from a childhood memory: sheets, blankets and nylon quilting, playing with dolls and their quilts too. I am curled heavy on the bed, sinking into it. Wanting it to swallow me up into the floorboards beneath me. I have no resistance. I am fragile and broken.

It is in this place that I find myself that I also imagine myself doing what I cannot physically do. I find some resistance. I imagine myself as the trapeze artist: strong and empowered. I imagine myself as the brave and majestic circus performer: conquering anything, risking everything, feeling everything. Fearless. The body doing what the mind wants it to. Tumbling through the air from the strength of her own momentum. An image of hope.

The images so strong in my mind through this time and after, determined a need to make it real. So, I become the work and the work becomes me. This is a work to reflect with.

I had anticipated that in the few minutes I had left to do some 'live' in-the-moment reflection that I would have things to say and that new reflection may emerge. I introduced this last part by repeating, 'So what does reflection look like?', and replying 'It looks like this'. But I became stuck, overwhelmed by seeing the work, listening to my voice, experiencing the work differently and finding it difficult in the moment to make the transition from reading my written reflection to being in the moment. My spontaneous live reflection amounted to: 'I think this space is perhaps not the space I imagined it might be'.

The reflective space I had made available at the end of 'Interview with Self Part II' was not as fruitful as I had hoped. The experience nevertheless influenced how I came to frame my practice. For example, being brave enough to experiment in the knowledge that it might not always 'work'. The artefacts arising from the process therefore became new material to reflect with.

Interview with Self Part III: Making Work to Reflect With

My artistic practice explores the spaces between research, making, writing, presenting and performance. Artefacts from this digitally enabled process were produced: through the process of 'becoming' an autoethnographer, through embodied experiences of autoethnography, and through long arcs of reflection. They became both significant artworks and 'tools' enabling a new articulation of my practice, which I found empowering.

In this chapter, I have reflected on three interconnected elements and layers of my work: digital autoethnography, self-interview and performance. Autoethnography is often described as both *process* and *product* (Ellis, Adams, & Bochner, 2010, my emphasis). However, reflection in autoethnography has not typically focused on the *making* of the product, and what happens *beyond* the process of the making. In doing so here, I have tried to show how autoethnographic artefacts became *vehicles to reflect with*, as well as stand-alone pieces and finished products. In addition to facilitating reflection, digital autoethnography and the work arising from it became ways to reframe my practice and one of several useful pedagogic strategies. The digital material became another product to work with and through it, and I was able to disrupt my usual patterns of working and thinking. At times, I became more attuned to all the elements of my making: drawing, materials, processes, feelings, emotions, and physical presence.

The self-interview technique provided a structure for my reflections. This was helpful as a means of ordering the messiness and complexity of 'data' from my digital autoethnography. Although I had written the questions myself, when I came to answer them, they felt 'unfamiliar'. Through navigating the questions, I was able to make sense of my experiences and create a new narrative of my personal experience of crafting a digital autoethnography.

By revisiting the self-interview through a performance and presentation to a live audience, I was able to further 'disrupt' my reflections on the process of artistic making. Opening up publicly in this way and reflecting with (and in view of) others felt vulnerable and uncomfortable. It also provided a dynamic space for reflection and helped me to dismantle the boundaries between making, presentation, performance, and reflection. This felt like slipping into the spaces 'in-between', in order to discover the 'cracks and erasures' (Sullivan, 2010, p. 116) in the process of making, thus resurfacing and making visible those aspects of the process which are typically hidden or unheard in our public accounts of the process of creating and crafting research, art, and autoethnography (including those elements that 'don't work' – or at least don't work as expected). Using digital autoethnography as an approach to facilitating reflective practice in my making and performing of visual art enabled me to embrace my identities as autoethnographer, researcher, maker, and performer.

While the set of questions above might offer a prototype or 'starting point' for others who wish to reflect on their artistic and/or autoethnographic practice(s), reflective processes are more complex than simply following a model or set of steps on 'how to reflect' and 'what to reflect on'. For example, documenting and reflecting on one's habitual practices using different media and in different settings creates new juxtapositions that do not fit easily into Schön's (1983) reflection 'in' and 'on' action model. For me, reflection did not just occur in the moment or even immediately after actions, but it was more complex and differentiated in its manifestations. Schön seems to assume an a priori confidence and competence in 'doing reflective practice' that reproduces the binary of 'thinking' and 'doing/ making'. Instead, digital autoethnography enabled my reflection to become a material and *dynamic* part of my making processes, offering multiple strategies for self-reflection that sometimes included others beyond the initial crafting of the autoethnography (i.e. the audience for the performance). Ultimately, reflexivity is about challenging what we have come to believe, what we have come to take for granted, and what has become routinised. It is a dynamic process in which makers are 'finding strategies to question our own attitudes, theories-in-use, values, assumptions, prejudices and habitual actions; to understand our complex roles in relation to others' (Bolton, 2018, p. 10).

Using digital autoethnography to revisit and re-see in a different medium or situation was initially intended to enable me to examine habits and familiar practices in my creative work. It disrupted familiar cycles and loops, replacing them with reflections that were playful, surprising, and unsettling. It was important to embrace the messiness and allow these strategies to become different each time, avoiding the 'returning to' – establishing new habits and cycles of reflection. Thus, a multi-layered reflective account on the process of *making* and *performing* a digital autoethnography demonstrates how we can bring the 'digital' into our autoethnographic practice(s) to facilitate further critical insights. By exploring how digital technologies and platforms could be introduced and embedded into my autoethnographic inquiry, I came to see where new spaces could be created for simultaneously observing, documenting, and reflecting on the practices I engaged in as an artist-teacher going about my creative making.

Notes

1 Artistic statements are commonly made to accompany personal profiles and applications for artistic opportunities. The use of statements about my artistic practice is reflected on in full in the blog post 'The Beginning' October 2013 https://feltlikeit. wordpress.com/2013/10/18/the-beginning/ (Neil, 2013).

2 My own experiences as an art student reinforced this; artists visiting to give a slide show about their work would often present a linear and seamless account of the work. The fear and uncertainty of making work was rarely spoken about.

3 Evernote is a commercial digital platform designed for note-taking, organising content and archiving. It enables users to store notes they have created which might include text, webpages and excerpts, photographs, voice memo's and attachments, these are organised in labelled notebooks.

4 The phrase 'Glassholes' for those early up takers of the Google Glass technology began to take root fairly quickly https://techcrunch.com/2013/01/28/glassholes/ (Lawler, 2013) amid concerns of invading privacy and generally looking a bit daft.

References

Barrett, E., & Bolt, B. (Eds.) (2007). *Practice as research: Approaches to creative arts enquiry.* London: IB Tauris & Co Ltd.

Bolton, G. (2018). *Reflective practice: Writing and professional development* (5th ed.). London: Sage.

Coffey, A. (1999). *The ethnographic self.* London: Sage.

Delamont, S. (2009). The only honest thing: Autoethnography, reflexivity and small crises in fieldwork. *Ethnography and Education, 4*(1), 51–63.

Dunn, T. R., & Myers, W. B. (2020). Contemporary autoethnography is digital autoethnography: A proposal for maintaining methodological relevance in changing times. *Journal of Autoethnography, 1*(1), 43–59.

Ellis, C., Adams, T. E., & Bochner, A. P. (2010). Autoethnography: An overview. *Forum Qualitative Sozialforschung/Forum: Qualitative Social Research, 12*(1), https://doi.org/10.17169/fqs-12.1.1589

Lawler, R. (2013). Get ready for even more Google Glasshole sightings. *TechCrunch, 23*(January 2013). Retrieved from https://techcrunch.com/2013/01/28/glassholes/

MacLaren, J., Georgiadou, L., Bradford, J., & Taylor, L. (2017). Discombobulations and transitions: Using blogs to make meaning of and from within liminal experiences. *Qualitative Inquiry, 23*(10), 808–817.

McNiff, S. (2013). *Art as research: Opportunities and challenges.* Bristol: Intellect.

Murray, D. C. (2015). Notes to self: The visual culture of selfies in the age of social media. *Consumption Markets & Culture, 18*(6), 490–516.

Neil, J. (2013) The beginning. Blog entry posted 18 October 2013. Retrieved from https://feltlikeit.wordpress.com/2013/10/18/the-beginning/

Neil, J. (2016) Interview with self Part II. Feminist Readings #3 'Feminist Writings' Conference 2016, University of Helsinki, Finland. [Unpublished].

Neil, J. (2017). Digital autoethnography: Interview with self. *Prism: Casting New Light on Learning, Theory and Practice, 1*, 46–72.

Pink, S., Horst, H., Postill, J., Hjorth, L., Lewis, T., & Tacchi, J. (2016). *Digital ethnography: Principles and practice.* London: Sage.

Schön, D. A. (1983). *The reflective practitioner: How professionals think in action.* New York: Basic Books.

Sullivan, G. (2010). *Art practice as research inquiry in visual art.* Thousand Oaks, CA; London: Sage.

8

STITCHING AS REFLECTION AND RESISTANCE

The Use of a Stitch Journal During Doctoral Study

Clare Daněk

Introduction

In this chapter, I consider how a piece of cloth, appliqued and embroidered, is used as an autoethnographic tool for both reflecting on and resisting the challenges of doctoral research.[1] The 'stitch journal'[2] (see Figure 8.1) began in April 2018 and concluded in April 2020, during which time I wrangled with PhD processes, went on holidays, grew flowers, and navigated family life. The chapter is divided into three sections: stitching as record, in which I explore how I worked within the constraints of small squares to express my feelings and experiences every day; stitching as resistance, in which the experience of engaging in a self-directed leisure pursuit of this nature is considered a way of subverting my daily experience through playful improvisation; and stitching as sharing, in which the practice of sharing the journal in its physical form and through digital interactions can be seen as a way of disrupting the solitary experience of doctoral study. The structuring of the chapter thus also indicates to the reader that this artefact, initially created as a distraction from engagement with the PhD, over time became a means of creating connection and community.

Stitching as Record

A large sheet of linen fabric is spread out across a table. It is the colour of clotted cream and smells somewhere between sour and musty. The fabric is covered with a grid of colourful squares of fabric scraps, each overlaid with embroidery, beads, sequins. The squares are consistent in size at 5 centimetres square, with 35 to a row and 21 rows, but their content ranges from the highly pictorial (rural landscapes, a bowl of tomatoes, a cup of coffee) – through to more symbolic images (blue and orange intersecting arrows, a square almost filled by a huge black spot),

DOI: 10.4324/9781003309239-12

FIGURE 8.1 The completed stitch journal in April 2020. Photograph by author

and, here and there, statements such as 'sit a while with the difficulty' or 'whose leisure should be prioritised?' A viewer might reasonably understand that there is a narrative to the squares, but how might the piece be read, and where should one begin? Is the piece intended for the viewer or the creator?

One day in April 2018 I read an article by Thomson (2018) discussing the idea of a 'red thread' as a line of coherence through a piece of academic writing; she considers this metaphor through the image of the red rope sometimes used on Norwegian mountain paths as a means of route finding. The idea of creating a 'stitch journal' came to me that evening as an opportunity for a distraction from writing, although I told myself it was a way of separating myself from what I'd come to think of, eight months into my doctoral studies, as 'the PhD machine'. I dug out a piece of finest Irish linen from my sizeable fabric stash, rummaged in my sewing box for some embroidery threads, and created the first square, a white panel with a broken line of red thread running through it. The stitches were uneven and the effect was crude. I decided to share this messy, unfamiliar stitching; I posted on Instagram saying that I had an idea for a *thing* (see Figure 8.2).

There are public and private versions of the background to my stitch journal: in public, my PhD rolled on from a Master's project in which I explored the experience of learning basic woodwork skills. I was curious about how we learn craft skills alongside others, and in a shared community space, and this enquiry formed the basis of my doctoral research. The Master's research had used autoethnographic methods, largely due to a desire to get my hands dirty or, as the cultural theorist David Gauntlett notes, to be 'actually doing the thing' (Gauntlett, 2014). Following an established model within craft ethnography of

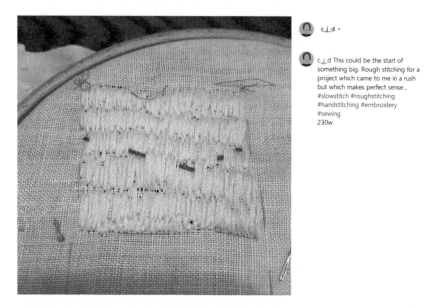

cj_d ·

cj_d This could be the start of
something big. Rough stitching for a
project which came to me in a rush
but which makes perfect sense...
#slowstitch #roughstitching
#handstitching #embroidery
#sewing
230w

FIGURE 8.2 The first stitched square, shared on Instagram. Photograph by author

researchers apprenticing themselves in a craft practice in order to gain experimental knowledge (Atkinson, 2022; Carr & Gibson, 2016) I planned to use the same approach with my PhD. As with any tale, however, there is the text and then there is the subtext. Many years prior, I had completed an undergraduate degree in Fine Art, and while my creative urges had been largely set aside in the intervening years, the desire to 'think with my hands' (Pallasmaa, 2009), expressing myself through material engagement rather than via words tapped out onto a screen, became increasingly hard to resist. I found myself dabbling with scraps of fabric, pulled by an urge to think in colour and to stitch instead of writing. This wish was rooted in sensory processes that were familiar to me: the feel of a threaded needle pulling through material, the juxtaposition of a particular colour and weight of thread against a particular colour of cloth, the sensation of using small, sharp embroidery scissors to cut precise shapes from stiff acrylic felt. The images I wanted to create appeared as snapshots in my mind, far more readily than the slowly coaxed sentences that would add up to form endless drafts of thesis chapters.

I had seen various challenges on Instagram inviting acts of repetitive daily creativity – for example InkTober (a drawing every day in October, for printmakers and sketchers), or MeMadeMay (in which amateur dressmakers share a homemade garment every day in May), and was interested in the idea of a daily habit, but my motivations were not so much about this as wanting to have the treat of tactile engagement after the hard work of each day as I pulled together thoughts on methodology and rummaged through endless papers for a literature review. While I had sewn for almost 30 years, this had largely taken the form of dressmaking; I had very little embroidering experience. The invitation I gave myself, to stitch a small square every day, was therefore deliberately modest. The first entries are crude and experimental, pulled together from materials already at my disposal, but I hoped that, as described in literature on craft learning, with regular practice I would develop competence (see for example Korn, 2013; Sennett, 2009). The idea of the textile-based reflective record is not original to me; it has notable recent precedent in work where simple repetitive stitching occupies a more considered, meditative space for reflection (Wellesley-Smith, 2022) or, in other examples, where daily entries record fluctuating temperatures or passing seasons (e.g. Harrigan, 2020).

It is important to note that while the stitch journal did not form part of the research itself but instead sat as an adjacent activity, in which I reflected *in, on* and *through* the action of stitching (Dewey, 1925; Schön, 1983), I started to use this particular form of making as a way of *coming to know* (Ingold, 2015) the processes involved in creating both the stitch journal and the thesis, and as a way of considering my research in more tactile, less textual terms. With each daily square, I was presented with an opportunity to try something new, whether that was a new style of embroidery, or a new challenge in interpreting a thought through thread and fabric. I began the project with fond thoughts of therapeutic mindful stitching each evening and intended that my writing practice would be influenced by the regularity of the stitch journal. I set myself two rules: that each entry occupied a sequentially placed square, and that there was an entry for each day, even if I had to go back and complete it later. This discipline echoed myriad pieces of advice on academic writing which exhorted the student to write little and often. However, as time went on it became apparent that the stitch journal would not be completed in a diligent consistent daily moment, but rather that it would be stitched in batches of five or six entries at a time, drawn from lists scribbled during busy days.

Stitching as Resistance: Escape Attempts

Despite the consumption of a plethora of 'How to' guides, and instructional seminars as part of my scholarship, it felt as if I fumbled my way through the processes of doctoral research, finding that, just as a key finding of my research into the processes of learning craft skills was about the necessity of improvisation, so, too, was it necessary to feel my way forward through the rarely straight path of the doctoral process.

Cohen and Taylor (1978) describe *'la perruque'*, in which the worker finds small ways to subvert his or her work experience – for instance via a private conversation conducted on work time, or a piece of stationery taken for personal use. In this way, the worker finds subtle ways to resist the system in which they are employed. The stitch journal offered me a similar escape route (Cohen & Taylor, 1978) from my 'employment', in that it provided a way of resisting the doctoral experience while simultaneously offering a route to reflection on both the day-to-day experience and my wider concerns. Through these stitched entries, I could share my triumphs and uncertainties with a wider audience, offering insights through metaphorical imagery.

Considering the journal as a form of 'side project' enabled me to frame it partly as a form of leisure; such pursuits can be considered forms of identity work, in that they exist outside employment and domestic commitments, and can offer a route to self-actualisation, enabling what Cohen and Taylor (1978) refer to as 'free areas' within a familiar world (p. 98). I was able to express emotions through the quilt that I did not find easy to articulate either at home or with my supervisors; it became a 'free area' in its own right, and also in the space and time its production and materials took up at home. As I became more involved in the process, I found myself accruing ever more shades of embroidery thread, scraps of felt, beads and buttons, and in choosing where to store these I was able to stake new claims on shared domestic space (Stalp, 2006a; Stalp, 2006b; Stalp & Winge, 2008).

I began the process of creating the stitch journal with very little experience of embroidery – previous hand stitching had been largely limited to sewing hems on garments, and everything else involved a sewing machine. I had to learn how to manipulate the tools and materials required to create decorative stitches and appliqued designs. As I gained more experience, I was able to refine my choice of tools, from larger needles to a tiny 5-cm long crewel needle, and to gain a nuanced understanding of the many weights and variations of embroidery thread. To use Polanyi's (1962) description of subsidiary and focal awareness, at first I had to focus on forming stitches, careful to notice how I was forming each stitch (subsidiary focus), but as time went on, my increasing proficiency moved me into the arena of focal awareness, where my stitching know-how had become tacit and I was able to make more ambitious decisions about the things I was creating *with* the stitching. This experience offered me a form of control that did not seem so apparent as I refined my academic writing skills, where meanings seemed slippery and harder to control. In succumbing to this uncertainty within the confines of the stitch journal, I was able to improvise more successfully (Hallam & Ingold, 2007).

The process of deciding on and constructing each entry became a form of 'playing' – 'a way to be otherwise' (Woodyer, 2012, p. 318), or a way of 'trying things out' in a liminal space (Turner, 1969). As with other forms of play, there are rules, boundaries, and constraints, but the subject for each entry could be whatever I felt was appropriate that day: it might involve a note on my research, an observation on the country's current political situation, a local landscape viewed from a particular angle, or a simple thought, caught before it vanished. The only link between each square and its horizontal neighbours was in the way that one day followed another, yet, in scanning across the piece two years later, I find that my eye is not led along each row but instead roves here and there, entries triggering memories in me, and, when displayed, prompting questions from others. While the genesis of the stitch journal had been as an escape from the doctoral process, in this juxtaposition of diverse entries the opposite is shown to be true – that the doctoral process is part of a wider life encompassing multiple overlapping spheres.

The stitch journal does not only serve as a repository for my ideas; through repeated handling, my bodily presence as creator remains present in this unwashable work, and in this way the stitch journal is not only autoethnographic – exploring, representing and reflecting my lived experience both within and through itself – but also an incidental repository of corporeal engagement (Rippin & Vachhani, 2019), in the scent accrued through its repeated passing through my hands, through needles threaded with saliva-wetted fibres, and through crumbs and cat hairs and the detritus of household existence. The tiny necessary steps of the stitching process – slicing, piercing, pinning, cutting (Parker, 2010) – can be considered tiny brutal acts in the creation of a new appliqued square on the body of the journal; there are obvious parallels with surgical actions performed on the human or animal body. I am thus able to create and recreate myself through these appliqued actions, stitching myself into being in ways over which I alone have control.

Stitching as Sharing

In writing this chapter, I find myself reflecting on some of the decisions I made. Many of the entries were deliberately oblique, as if there was a code that only I could crack; in this way, I suggested to myself that I could somehow hide in plain sight, offering a narrative to the world (which, I should note, the world had not actually requested). In a similar way, by choosing to illustrate just one scene, thought, reflection from a day, I felt myself able to conceal all sorts behind that single square. I presented the stitch journal at a symposium when it was at a very early stage and, when somebody asked me how I'd remember what each square referred to, I said that contextualising the experience wasn't important and that the meaning behind each entry could drift into the ether. However, as soon as I got home I wrote down an explanation for each entry while I could still remember it; in this instance, the experience of sharing with others prompted a new step in my relationship with the piece and its relationship with the wider world. Through proving one's credentials, showing work enables connections and can offer a route into a creative community. Sharing the stitch journal in its earliest stages was an exercise in curiosity: 'this is a thing that I am doing; what do you think?' I first shared it on Facebook, a more private network made up of friends met in various life contexts; most know that I am 'creative' but few knew, initially, quite what to make of this particular manifestation. I shared it on Instagram, where, through careful use of hashtags I drew a new audience of fellow stitchers. On Twitter, which I used predominantly for academic conversation, I used the entries as a way of starting conversations.

Despite an explosion in 'hoop art' driven by Etsy and Instagram, and notably more political and expressive work being shared, to the uninitiated needlework still retains an aura of suspicion-arousing folksiness not shared by other amateur leisure pursuits such as cycling or running. Stitch journal kits are now sold at Hobbycraft, inviting the stitcher to mark each day with some small motif as part of a pre-printed circle; stitched self-reflection has been commodified, in a similar way to bullet journaling. When I began to share my work on social media, I was nervous: will it be considered twee? Will people cringe? A couple of friends told me they'd reserved judgement about my stitching for quite some time, the unspoken observation being that they wanted to see whether others approved first: 'is this something to mock?' There is a risk involved in sharing, but also a defiance: this is who I am.

When photographed, the individual squares looked strange and abstracted to me as they filled the screen, scaled up massively from their original 5 centimetre squares. I realised that the entries would benefit from being framed in the wider context of the whole piece, so I created a website, began to pull together notes explaining the entries, and after the first couple of months I shared a monthly link in which I offered an explanation of each entry. The link to the website thus provided a way both to capture and to explain the work as it progressed. The gap between sharing individual entries online and gathering entries for the website offered time to refine thoughts about each day, so that many explanations were expanded. I also shared the work in progress at academic conferences, first spreading it out across a table when there were fewer than 50 of the eventual 735 entries; in hindsight, this felt like a bold strategy, but it enabled people to participate in a journey as the piece developed.

I continued to share entries as the work gathered momentum, seeing each square as a new opportunity. Gauntlett (2018) describes ways in which making is connecting, in that the act of making can offer a common ground, whether in the shared workshop (the subject of my doctoral study) or via the act of sharing online. The connection can lie in sharing the *process*, or sharing the *product*. I was not simply sharing the image of the embroidered and appliqued work, but the narrative accompanying it, which meant embracing vulnerability, risking opening myself up to critique, and enabling conversations about the doctoral experience. The making process offers the maker a particular power in the production of social relations: while my research is 'hands-on', involving ceramics and printmaking activity, it was through sharing the progress of the stitch journal that I felt able to take up a space as a scholar of craft: through sharing my practice I was proving my credentials and establishing my right to inhabit this space (Price & Hawkins, 2019). Parker (2010) observed that embroidery offers opportunities for defiance: if for second-wave feminists the personal was political, here, the personal is universal. If I was finding the doctoral process challenging, then surely others were too? People would message me privately to say that they shared my troubles but were reluctant to admit this in public.

As I committed to a habit of sharing (most) entries, I began to consider what I shared: would I choose something highly pictorial, a bowl of cherry tomatoes recreated with thread as accurately as my skills permitted, or would I focus

FIGURE 8.3 A bowl of tomatoes and a bias-bound seam. Photograph by author

on the subsequent entry, which appeared to be an abstract form comprised of ing two pieces of denim joined together, their seams concealed beneath bias binding – the second, in fact, held far more relevance for my research into craft learning as it represented a new dressmaking technique, while the entry featuring the tomatoes holds no more profound meaning than might a casual snapshot (see Figure 8.3).

Elsewhere, the content expressed my thoughts more directly: for instance, 'am I stupid or is it difficult?' (see Figure 8.4) or 'how can we make knowledge visible?' (see Figure 8.5). I saw repeatedly that, particularly on academic Twitter,

FIGURE 8.4 Questioning the academic writing process. Photograph by author

FIGURE 8.5   Trying to articulate the processes of craft ethnography. Photograph by author

there is resistance in some quarters to expressing anything other than one's most professional thoughts, as if public confession of struggles was to be taken as a sign of weakness or, worse, dilettantism. The decision to share my experiences in this way in public offered a counterpoint to discussions in online spaces of 'impostor syndrome', where a person does not feel they deserve to inhabit their role; the stitch journal offered a metaphor-laden route to sharing my lived experience, an act of deliberate resistance consciously fracturing the professional façade seemingly expected of doctoral students performing their identities in public online spaces.

Conclusion

The passing of months permits me to inhabit a hybrid space as both author and viewer of the work; while the creation of some images lingers in my mind, as much due to wherever I might have been while stitching as to their specific content, others fade into memory, and I find my eyes being led up, down, across, rather than in the order of fabrication, working row by row from top to bottom. From the vantage point of two years later, while some entries are obvious, others are now mysterious to me – what might a single curved golden line refer to? A square filled with buttons? Four orange felt arrows, each pointing to a corner of the square? I finished the last entry in mid-April 2020, as the country experienced its first Covid-19 lockdown, and though many others sought solace in stitching, I found myself watching their endeavours with some detachment.

It did not take long for the daily obligation to conjure up an entry to fade, and the stitch journal now lies folded in a box, an independent entity already functioning as an artefact of a particular time. Reviewing the physical piece is akin to pulling a diary from a shelf and wondering over names and events whose full significance is now uncertain; the complete picture is accessible only through the digital record of its creation.

Through the repetitive practice of manipulating threads and materials, my competence has improved – in Dreyfus' (2004) parlance of skill acquisition, I can consider that I have shifted from novice to amateur – but through sharing the development of the work, and subsequent pieces, I have been able to participate in conversations not only as a scholar of craft practices, but as a practitioner. In sharing work and demonstrating this willingness to be vulnerable I embody Pye's 'workmanship of risk' (1995 [1968], p. 20), where the craftsperson is constantly evolving and refining their skills, always mindful that stumbles, glitches and failures are vital parts of this improvisatory process.

In reflecting on the process I remind myself of the ways in which, at different points, the stitch journal became distraction, conversation, retreat, and even performance. If there is a 'red thread' that runs through the practice of its creation, it perhaps lies in the ongoing experience of its sharing, whether online, at conferences, or in contexts such as this chapter. In each engagement I am compelled to relate the artefact back to myself and my process of creating it. Ingold (2014) describes an idea of 'following the material' as a mode of skilful engagement with making processes, whereas Brown (2021) observes that 'unfolding' might be more apt, this notion carrying with it the combination of skill and adaptivity to an ongoing situation. The stitch journal has thus allowed me to continue to unfold into my experience of doctoral research while simultaneously constructing a new identity for myself as a stitcher.

Notes

1 This research has been funded by the AHRC through the White Rose College of the Arts & Humanities, grant no. AH/L503848/1.
2 The stitch journal can be seen in its entirety at http://www.claredanek.me/stitch-journal.

References

Atkinson, P. (2022). *Crafting ethnography*. London: Sage.
Brown, A. (2021). The mark of the researcher's hand: The imperfections of craft in the process of becoming a qualitative researcher. *Management Learning, 52*(5), 541–558.
Carr, C., & Gibson, C. (2016). Geographies of making: Rethinking materials and skills for volatile futures. *Progress in Human Geography, 40*(3), 297–315.
Cohen, S., & Taylor, L. (1978). *Escape attempts: The theory and practice of resistance to everyday life*. Harmondsworth: Pelican.
de Certeau, M. (1988). *The practice of everyday life*. Berkeley, CA: University of California Press.

Dewey, J. (1925). *Experience and nature*. Chicago, IL: Open Court.

Dreyfus, S. E. (2004). The five-stage model of adult skill acquisition. *Bulletin of Science, Technology and Society, 24*(3), 177–181.

Gauntlett, D. (2014). *Actually doing the thing*. Retrieved from https://davidgauntlett.com/creativity/actually-doing-the-thing/

Gauntlett, D. (2018). *Making is connecting: The social power of creativity, from craft and knitting to digital everything* (2nd ed.). Cambridge: Polity.

Hallam, E., & Ingold, T. (2007). Creativity and cultural improvisation: An introduction. In E. Hallam, & T. Ingold (Eds.), *Creativity and cultural improvisation* (pp. 1–24). New York: Berg.

Harrigan, L. (2020). *Calendar project*. Retrieved from https://dreamstate.to/harrigan/index.htm

Ingold, T. (2014). The creativity of undergoing. *Pragmatics & Cognition, 22*(1), 124–139.

Ingold, T. (2015). *The life of lines*. Abingdon: Routledge.

Korn, P. (2013). *Why we make things and why it matters: The education of a craftsman*. London: Square Peg.

Pallasmaa, J. (2009). *The thinking hand: Existential and embodied wisdom in architecture*. Chichester: John Wiley & Sons Ltd.

Parker, R. (2010). *The subversive stitch: Embroidery and the making of the feminine*. London: I.B. Tauris.

Polanyi, M. (1962). *Personal knowledge: Towards a post-critical philosophy* (2nd ed.). London: Routledge & Kegan Paul.

Price, L., & Hawkins, H. (2019). Towards the geographies of making: An introduction. In L. Price, & H. Hawkins (Eds.), *Geographies of making: Craft and creativity* (pp. 1–30). Abingdon: Routledge.

Pye, D. (1995). *The nature and art of workmanship* (2nd ed.). London: Herbert.

Rippin, A., & Vachhani, S. J. (2019). Craft as resistance: A conversation about craftivism, embodied inquiry, and craft-based methodologies. In E. Bell, G. Mangia, S. Taylor, & M. L. Toraldo (Eds.), *The organization of craft work: Identities, meanings, and materiality* (pp. 217–234). Abingdon: Routledge.

Schön, D. A. (1983). *The reflective practitioner: How professionals think in action*. London: Ashgate.

Sennett, R. (2009). *The craftsman*. London: Penguin.

Stalp, M. C. (2006a). Hiding the (fabric) stash: Fabric collecting, hoarding and hiding strategies of contemporary U.S. quilters. *Textile: The Journal of Cloth & Culture, 4*(1), 104–125.

Stalp, M. C. (2006b). Negotiating time and space for serious leisure: Quilting in the modern US home. *Journal of Leisure Research, 38*(1), 104–132.

Stalp, M., & Winge, T. (2008). My collection is bigger than yours: Tales from the hand-crafter's stash. Home Cultures: The journal of Architecture, *Design and Domestic Space, 5*(2), 197–218.

Thomson, P. (2018). *Thesis knowhow – "the contribution" can create coherence*. [Online]. Retrieved from https://patthomson.net/2018/04/02/thesis-knowhow-how-the-contribution-can-create-coherence/

Turner, V. (1969). *The ritual process: Structure and anti-structure*. London: Routledge & Kegan Paul.

Wellesley-Smith, C. (2022) *Claire Wellesley-Smith*. [Online]. Retrieved from http://www.clairewellesleysmith.co.uk

Woodyer, T. (2012). Ludic geographies: Not merely child's play. *Geography Compass, 6*(6), 313–326.

9

MAKING *THE DREAMER*

Cut-ups, Découpage and Narrative Assemblages of Interbeing and Becoming

Mark Price

> *There's a crick in my neck, as I try to look back.*
> *I got what I wanted, but I miss what I lack.*
> *The gap between what we loathe and we treasure*
> *Is hard to accept – it's even harder to measure*
> From the revisionist by The Revisionist (words and music
> by M. Price) Red Black and Blue Records (2017)

Introduction

Years ago, I was given a reproduction statuette of Rodin's *The Thinker* from a cohort of students at the end of their degree – a gift so kindly meant. And when in the pandemic depths, I left my academic role of over 20 years and cleared my office, *The Thinker* came home. Locked-down and zoomed-out, relationality became dislocated and cut up. Muted text. On hold. Eye contact rendered impossible.

Over the coming months, and as an act of agentic recreation, I began to cover the statuette with images from magazines I'd bought and read during lockdown, and added cut-out words later – over time, *The Thinker* becoming *The Dreamer*. The autoethnographic *making process* and *crafted product* became entangled and entwined with *rhizomatic* methodologies of meaning-making: *deconstruction, defamiliarisation* and *intertextuality* of text.

This chapter presents a découpage autoethnography of 'cut up' assemblages of found texts and images applied to a three-dimensional object, as an exploration of self-storying life transitions and transformations. Over the course of the chapter, I render the 'making process' explicit, evoking the shape-shifting, fluid liminality I experienced betwixt teacher and student; researcher and writer; thinker and dreamer.

DOI: 10.4324/9781003309239-13

The narrative presented is sequenced and revisioned, presenting an evocative, embodied creative-relational re-positioning, re-selfing, re-wilding, through the cutting-and-gluing experience.

Texts are chosen for association and resonance in order to illuminate this cut-up, derivative representation – a personal narrative of becoming – layering identities – arriving, not finishing. Through the storying of the assemblage, the chapter writes my process from *Thinker* to *Dreamer*. Rather than 'theorise' the autoethnographic process, it touches on the reference points that spoke to me *en route*: 'touchstones' that influenced and 'texturised' the assemblage in a felt sense.

Déjà écrit

So much storying and narrative development seems to be orientated linearly. Even accounting for 'flashbacks' and 'prequels', book chapters (like this one), conference presentations, TV drama series, film franchises and more, are all sequenced. CVs too. And yet whilst everyday time appears chunked in terms of hours, days and years, when it comes to storying ourselves, it never quite feels to be this straightforward.

My CV tells a story of sorts. I have played many parts – playworker, teacher, youth worker, psychotherapist, academic and writer – and whilst there is a temporal array here, there is so much ebb and flow too. Waves fold over, layering scenes across time and space. A bleeding through of influences; echoes of relationships still sounding at times.

And as so often in the past, even here and even now, I write to 'make sense'; to find meaning in my present and yet-to-be-lived life. And I began to notice too – even though I never set out to do it like this – that my writing appears to be chopped/chunked. Half-formed sentences. Cherry-picking fragments of meaning, like glossy waxwings, our occasional winter visitors, out for what they can get.

In this piece, I aim to write into a process of *'becoming'*. The Möbius strips of life, experience and desire (Alagappan, 2021), represented, re-presented in cut-up form, pasted over one another.

déjà rêvé already dreamt
déjà vécu already lived
déjà vu already seen

This writing explores creative-relational imaging and imagining in the field of what Erin Manning calls *'relationscapes'*, where the emphasis is 'on the immanence of movement moving: how movement can be felt before it actualizes' (2009, p. 6). Or perhaps what might be felt to be, considered as *thoughtforms* – ideas and desires made manifest, through the making, through this writing.

Both this writing and the making process, re-presented and sequenced within this chapter, are evocations and responses to the relational shifts I have experienced over recent time and times. There's no clear destination here – only a revisionist's reclamation. The focus is to explore cut-up, derivative and visually graphic techniques as a process for creating and re/presenting personal narratives of identities in transition; processes of *becoming*. The notion of 'narrative' here is considered through lenses of *life as narrative* (Bruner, 2004), *narrative capital* (Goodson, 2013) and *writing as inquiry* (Richardson & St Pierre, 2005).

Process and Product

The *'product'* of the narrative presented and the *process* of creating and presenting the narrative, are entwined and entangled. *'Rhizomatic'* (Deleuze & Guattari, 1987) methodologies of meaning-making are considered/deployed, alongside *deconstruction* (Derrida, 2001), *defamiliarisation* (Shklovsky, 2017) and *intertextuality* (Kristeva, 1986) of found and written text. In reaching for and finding meaning, I aim for and invite a co-constructive ontological dialogue. Hence, I am writing alone but in relation to others.

The form of the narratives presented is visioned and fashioned from two-dimensional assemblages of found text, into a three-dimensional *découpage*. The source texts are chosen for specific meaning and resonance. The final piece is seen always as a work in progress, the form lending itself to a non-linearity of reading, with an invitation to 'have-a-go', 'do-it-yourself'.

The 'product' is a narrative of reclamation and re-wilding. An embodied projection of a narratable self in transition. At times, in and out of time, I have experienced this as painful and dislocating, liberating and energising, and full of potential and self-doubt and recrimination. But fundamentally this transition and now this project have become processes of re-positioning and re-presenting myself, my *self*. My shifting narrative. My becoming. A process of relational *inter-being* (Nhat Hanh, 2017) – encountering myself through and within relationship with others, human and non-human.

Découpage

All research and all storytelling follow trails laid down by others (see Plummer, 2016). Découpage, the cut-out and stuck-down assemblage of found images and other decoration on three-dimensional objects can be traced back centuries to China and Eastern Siberia, with more latter-day examples from Poland and Italy (Découpage Artists Worldwide, 2020). And of course, the punk aesthetic of the 1970s drew on cut-out re-assemblages as an oppositional disturbance to accepted style and form (see Hebdidge, 1979). Visually, Georges Braque and Pablo Picasso developed *papier collé,* or cut paper techniques at art, whilst William Burroughs and David Bowie, among others, used cut-up techniques with words and verse. Everyone's at it now. In music, the 'sampler' is a creative instrument in its own right. 'Cut and paste' is the click of button away.

Such assemblages – creative placing of found materials to form a new piece – may also be termed *'bricolage'*, a term coined by Lévi-Strauss (1966) to refer to the process of re-making and re-modelling mythological thought from diverse sources. Hebdidge (1979) explores bricolage in relation to the development of style within subcultures, whilst the concept is applied to research inquiry by Kincheloe (2001).

Within qualitative research, collage and related assemblages have begun to be deployed in different contexts, particularly as a way of storying identity experience and meaning-making (e.g. Butler-Kisber, 2008; Lahman et al., 2020 (collage as inquiry); Vacchelli, 2018 (collage making with the migrant and refugee/asylum-seeking women)). Use of découpage specifically, as *making autoethnography*, is less developed. In this chapter, the cutting, glueing and crafting are both conceptually and theoretically positioned, and contextualised personally, as I am living and transitioning through the Covid-19 pandemic, making *The Dreamer*.

Starting Out: The First Cut

I worked in the same UK university for over 20 years – over a third of my life. My work changed during this time, and I'd grown into it, more and more. But I had become root-bound too, ivy entwined my limbs. I knew I had to leave and it was during the first lockdown that it came to an end. I was lucky, I know – I chose to leave. But it was one of the hardest things I've done. It still is.

As a starting point and as an exercise in self-revisioning, I took my recently revised CV and plundered it, poetically (see Figures 9.1 and 9.2).

Recent Study of Personalised Academic
Becoming vulnerable,
Professional identities frame a narrative.
Changing careers,
A new model of boundary crossing
of a shared space
Challenging validation;
Constructions and implications.
Becoming you,
Between a rock and a hard place.

Critical debates about
personal, social partnerships and relationships.

Learning collaborative agency and reading and writing.
Conscientious roles of 'good-son' and 'love-less'.
Dreaming of congruence
and qualitative participatory development.

What would my dad think?
Let's get changed.

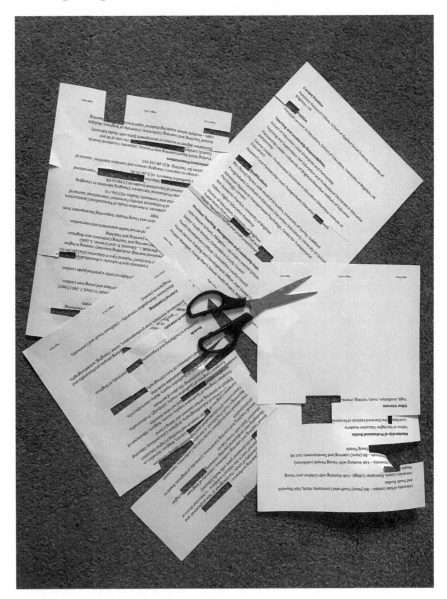

FIGURE 9.1 Cut–up CV alongside. Photograph by author

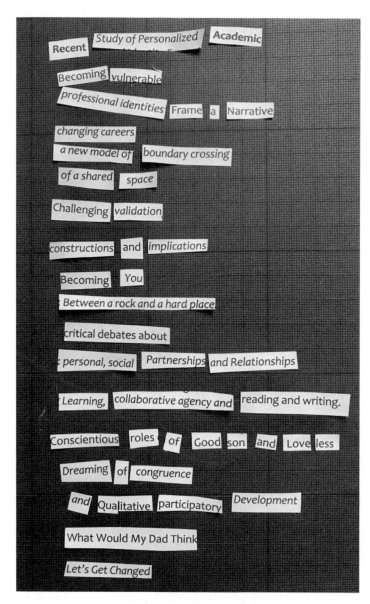

FIGURE 9.2   CV poem. Photograph by author

This was cathartic. Setting the words free of their contextual meaning, something both playful and resonant emerged. Only I knew the references, though I have misplaced several of them now. Seen here, they appear like worn and torn suitcase stickers or faded passport stamps.

And this got the thinking part of me thinking more. *The Thinker* became the focus of transformation; of a relational becoming (see Figure 9.3).

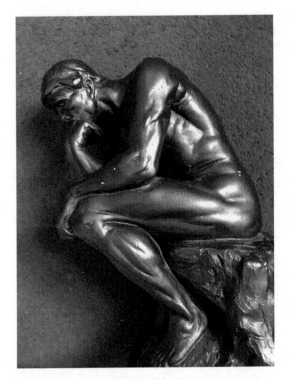

FIGURE 9.3   The Thinker. Photograph by author

Forming and the Form

I started by saving magazines that I was reading at the time: news magazines, landscape and nature magazines, psychology, 'lifestyle' and well-being magazines, and music and guitar magazines (see Figure 9.4). No sport magazines (though I do like some sport) and no travel magazines (though I do like travel). There was little sport or travel during lockdown and so my choice of sources – both what I was drawn to and what made the final 'cut' – was contextually constrained.

First, I covered the statuette with cut-out images and then later added words (see Figure 9.5). The images I collected were all rectangular in shape. I hadn't consciously planned it that way but that's how I cut the pictures out. Formed and bounded by the scissors' severance. And in the layering, you can't always see the whole of each picture. I didn't have the whole picture. Who does?

And of course, with the statuette there are no flat, rectangular surfaces. This means I had to 'stipple' (is that the right word?) the cut-up images into *The Thinker's* cracks and crevices, the nooks and crannies.

FIGURE 9.4 Magazines. Photograph by author

I used a mixture of PVA glue and water. It was runny, messy and tactile; sensual, partial and liminal; fun to do; therapeutic too.

Overall, it took me about six weeks. The process had urgency and agency but I tried not to rush. There was no rush; there is no rush, with any of this.

And *The Dreamer,* as *The Thinker* became, can be read any which way (see Figures 9.6 and 9.7).

FIGURE 9.5 In progress. Photograph by author

FIGURE 9.6 The Dreamer 1. Photograph by author

Here's one reading from an earlier time:

> your skin   a permanent shadow
>   the new vegan
>
>   stories   at the break of dawn
>   the stillness within   an autumn retreat
> ridge of myths carved by ice   great rail journeys
>   a place to make yourself at home
>   once in a lifetime!   years   recover
>   life's too short to ignore your talents
>   lockdown   re-wilding
>   restorative song   chasing the blues away
>   thank you

But even this loses something in the telling. You had to be there, you see.

FIGURE 9.7 The Dreamer 2. Photograph by author

Making the Dreaming Body

There is something very fundamental about validating one's own life experiences, regarding them as a legitimate source of knowledge, all the while recognising the inevitable limitations or what we know personally, and even what can be known. When we become familiar with the rock upon which we ourselves stand, a secure footing can afford us a sense of orientation to the world around and beyond us.

Andrews (2012, p. 33)

The new academic year started. I had no new work schedule. No new teaching responsibilities. No management meetings to attend. No planning meetings. *The Thinker* sat on the floor next to my bookcase. Heavy – though not particularly attractive. Picking it up, feeling its weight, its curves, its form, I remembered the students who'd given it to me – and so many other students before and since them, since then. Students, tutees, supervisees – I had sat with them all; walked with them too.

And now I had none. Both set adrift and set free, I wondered. Daydreaming at times through the ebb and flow of lockdowns, wondering what it might be like to reclaim or situate the figure, as an act of personal reclamation. I knew it would be instinctual – feeling my way into it. We would come and go – together.

Collecting images from magazines at hand, I realise now that magazines have always felt like a treat. When I was young, we had 'summer special' magazines at the start of the holidays. Times of promise. And I still associate magazines with holidays and travel. Train stations and airports – browsing at the racks. Choosing the images was such a delight. Whatever caught my eye – to be ripped first, then trimmed.

And the glue: PVA mixed with water. Playfully. It felt so daring too. It wasn't exactly 'desecration', but for a while, secretively, I didn't tell anyone what I was doing. It felt both private and subversive. The first few images stuck across at angles – avoiding the linear. I lost track of time.

I remember seeing scrap books covered like this – and boxes and table tops too, as I recall. I imagined how *The Thinker* might look, covered in cut and pasted magazine images: reclaimed and rewilded. Wow!! I could choose any-thing!! And yet of course, the choice was limited. As I chose the images and began the layering process, I took delight in the sense of freedom it seemed to evoke. Birds; colours; trees; landscapes; interiors; yoga; music; pallets and patterns of colour. Random and yet arranged. De-cluttering. This was MY process. And remembering more, the different groups of students. And places where I'd taught too. Hopes and dreams. Rushes of excitement. Conferences, lectures, seminars, tutorials. Sifting through it all; a cut-and-paste *memento mori*. And in there, loss too; and vulnerability. Things would be, can never be, the same.

Waking dreams: sometimes the images didn't stick. And it got SO messy. It was easy on *The Thinker*'s back and thigh – smoother, more open expanses. But there were other areas where it didn't come easy. I had to work the chosen images into and across more complicated edges and corners. At times it didn't happen as I wanted it to, but that was all ok too. I just cut again, re-edited and covered it up.

Choosing the words felt different somehow. The resonance was more lit-eral. But I wanted balance too. Representations of interests and identities. Aspirations and affinities. I was re-presenting who I was and who I wanted to be. And the spacing and layering over all became part of it – the ontological assemblage.

It had purpose and affordance. This felt so personal. Frame by frame, word by word, I was becoming. *The Thinker* was becoming *The Dreamer*.

Becoming and Interbeing

I can do this again if I wanted to; if I want to. I haven't added to it for a while, although recently (and probably as a result of writing this), I have begun to think about, dream about it all again. But what can I, could I, dream of next? Where does this process of dreaming, of becoming, take me?

The process and the form itself can never be linear. The 'rhizomatic' nature of my life subverts linearity. I have wondered and wandered so much and yet the wandering is never completely random. But only with distance can I see this. To stand back from the form and process; meaning-making with hindsight – after the event. And yet there is never an 'after' – everything is in process; both being and becoming.

Barthes (1981, p. 39) provides the clarion call for this:

> Any text is a new tissue of past citations. Bits of code, formulae, rhythmic models, fragments of social languages, etc., pass into the text and are redistributed within it, for there is always language before and around the text. Intertextuality, the condition of any text whatsoever, cannot, of course, be reduced to a problem of sources or influences; the intertext is a general field of anonymous formulae whose origin can scarcely ever be located; of unconscious or automatic quotations, given without quotation marks.

With *The Dreamer,* there is no beginning and end, but rather a narrative chronotope of 'intrinsic connectedness of temporal and spatial relationships' (Bakhtin, 1981, p. 84). Gomel and Shemtov (2018) coined the concept of *limbotopia* to represent a narrative without end or closure, and where the chronotope, rather than being chronological in nature, is experienced durationally. Hence, *The Dreamer* is a representation, and embodiment of my own limbotopia – dreaming a present, where a created future is assembled through a découpage of found images and words.

And this dreaming and entanglement is perhaps an identification of becoming. *The Thinker,* originally gifted and then changed through the découpage process of cutting-and-gluing, becomes layered with meaning and dreaming becomings. Shining through the cracks of *interbeing* between me and *The Dreamer,* I become an embodiment of dreaming. I make the dreaming body. As Gomel (2021, p. 2) suggests, 'the temporal aspect of narrative can be subsumed by its spatial dimension', creating (potentially) an infinitely narrative, Möbius strip. I am not *The Dreamer,* but through creating and engaging, intentionally, episodically, rhizomatically, I am able to dream.

So, what is the story? Is it one of crisis and catharsis? Or one of cut-up and making? Or of writing a chapter and giving a presentation? Phillips and Bunda (2018, p. 7) gave us this:

> It is our position that stories are alive and in constant fluidity as we story with them. In research, we see storying as sitting and making emergent meaning with data slowly over time through stories.

Can I plunder this? Can I cut this up and sample and paste it here?

I want to take a position that my stories are alive and in constant fluidity as you and I story with them. I want this storying to sit and make emergent meaning with data (the writing and reading of our stories – yours and mine) slowly over time.

In doing so, I reach for a place of relational intersubjectivity and interbeing, where 'we each take possession, as part of our selves, of the space(s) between "us", or indeed "them"' (Dunlop, 2019).

In crafting my autoethnography, it is through reaching into the liminal space between the writer and the reader, the maker and the object, *The Thinker* and *The Dreamer,* me and you, that resonance and meaning are created. This state of interbeing, where intention connects the blacksmiths' eye, the hammer, the metal, the anvil and the forge.

My storying through making is 'a gesture of longing to recover the past in such a way that one experiences both a sense of reunion and a sense of release' (hooks, 2015, p. 158). The form and process of crafting the autoethnography providing an affordance to dream again. Gluing one fragment onto the next, putting one foot in front of the other; baby steps towards becoming. My becoming was and always is a process of interbeing.

Déjà rêvé

Bellingham (2020, p. 88) proposes that reality 'only emerges via entities in relations and the particular ways of (human and non-human) knowing that are brought to these relations'. But when did I start dreaming again? How was interbeing made becoming?

In the beginning there was diffusion. Meaning-making had become dispersed. Locked in and then locked down. I remember being at a conference in early 2020, just before the pandemic really took hold. We'd been out for dinner somewhere. It was a lovely evening and we were sharing a minibus taxi back into town. Some people I knew well, whilst others I had only met recently. The next day I was presenting a workshop at the conference and I knew I really should get an early night. I asked if I could be dropped off as my apartment was close by. I bade hurried farewells and jumped out of the taxi. But I was wrong. I was nowhere near my apartment. I was lost. I had misjudged all the signs. It was completely the wrong place.

When I left my role of 20 years – 20 years of becoming – my world didn't come crashing down, but rather a lost stillness settled. Everything in its place, but none of it seemingly of my making. But nothing is permanent. I have learned this over and over. That sense of gradually letting go. Gradually disappearing. Sooner or later everyone leaves. To say things are forever is such a mistake and to think otherwise is foolish. And still it happens.

The ancient Greek concept of *Kronos,* sequential, linear time, should be seen, felt, experienced, differently to *Kairos,* the time of festivals and epiphany, when time dances and conjures, and we become lost and found. Kairos is the time of entanglement and enchantment – and Kairos is the *right time:* the propitious time. A time of fecundity and new beginnings.

Leaving my job; getting locked down; cut-ups and stick-ups; from *The Thinker* to *The Dreamer.* This was, this is, an autoethnography of my making.

Traditionally, narrative analysis might anticipate some kind of beginning/middle/end to storying. The découpage process of reclamation explored in this chapter affords a more fluid, iterative, limbotopic autoethnographic process. The mountain shifts its gaze and the river alters its course accordingly. Everything in dynamic movement. The birds still go about their lives. New wild growth comes again through the cracks. Breathing again. And always the cracks.

The découpage process became one of pushing and working into my cracks and creases, as *The Thinker* became *The Dreamer.* In *Kintsugi* – the Japanese art of gluing broken objects and vessels together – rather than hiding the cracks, they are filled with gold, so the broken whole shows its scars and fractures. In coming to this place now, of interbeing, of becoming, I've been working into the cracks, mining for gold.

Holding *The Dreamer* again now, in both hands, turning it, reading it, feeling its heft, I'd like to think/dream that the students who presented me with the statuette would understand and approve of what I've done with it, and the part it's played in my becoming; and with this chapter too. And so now again, 'first I am touched, caressed, wounded; then I try to discover the secret of this touch to extend it, celebrate it and transform it into another caress' (Cixous, 1991, p. 45).

References

Alagappan, S. (2021). The timeless journey of the Möbius strip. *Scientific American*, January 16, 2021. Retrieved from https://www.scientificamerican.com/article/the-timeless-journey-of-the-moebius-strip/

Andrews, M. (2012). Learning from stories, stories of learning. In I. F. Goodson, A. M. Loveless, & D. Stephens (Eds.), *Explorations in narrative research: Studies in professional life and work* (pp. 33–42). Rotterdam: Sense Publishers.

Bakhtin, M. (1981). Forms of time and of the chronotope in the novel. In *The dialogic imagination* (pp. 84–258). Austin: University of Texas Press.

Barthes, R. (1981). Theory of the text. In R. Young (Ed.), *Untying the text* (pp. 31–47). London: Routledge.

Bellingham, R. (2020). Posthuman poetics and the transcorporal, hypercorporeal chronotype. In M. K. E. Thomas, & R. Bellingham (Eds.), *Post-qualitative research and innovative methodologies* (pp. 85–101). London: Bloomsbury.

Bruner, J. (2004). Life as narrative. *Social Research, 71*(3), 11–32.

Butler-Kisber, L. (2008). Collage as inquiry. In J. G. Knowles, & A. L. Cole (Eds.), *Handbook of the arts in qualitative research: Perspectives, methodologies, examples, and issues* (pp. 265–276). Thousand Oaks, CA: Sage.

Cixous, H. (1991). *Coming to writing' and other essays.* Cambridge, MA: Harvard University Press.

Découpage Artists Worldwide (2020). *History of découpage.* Retrieved from https://www.decoupage.org/home/history-of-decoupage

Deleuze, G., & Guattari, F. (1987). *A thousand plateaus: Capitalism and schizophrenia.* London: Continuum.

Derrida, J. (2001) *Writing and difference* (2nd ed.). Abingdon: Routledge.

Dunlop, M. (2019). Inter-subjectivation: cultivating intersubjectivity within cultures of immersive individualism. Panel presentation to *European Congress of Qualitative Inquiry,* Edinburgh, 13th–15th February 2019.

Gomel, E. (2021). Moebius future: The carceral city as a chronotope of post-history. *Academia Letters,* Article 205.

Gomel, E., & Shemtov, V. K. (2018). Limbotopia: The 'new present' and the literary imagination. *Comparative Literature, 70*(1), 60–71.

Goodson, I. (2013). *Developing narrative theory: Life histories and person representation.* Abingdon: Routledge.

Hebdidge, D. (1979). *Subculture: The meaning of style.* Abingdon: Routledge.

hooks, b (2015). *Talking back: Thinking feminist, thinking black.* Abingdon: Routledge.

Kincheloe, J. L. (2001). Describing the bricolage: Conceptualizing a new rigor in qualitative research. *Qualitative Inquiry, 7*(6), 679–692.

Kristeva, J. (1986). Word, 'dialogue and novel'. In T. Moi (Ed.), *The kristeva reader* (pp. 34–61). New York: Columbia University Press.

Lahman, M. K. E., Taylor, C. M., Beddes, L. A., Blount, I. D., Bontempo, K. A., Coon, J. D. … Motter, B. (2020). Research falling out of colorful pages onto paper: Collage inquiry. *Qualitative Inquiry, 26*(3–4), 262–270.

Lévi-Strauss, C. (1966). *The savage mind.* Chicago, IL: University of Chicago Press.

Manning, E. (2009). *Relationscapes: Movement, art, philosophy.* Cambridge, MA: Massachusetts Institute of Technology.

Hanh, N. (2017). *The art of living.* London: Rider.

Phillips, L. G., & Bunda, T. (2018). *Research through, with and as storying.* Abingdon: Routledge.

Plummer, K. (2016). A manifesto for social stories. In L. Stanley (Ed.), *Documents of life revisited: Narrative and biographical methodology for a 21st century critical humanism* (pp. 209–220). Abingdon: Routledge.

Price, M. (2017). 'The revisionist'; on *the revisionist ep* recorded by The Revisionist on Red Black and Blue Records. Retrieved from http://therevisionist.co.uk

Richardson, L., & St. Pierre, E.A. (2005). Writing: A method of inquiry. In N. Denzin, & Y. Lincoln (Eds.), *The sage handbook of qualitative research* (3rd ed., pp. 595–578). London: Sage.

Shklovsky, V. (2017). Art as technique. In J. Rivkin, & M. Ryan (Eds.), *Literary theory: An anthology* (3rd ed., pp. 8–14). Chichester: Wiley Blackwell.

Vacchelli, E. (2018). Embodiment in qualitative research: Collage making with migrant, refugee and asylum seeking women. *Qualitative Research, 18*(2), 171–190.

SECTION IV
Creating Class

10

HIDDEN TIME

An Autoethnographic Narrative on the Creation of *Seven Working-Class Time Pieces*

Aidan Teplitzky

Introduction

During August of 2021, I wrote a collection of pieces for keyboard and metronome called *Seven Working-Class Time Pieces*. The collection explores how time is experienced by working-class people, focusing on areas such as work, personal possessions, commuting, and leisure time. Drawing on my own experiences of being working-class and placing these experiences in the context of earlier research on class and time (Bond, 2020; Cruz, 2021), I provide a wider consideration of how working-class experiences of time are shaped: positively, through the affective 'gift of attention over time' (Skeggs, 2004) and negatively, due to the lack of security related to low wages/part-time work. What follows is a narrative that explores the process of the compositions' making – the hidden thoughts and feelings I had in creating these pieces, and my reflections on their making. Each of the seven pieces draws on me and my family's personal experiences of being working-class. These experiences were then considered in greater depth by examining the larger context of how other working-class people's lives and times(s) are ruled by financial constraints (Cruz, 2021; McKenzie, 2015). A performance of *Seven Working-Class Time Pieces* can be found here: https://www.youtube.com/watch?v=voxr_8cSTc0&t=4s

1. Expiration Date

It all started with the shirt below (Figure 10.1). I found it in the Glasgow Vintage Co. on Great Western Road around eight years ago. I paid nine pounds for it because I got a student discount of ten per cent. I can't explain why it's my favourite shirt because I don't think there is a particular reason anymore. When I first saw it, I was drawn by the pattern of different shades

DOI: 10.4324/9781003309239-15

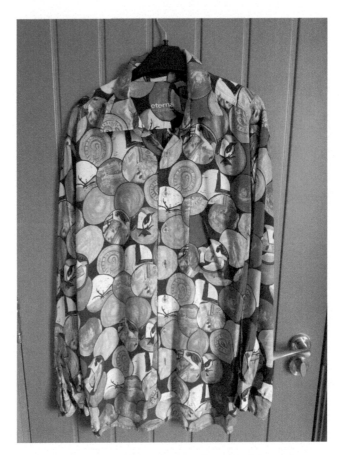

FIGURE 10.1   A blue and white patterned shirt. Photograph by author

of blue with moments of white, like an ocean made of coasters. Now it's my favourite shirt. So much of my life has been lived in this shirt. I need to keep wearing it. I've performed *Seven Working-Class Time Pieces* a number of times now and whenever I am getting ready to do so, I'll look at the shirt. I'll see the frayed threads on the inside of the sleeve. I'll notice the faint creases from the past where I was lazy with my ironing. I'll ignore how much the collar has lost its crisp edge. These moments, which were my private concerns of whether the shirt can last another month, have now become public through *Seven Working-Class Time Pieces*.

And, it all started with this shirt.

I began making *Seven Working-Class Time Pieces* while stuck, staring out the window of my old bedroom in the middle of 2021. In my staring, because of Covid-19, I was waiting for the world to change back to normality. I was stuck because I was alone and feeling worthless. My productivity had disappeared with my job as well as the social networks I relied on to make new work. I forced time to pass me by through watching the clock tick down another day, hoping it might be counting down to the world going back to normal.

I was wearing this shirt.

I had been wearing this shirt for long periods of time – longer than I usually would. I would ignore if it started to smell because it was a little piece of life before everything had closed off. It was the meetings, the nights out, the minutes and hours walked across Glasgow getting the weekly shop in for my mum. It was a life that was past because of Covid and so the ragged threads hidden on the inside of this shirt became a way for me to have that life back.

The shirt became a prime example of Bev Skeggs' idea of affect being the 'gift of attention over time' (Skeggs, 2004, 2011). Skeggs' concept is derived from the idea of affectual significance and considers the time invested by the working-classes into objects and/or pastimes as a way of identifying what is valued by the working-classes, which may be devalued by those outside of their class. We may also take Gershuny's (2002) political economy approach to time, in which he adds in what Marx omitted, namely the nature and distribution of time spent outside paid work. This shirt held both the good and bad times – times spent in *and out* of paid work – that constituted my life for seven years; in having a life lived in this shirt, it became something more to me.

I decided I needed to make something of this shirt and would do so via *Seven Working-Class Time Pieces* for keyboard and metronome. The shirt had become a symbol for what my life was and those experiences needed to be remembered. It came to represent a need to get the most out of everything because thriftiness was a necessary part of being working-class for me. I figured out how much the shirt had cost me to wear per day. I figured out how often the fabric had been on my skin. I figured out a chord that captured the beauty I found in its sea of coasters. But this wasn't enough. I needed to make the time it had been worn coincide with the feelings I had experienced when wearing it – the moments I had of doubting whether I could keep this life. The times I worried about my poverty being seen and judged. The times I questioned whether my money had gone to the right thing, whether I had been correct in how I navigated my relationship to capitalism with what little I had.

The piece became a counting down of the shirt's time. A metronome became time's presence. This decline was subtle before it wasn't any longer. I decided the ambiguity of music was not enough to explain the interconnected threads that built this shirt into becoming a representation of my life. I wanted to explain everything this shirt meant to me so that I was no longer concealing the often hidden class-based relationships that shaped my sense of self in contemporary society. The piece came to stand in for the inherited jewellery, the weather-beaten coats, the sturdy shoes: every purchase that became something more than the object itself because of the 'what-ifs' that surrounded the decision to buy it. The piece made the decline of my shirt, once an ocean made of coasters, into a metaphor for living with the concerns of economic, cultural, and social capital (Bourdieu, 1984; Skeggs, 2004).

It all started with a shirt and ended with that shirt becoming the meeting point of all the threads that connect the individual with the realities of being working-class in this society.

After the first performance of the seven compositions, somebody came up to me and told me they had never thought of a shirt that way before.

I envied them.

2. Off-Time

I was sitting, moving between different technicolour screens hoping for some sense of direction: the TV, my phone, my laptop. Scheduled entertainment in front, social media to the side, and a slow treadmill of unnecessary 'admin' across my thighs. The ritual of moving between different pixelated panes of glass lost its charm quickly in lockdown. I wanted something to appear, suddenly, to shake the habitual into a focus for my mind. Instead, I was left with a brain jogging on the spot for a race that wasn't going to start. I can't say how long I sat like this.

The guilt I felt about 'relaxing' was something I developed in school. I would spend my lunchtime writing music rather than socialising with friends. It seemed more important that I keep working because I believed in meritocracy. Ten years on I still can't relax, even though I know I should. Relaxing seems like a luxury I haven't earned because the rewards came with conditions in the fine print, in which I would never meet the unrealistic expectations of working hard enough to be worthy of meritocratic approval. With an expectation of never earning the right to relax, I lost the ability to fully switch off.

This 'suspension' of myself in a liminal space between working and inactivity translated easily into suspension in harmony – musical notes leading to unsatisfying chromatic dissonance, while a steady pulse kept time slowly moving. Text was restricted to a word per beat, regardless of syllables, in order to create a tension between stability and sudden rushes of immediacy – like the tension felt before the start of a race. The feeling of emptiness I experienced when struggling to find a goal in the constant shifting between pixeled screens became a measured silence in the composition with nothing happening except a sense that time was passing with every swing of the metronome's arm, each moment bringing the recognition that I was hollow when staring from TV to phone to laptop.

I find this piece the hardest to experience. I want it to push on, for fiction to creep in and for the feelings of being/not being I have in trying to relax to be cast aside for something with direction. But that would be lying. I have grown with an expectation that I cannot free myself from not doing enough to earn the right to relax.

I still can't be fine with being 'off-time'.

3. Needed Time of Arrival

Commuting takes up so much of my time. Whether that is in the planning needed either to make sure I can get the cheapest ticket or to find the shortest journey time from A to B.

This piece came about via a combination of two things: wanting to have more time with people I cared about and wanting to be free from the economics of commuting.

I had ended a relationship with someone in Manchester a month before writing this piece and one of the issues we had was the distance between us. It was a three and a half hour journey from Glasgow to Manchester, four and a half door-to-door. Because of this, there was the feeling that we needed to spend our time wisely to make the commute worthwhile. This led to me spending more time with him than I should have at the start of a relationship.

Alongside this came my fascination with superpowers. I don't care that it's childish; the possibility of escaping reality through some innate gift is something I keep on coming back to. I want the ability to teleport anywhere instantly. The removal of the journey to my destination was because so much of my life was focused on 'getting things done'. I didn't have the luxury to *enjoy* travel because time was not on my side. I couldn't savour the journey because I needed to focus on reaching the destination. In the piece, I talk about not wanting to even be able to *control* time, all I want is to be able to teleport anywhere with no *loss* of time. The ridiculousness of this is not lost in hindsight: It would be so much more beneficial for me to be able to control the *measurement* of time, to have a tangible means of controlling this thing that measures out my life. Still, I would rather be able to teleport – to get an instantaneous resolution to whatever goal my time spent on a train, a bus, on foot, or taxi was designed to achieve. I reflect on whether this shows how much of an effect my working-class origins have had on me – that even in fiction, the economic constraints I live under are stifling the fantastical ways I try to escape. The urgent need to keep ahead of work holding my focus so that I cannot see beyond the next task in hand.

The piece expresses the conflict I experienced when attempting to compress time spent travelling. A rising scale provides direction and motion towards a goal. The speed the scale is played at is shortened over the duration of the piece to try and compress the time needed to get from A to B. Alongside this is regimented text. A syllable a beat to provide the reality that no matter how much I try to compress time, I will always be living to the dictates of a ticking clock.

The text also goes into the complexity of the economic costs of different modes of transport and debating which services you can afford. I can't stand using taxis because I can *see* how much they are charging me. I have had enough painful moments watching the little eight-pointed star moving like a clock, adding another 25p to my journey, each completed rotation a marker of distance through time, providing further reasons to question: 'Why didn't I just walk home?' The guilt and annoyance associated with travel costs have often led me to leave nights out for the last train or to walk the hour and a bit from town to my house rather than get a taxi, losing out on both leisure and recovery time.

The piece ends with an acknowledgement of the time I have lost in commuting – time otherwise available to spend with a romantic partner, with friends, or with my mum. Would an ability to teleport have saved my previous relationship or deepened the connection I have to my friends and my family? Impossible to know, but this goal-orientated fantasy is something that drives me to spend as little time on the 'to/between' A and B as possible. To try and make the most of the time I have.

4. Part Time

This piece is about a family member's attempts to participate in a capitalist society. They are referred to as an 'aunty' in the piece. I chose not to specify who they were because I realised they might feel shame over the fact they do this and I didn't want to expose them.[1] What this family member would do is buy something, maybe a dress or some bit of tat for around the house, and own it for a couple of days before returning it. I thought a lot about Bourdieu's (1984) theory of different kinds of 'capital' when composing this piece: his idea that members of the working-class lack access to the kind of resources that society values and this affects their ways of being, confining them to live within an 'adapted habitus'. I thought a lot about how personal choice is constricted by a life defined by precarity. Was my aunty's part-time ownership of items of clothing an active personal choice or an 'adapted' response to the precarity of an inadequate income? The question remains unresolved in the composition; it is left open as an act of 'conferring choice' on someone for whom it is typically limited.

I would like to see their act as one of defiance, a rejection of the idea that a person's value rests on their ability to consume. I would like to see it as a rude gesture to the 'prosthetic lives' represented in advertising, to celebrities who are famous because of their conspicuous consumption (Hebdige, 1994; Veblen, 1912), to people for whom owning something new gives them a sense of purpose (Miller, Jackson, Thrift, Holbrook, & Rowlands, 1998). To reflect this idea of a 'throw away' society, the piece is made up of a myriad of new musical ideas and sounds. Each line starts with a new idea and with a new musical voice before being discarded for the next thing. The lack of regard for making the most of these ideas is to show that newness (see Bell, 1972) is something we are told we need, because capitalism thrives on making us believe the next thing will make us feel whole.

My need to see my family member's act as one of defiance is due to the shame I experience on their behalf – and a sense of frustration that their life is characterised by worry and uncertainty. I need a 'borrowed' defiance to confirm for me a belief that capitalism doesn't provide answers to society's ills, and that chasing short periods of time when we can make ourselves 'new' won't make us content. But this doesn't relieve me from a desire to enable my family members to be free of worry, to be able to spend beyond pure necessity, to enjoy the sense of freedom unnecessary spending can bring. I want them to have that opportunity to *choose* between full-time and part-time ownership, to be able to have something *of one's own,* a life of one's own rather than one that is temporarily rented.

I want them to live a life in which they have 'active' agency, rather than being 'reactive' to the pressures of precarity.

5. Queuing

I am pondering how much time we waste in waiting. In meetings, offices, endless sites of bureaucracy that often seem to me to exist solely to limit me. For three years during my undergraduate and Masters degrees, I worked as the vice-president of a student union. A lot of time was spent listening to wealthy senior staff trying to figure out how to make arts education more like a business. I thought some were brilliant, but that their brilliance was stifled by the demands of the organisation's 'management priorities'. The three years I spent in meetings, hearing people repeat bullet points from 'mission statements' and 'vision workshops', made me realise that most of these people had never lived a personal life driven by deadlines, even if they were familiar with them at work. They never had to worry about the five weeks between losing a job and waiting for Universal Credit to come in. They didn't have to work miracles in their weekly budgeting. They had never lived with the fact their savings will have to save them and not be an extra holiday in the summer.

Am I being too flippant? If so, it is a flippancy born of living a deadline life outside of work as well as inside. If people in management positions had shared such experiences, would they waste the hours and days going over the same ground, I wondered to myself? Would they continue to see the simple passing of time as a marker of progress just because the hours add up? As I think how privileged they are, I wonder whether the social relationships that formed them would equip them with the resources to cope in more economically deprived circumstances, and I question whether they are nevertheless capable of empathy, and my thoughts turn to queuing. Queuing as an attempt to make things fair. Queuing and its effects on the experience of time.

Time does a weird thing when you're stuck in a queue. It is both slow and fast, moving and not moving, present and absent. Thoughts arise of all the times I've sat 'on hold'; shuffling across the laminated floor of a bank; trying to catch the eye of a server working at a bar.

Then again, I *did* make that choice: I made the choice of signing up, campaigning, attending these meetings because I felt there were issues that weren't being addressed in relation to the needs of working-class students. So I chose to spend my time waiting, with other people with points *they* felt needed to be heard. I chose to join that queue. I could have avoided it. I could have hoped someone else would spare the time to deal with these issues and hoped someone else could (and would) spare the time waiting to make their point. But I was in a conservatoire where working-class people were in short supply and I chose to give my time in the hope of making a difference. So I waited in the queue to make my points. It felt like an endurance test. The way time mutated in that queue made me question the validity of my choice: Is my issue actually important? Can I live with this not being resolved? Is someone in greater need behind me? Am I being selfish? Balancing the amount of time you can invest in something against the prospective benefits is crippling for working-class people (see Tyler, 2015). The upper/middle-classes can afford to wait, to bide their time, because they have more flexibility, more time to spend. Their savings don't have to save them.

So I was left thinking about how long things should take, measuring out the stages of life, and trying to evaluate what a suitable amount of time is to get the task completed. It shouldn't take thirty minutes to say an organisation needs to improve its reputation. It shouldn't take five weeks to get your first payment of Universal Credit. But for those living with the realities of being reliant on Universal Credit, such calculations are constant, but change nothing. Those who won't be penalised for spending time queuing don't need to make such calculations.

I translated this into a metronome by itself, beating as slowly as possible. I wanted the time to be seen, to be able to feel its weight, to be able to mimic the queues I have sat in, stood in, inched through. I had initially wanted a metronome that could beat one crotchet a minute, but this proved impossible for a physical metronome. Instead, I physically stopped and started the metronome. This wasn't ideal since it implied that I controlled the time in question – that it was by choice I was stuck listening to senior management waxing lyrical about the latest plans that didn't incorporate the needs of working-class students.

6. Per Hour

I had a routine on the go for eight months. I would have dinner at around five, be finished by five-thirty, then go scrawl through every job search website I could find for about an hour. I'd lost my main source of income as a waiter because of the pandemic. I'd apply to everything I could and then log it all onto the Universal Credit website. A key requirement from Universal Credit is that you need to log all of your job applications and any part-time hours worked in order to get the financial aid. I started out being very selective, only picking jobs I would want to do and that I thought I had the appropriate education to do. This stopped at about the two-month mark, after which I would just apply to anything that I could. When checking through websites, I was desperate to find out how much a job would pay me.

I was stumped by what a pro rata salary actually meant because I didn't finance my life on a yearly basis. I was, at best, living with a per month figure but even this was a compromise in that I wanted to know how much I'd be paid per hour.

I would take the time to figure out what this large number broke down into, in terms of an hourly rate. It was often less than what I was expecting.

I still don't understand why businesses frame a salary as a yearly rate. A year is a long time and it seems strange to think about all the bills, expected and unexpected, that would pile up over a year and how you would determine whether your salary could actually cover everything. It feels like they are tricking you into being amazed by a large number and hoping you wouldn't bother to break that down into the realities of living. I doubt I will ever earn enough to be able to look at my yearly salary and know that I can survive on it. That is part of the reason why I like being paid per hour. When you're paid per hour, you can better quantify how work translates into living. When buying anything, I would think about how many hours it would take for me to earn whatever it was I was buying. The cost of food, bills, rent, travel, all became qualified by the hours I had spent running back and forth across the restaurant floor, picking up hot plates, taking orders, checking customers were okay. I could see how much I was worth with my per-hour living. I could feel as though I had earned everything I bought. I didn't mind that I was living per hour because I could be proud of how hard I'd worked.

While I was working, I would think about how much I was doing and how much that had earned me. I am a hard worker and would strive to do as much as I could, to be as good as I could be. Looking back, such a desire for excessive quality (of work) in exchange for a minimum quantity (of wages) makes me realise just how naïve I was in believing in meritocracy. I wanted to believe that working hard was worth something, that making the most out of my time on the clock was in some way an investment for the future. Such an idea is ridiculous when applied to the six years I worked as a waiter – time spent thinking that my hard work would amount to something, time when my work meant more to me than the value inherent in what I was paid.

Still, I wanted to make the most of every hour I could. I took pride in the quality of my work, how much I could do and the skill I had in doing it, even though I was only being paid minimum wage, including tips. I knew how valuable I was, even though such value was not reflected in what I was paid.

Working on a per-hour basis gave me a complicated sense of understanding of value and worth. I knew how valuable I was, but being limited to only thinking on a per-hour basis shaped my struggle to find work commensurate with my worth, to find a job in which hard work and excellence actually translated into pay that valued my worth as I did.

This complex set of personal and economic relations shaped the music for this piece. Moving between two beautiful chords that represented being free from the physical sense of time and mirroring my love of hard work, only to be rushed when faced with the reality of per-hour living, the piece ending with the chords now restricted by the ticking of time, in an acknowledgement of the fact that even now, I think about how many hours it would take for me to earn whatever I purchase.

7. Repetition

While travelling to Manchester from Glasgow, I was in the in-between bit before Manchester Oxford Road while reading Cynthia Cruz's book 'The Melancholia of Class' (Cruz, 2021). I had finished six of the working-class time pieces but felt there was something missing from the collection. I was concerned I had missed something vital that meant the collection was not good enough to express the realities of how time is experienced in a working-class life. In front of me were two girls who had joined the train at Preston. They were getting off at Manchester Piccadilly and to kill the final ten minutes before pulling into the station they asked each other a question:

'Would you rather have two million pounds or two pound every time I pissed you off?'

'Two pound every time you pissed me off.'

'Would you rather have two million pounds or two pound every time I stressed you out?'

'Two pound every time you stressed me out.'

In that apparently insignificant moment, these two girls showed me what I had been missing in the collection: I had not addressed the reality that working-class lives kept on repeating themselves. In that moment of understanding that each of them believed they would earn more money being pissed off and stressed at each other, the reality of all the previous pieces became clear. I interpreted them to myself anew:

1. I would continue to repeat the need for sustainability in every purchase I made.
2. I would continue to repeat the struggle of feeling unworthy of being off time.
3. I would continue to repeat the challenge of making the most of my time.
4. My family member would continue to repeat the act of owning things part time.
5. I would continue to repeat the anxiety of living with queuing.
6. I would continue to repeat the feeling I was living a per-hour life.

Each of the pieces held an understanding that much of my working-class experience would shape my future, that the way I experienced time would repeat itself in how I lived my life. The piece evolved into a way of measuring out the grim reality that the two girls would earn more from the repetitions of their conflicted relationship than a two million pounds lump sum. Music crept in to measure each financial gain through their trauma: two notes, dissonant but still connected, repeating for each pound they earned.

I didn't want this piece to be the end of the collection. It spoke too much of the painful reality of working-class lives in which the trauma of your past will creep into your future.

I wonder where those girls are now.

I hope they haven't earned as much as they thought they could by pissing each other off and stressing each other out.

After the End

Seven Working-Class Time Pieces provides an exploration, through musical movements, of various ways in which I and other working-class people close to me experience time. They illustrate: the need for belongings to last as long as possible; being unable to switch off from working because you feel you have not earned the right; negotiating different ways of reducing your commuting time; having to purchase things solely through need rather than want; the endurance test of working towards change; how a minimum wage inhibits how you value yourself; and knowing the problems of a working-class life will repeat themselves – all constituting what Bourdieu and Passeron (1977) refer to as social reproduction; that is, the social processes through which culture is reproduced across generations through the socialising influence of major institutions. In this chapter, I have described the process behind the composing of the pieces and have revealed the hidden class-based thoughts that underpin perceptions of and relationships with time for those whose lives are characterised by precarity.

Seeking to rectify a gap in research, Blyton, Hassard, and Starkey (1989) commented that:

> ... studies which access the heterogeneous and recursive nature of time ... are scarce. Few writers document how actors experience working time as qualitative and heterogeneous: that is, how they obtain meaning through the recurrence of temporally ordered events, and how they construct their own time reckoning systems.
>
> *pp. 13–14*

Seven Working-Class Time Pieces aims to contribute a better understanding of class-based experiences of time; and the elaboration here of the work's 'making' illuminates autoethnographic approaches to this field.

I don't know how I feel about *Seven Working-Class Time Pieces*. I think I am happy with them, but I am aware of how melancholic and hopeless they are. I wish I could have written some movements that didn't feel so sad, that expressed a belief that things can change and that this period of time will pass. I hope there *is* some change, that there will be less fruitless repetition in the lives of working-class people, that we will be relieved of the challenges we currently face.

But I don't know. I speculate that this is another element of working-class lives: to be stuck in the present, trying to recover from the past, and hoping to live more freely in the future. It is certainly in line with research showing that the role socio-economic status plays in shaping individuals' experience of the world includes influencing the self that people envision for the future (Antonoplis & Chen, 2021).

Until change comes, we deal with each day as it comes.

Note

1 A significant concern of autoethnographical research is ensuring an ethical approach to the narratives of others that connect with your own (Edwards, 2021) and even strategies aimed at such safeguarding (e.g. 'process consent' [Ellis, 2007]) may cause more emotional harm than good due to the subject matter in question. In my own attempts to provide respect and dignity to the family member mentioned, I emphasise my own interpretation of their actions without drawing any conclusions about their intentions. In doing so, I see my use of autoethnography as consistent with Lee's 'striv[ing] to achieve a version of the self and an account of events that is consistent and acceptable to their own conscience' (2018, p. 313).

References

Antonoplis, S., & Chen, C. (2021). Time and class: How socioeconomic status shapes conceptions of the future self. *Self and Identity*, *20*(8), 961–981.

Bell, D. (1972). The cultural contradictions of capitalism. *The Journal of Aesthetic Education*, *6*(1/2), 11–38.

Blyton, P., Hassard, J., & Starkey, S. (1989). *Time, work and organization*. London: Routledge.

Bond, C. (2020). I have measured out my life with coffee spoons. In J. Van Galen, & J. Sablan (Eds.), *Amplified voices, intersecting identities: Volume 2*. Leiden: Brill.

Bourdieu, P. (1984). *Distinction: A social critique of the judgement of taste*. London: Routledge.

Bourdieu, P., & Passeron, J. C. (1977). *Reproduction in education, society and culture*. London: Sage.

Cruz, C. (2021). *The melancholia of class: A manifesto for the working classes*. London: Repeater Books.

Edwards, J. (2021). Ethical autoethnography: Is it possible? *International Journal of Qualitative Methods*, *20*, 1–6.

Ellis, C. (2007). Telling secrets, revealing lives: Relational ethics in research with intimate others. *Qualitative Inquiry*, *13*(1), 3–29.

Gershuny, J. (2002). Service regimes and the political economy of time. In G. Crow, & S. Heath (Eds.), *Social conceptions of time*. London: Palgrave Macmillan.

Hebdige, D. (1994). *Hiding in the light*. London: Routledge.

Lee, C. (2018). Culture, consent and confidentiality in workplace autoethnography. *Journal of Organizational Ethnography*, *7*(3), 302–319.

McKenzie, L. (2015). *Getting by: Estates, class and culture in austerity Britain*. London: Policy Press.

Miller, D., Jackson, P., Thrift, N., Holbrook, B., & Rowlands, M. (1998). *Shopping, place and identity*. London: Routledge.

Skeggs, B. (2004). Exchange value and affect: Bourdieu and the self. In L. Adkins, & B. Skeggs (Eds.), *Feminism after Bourdieu*. Oxford: Blackwell.

Skeggs, B. (2011). Imagining personhood differently: Person value and autonomist working-class value practices. *The Sociological Review, 59*(3), 496–513.

Tyler, I. (2015). Classificatory struggles: Class, culture and inequality in neoliberal times. *The Sociological Review, 63*(2), 493–511.

Veblen, T. (1912). *The theory of the leisure class*. New York: Macmillan Company.

11

COMING BACK TO CLASS

The Remaking of an Academic Self

Chrissie Tiller

April 2013

I walk into Richard Hoggart Building 150 in Goldsmiths, University of London, the room we use for the MA I set up and run in Participatory and Community Arts in 2004. Whenever we work here we move the desks to the sides and place the chairs in a circle: determined to mirror the inclusive, dialogic, collaborative nature of the practice itself. Some of my students are already setting up their materials (bamboo sticks, paper cups, coloured string), for their workshop looking at balance as a practical introduction to exploring equality, equity and mutual exchange. This is the way we work. We make, we do, we move from the physical and experiential to the reflective (Dewey, 1939): sharing and drawing on the theoretical where it aids that reflection. Since we left the space yesterday, someone has written on the whiteboard, in large angry capital letters: 'Put the chairs and tables in this room back into rows facing the front when you have finished. TEACHING happens here!' As I come through the door one of my students, applauded by the others, is adding an exclamation mark to her response: 'Yes, but LEARNING happens in our sessions!'

Nine years into the MA in Artists in Society: Cross-Sectoral and Community Arts I established in 2004, to provide an education for artists working in more social contexts, it seems my students and I are still engaged in a struggle with the neoliberal academy's dominant, often patriarchal, forms of teaching and learning. I find myself momentarily revisiting the doubt and uncertainty that filled me the first day I walked into what I realised was 'my office' in this building. How on earth was I, a working-class woman, with a 2.2 in English and a Post-Graduate Certificate in Education in English and Drama, whose most recent brush with the world of academia was teaching practice-based modules, ever going to create an MA curriculum? Especially as some of senior management

DOI: 10.4324/9781003309239-16

had already questioned whether, as I didn't have an MA myself, I was the right person. As I looked at the green leather covered desk and dark oak book-filled shelves behind it, I tried to reassure myself I wasn't here under false pretences.

I was 55. I had taught English and Drama in the 1970s, gone back to Theatre School and led a Theatre in Education company in the 1980s, set up and run networks and training programmes for artists for National Theatre Education Department, the European Cultural Foundation and other funders across Central and Eastern Europe in the 1990s. In 1998, I had even persuaded the Portuguese Leader of Directorate General V at the European Union to invest over half a million euros enabling me to research possible learning models for artists working in more collaborative and social contexts.[1] The MA was the result of this research: research I had been asked to share across the European Commission to describe the contribution artists might make to intercultural dialogue, participatory governance and social inclusion. And yet, here I was, sitting behind this desk, feeling, as so many post-1944 Education Act, eleven-plus, first-generation university girls from working-class backgrounds have done, 'like a fraud' (McIntosh, 1985) and an imposter. Waiting for the institution to expose me.

22 March 2022

I have confidently declared in the framing statement for my PhD by practice and prior publication, that it will situate the past decade of my work within Gramscian theories of hegemony and counter-hegemony, proposing it is at the crucial intersection of critical and feminist pedagogy, radical theatre practice and gender and class-based activism, that a distinct critical voice has emerged. One that has enabled me to adopt a positionality as determined agent of change, on one hand, and influence cultural policy, on the other.

So far, so good. Sixteen years after I entered that room in Goldsmiths, I have learned to play the academic game (Bathmaker, Ingram, & Waller, 2013). I understand how to allude to Gramscian theories, to reference feminist ethnography and autoethnography. I have learned to use words such as 'situate' and 'positionality' (Miss Lord, who used to mark our compositions at school by ticking how many long words we used, would have appreciated this). My proposal has been accepted by the academy. All I have to do is sit down and write.

On my daily walk to the British Library, everything seems possible. Striding purposefully along the canal path, I rehearse what I want to say. I repeat it in different registers (I have always liked the fact the French word for rehearsal is répétition). I am clear and decisive. I give my 'self', (sensing the need to question whether in a post-structural, post-Derrida, Foucault, Levinas world such a self can even exist) a good talking to. I tell this 'self', I write. This is what I do. I write to share learning, make the theoretical accessible and provoke critical thinking. I write to empower artists and activists to better understand how they might draw on action and reflection as part of their praxis (Freire, 1970). I write to encourage curators, producers and arts organisations to question what quality might mean in the context of more relational aesthetics (Bourriaud, 1998), and as engaged with 'authenticity of process, empathy (and) relationship' (Kester & Lacy, 2011, p. 12) as with product. I write to persuade policymakers to abandon the 'chimera of social inclusion' (Cultural Policy Collective, 2004), for greater systemic change and 'a radical rethinking of funding structures' (Tiller, 2017, p. 12).

In the past few months, I have been commissioned to write a foreword on community leadership (Tiller 2022, p. 3), a provocation on cultural democracy for the Ministry of Culture in Oslo, an evaluation of English PEN's centenary, a (deliberately provocative) literature review for *Considering Co-Creation* (Heart of Glass and Battersea Arts Centre, 2021) for Arts Council England and 'Care as a Radical Act', a call to action, in response to Covid-19, in which I challenged the UK arts sector, 'to dare to think collectively' and 'reclaim the radical space and create a new blueprint for the society we want to live in' (Tiller 2020, p. 6).

I Write

'I write. This is what I do'. Why then, each time I pick up my pen to write this thesis (I am of course typing but picking up the pen feels a much more effective poetic metaphor), do I remain filled with anxiety and dread? Why is there an ever-growing series of documents labelled 'starts, false starts and restarts' in the PhD folder on my laptop? Why am I still affected by those 'structures of feeling' and 'psychic economies' (cited in Goode, 2019, p. 350) of class and gender, waiting for someone to trip me up and prove women like me will never 'inhabit the norm'? (Ahmed, 2017, p. 115)

Starts, False Starts and Restarts: One

> Even the greatest forces of intimate life - the passions of the heart, the thoughts of the mind, the delights of the senses - lead an uncertain, shadowy kind of existence unless and until they are transformed, de-privatized and de-individualized, as it were, into a shape to fit them for public appearance.
> *Arendt (1958, p. 50)*

In a letter to my supervisors after a particularly painful tutorial, in which a piece of work I had felt quite proud of turns out to be clearly off the mark, I try to explain why my progress is so stuttering, diffident, hesitant and painful. I describe how the fear of having 'nothing to say of any value or importance' and of being 'incapable of getting it right' (Kuhn, 1995, pp. 97–98) has become painfully reminiscent of how I felt as an undergraduate over 50 years ago.

I tell them of the 18-year-old, working-class 'clever girl', who frequently felt out of place, out of her depth and never quite academic enough. I relate the way I turned up to my first university interview at Durham University wearing a hat (albeit one bought from the Leeds equivalent of Biba) because I thought it might make me look 'posh'. I speak of my humiliation when the Professor asked me if my grammar school, Notre Dame, was a boarding school, because 'although it isn't a prerequisite to coming here it prepares people so much better for college life'. I explain how socially inadequate I felt (long before I understood Bourdieu's (2019) notions of habitus, field, and cultural capital) when I met my first tutorial partner, Ginger, who was American, was married to an England cricketer who taught in the Philosophy Department and was erudite in a kind of American novelist way, constantly made references to books and writers and music and theatre and dinner parties I knew nothing of. I confess the cyclical shame of hiding one's family roots, of lying about what my parents did (Skeggs, 1997), of never revealing my Dad's mental health issues, which meant he was rarely in work, or that my Mum was a cleaner at a university hostel in Leeds.

I describe to them how, after my Dad died in my first university vacation and I spent most of my time at the Social Security office helping ensure my mum had enough income to support her and my younger brother and sister, I wrote to my tutor, and he told me I could take an extra week for my essay. And how I only got a 2:2 in the end because I started to feel less and less confident that I had a right to be there or even understand what was needed.

It is at this point, as I consider giving up my struggle with 'getting it right', a fellow student, Mary Ann de Vlieg, sends me a copy of Jackie Goode's book, *Clever Girls: Autoethnographies of Class, Gender and Ethnicity* (2019). I skim read the first chapters which explain the book's positioning in a line of British scholarship on class and culture from 'Richard Hoggart's *The Uses of Literacy*'...to 'Valerie Walkerdine and colleagues' *Growing Up Girl*' (Goode, 2019, p. ix). Working in the arts sector where social class remains the elephant in the room, or the 'coffin that stays empty' (Hanley, 2016), I think I might always add Williams' *Culture is Ordinary* (1958) to that lineage. But it is the 'clever girl' stories rather than the theory I am hungry for at this moment; recognising a need to find myself within these pages and discover a sense of 'belonging' to this 'community in the making' (Lewis, 2009, p. 6) of working-class women for whom the struggle to find their place has, like mine, been central to their formation.

It is not difficult to find those echoes. If Thomas' eleven-plus experience differs from mine, her feigning of disinterest in (paid) school trips, discomfort at playground taunts that 'Council houses are where common people live!' (Thomas, 2019, p. 76) and her scorn for a 'careers education' that consists of 'tired floppy prospectuses for teacher training colleges' (Thomas, 2019, p. 81) are almost unbearably familiar. But it is Goode's reminder of her 'yes, yes' experience of first reading Hanley's *Respectable: The Experience of Class* (2016) that drives me to write her an email:

> Although your family was clearly different to mine, I began to recognise my own experience of growing up on a council estate in Leeds in so much of the writing. Then I got to the part where you describe your interview at Durham and your subsequent acceptance of a place at Newcastle and

the floods of tears began. I also had a disastrous interview at Durham at 18 and nearly gave up on the idea of university but then like you went to Newcastle.

Tiller (2021)

The disdain Goode senses in the interviewer's voice is unnervingly recognisable, as is the response of her 18-year-old self, who like me at that age, understands social class as something to do with 'the binaries of *posh* and *common*' (Goode, 2019, p. 103, original emphasis). My mother's fierce dismissal of two older female cousins, who were not only smoking but also wearing scarves over their rollers in Leeds Bus Station, is my own introduction to those binaries. Goode's note that it took another 30 years for anyone to write about the role of clothes and style (Reay, 1997), along with vocabulary and accent (Hey, 1997) in creating self-doubt, underlines my own sense of insecurities played out in needing to wear the right thing as much as use the right language.

I recognise, like Goode, that I am the product of a particular historical time and space for 'clever' working-class women, born into what Hall and Massey (2010) identify as the social reform ethos of a post-war conjuncture filled with working-class aspiration and idealistic notions of social mobility through education. I also recognise Goode's analysis of the complex and contradictory nature of this space, where the fear of failing or being found out (Walkerdine, Lucey, & Melody, 2001) looms large, and where, as so many of these 'clever girls' note, one is also haunted by a lack of self-worth that comes from the cyclical shame of hiding one's family roots that has felt part of that process (Skeggs, 1997). A space Hoggart (1957), writing about the feelings of uprootedness and anxiety, experienced by an earlier generation of 'scholarship boys', suggests comes from the sense that one never belongs fully to either the world one has left or the world in which one has arrived. Or which Reay (2017) speaks of as the 'oscillation, ambivalence, guilt and inauthenticity' which are a constant feature of upward social mobility and the 'affective aspects of class' (p. 114).

In the introduction to *Power Up* (Tiller, 2017), which is one of the few times I dare to use the autographical 'I' within my texts, I share the story of a visit to Leeds to see my cousin Pauline (she of the cigarettes and rollers) before she died. Revisiting the description of what I 'gave up' when I made the journey away from my Leeds roots, I now find it disconcertedly flippant: 'My Yorkshire accent, a sense of where I belonged and proper custard slices, Saturday afternoons at Auntie Mary's...' (Tiller, 2017, p. 6). A year later, in a review of Anu's immersive theatre piece, *Torch*, which shares stories of working-class women in St. Helens over the same period, I speak of a blurring of time and place which reconnects me with those women I left behind. Women whose lives were 'lived out, unnoticed and unrecorded'. Women such as the desperate 'young mother who nearly had her sons taken away from her because one day she fell asleep on the sofa, let a cigarette end drop, and almost burnt her house down: taking ours with it', or my own mother 'spending all day in the Social Security Office or waiting for handouts from the St Vincent de Paul to buy Christmas presents'. Women who somehow 'became the glue for each other's splintered lives' and in doing so held on 'to their vitality and their anger at the injustices of this world' (Tiller, 2019).

Starts, False Starts and Restarts: Two

> As a radical standpoint, perspective, position, 'the politics of location' necessarily calls those of us who would participate in the formation of counter-hegemonic cultural practice to identify the spaces where we *begin* the process of revision.
>
> *hooks (1989, p. 15, emphasis added)*

If on that day in 2004, one 'self' was sitting in that office writing out ideas for the curriculum in pencil, in order to rub them out if the 'real' academics in senior management questioned them, there was another 'self' present. The 'self' who, like my mum, is well practised at 'giving a good talking' to the other one. This is the 'self' who grew up among those women on a Leeds council estate, was schooled in class-consciousness and feminism in the 1970s and 1980s and has built a lifetime's practice informed by feminist, transformative, pedagogy (hooks, 1994). It was this 'self' who decided to tear up the notes I had made for a phantom lecture-based MA, place them in the litter bin in Goldsmiths' quadrangle and determine to resist the traditional model I had been offered by locating the curriculum within the 'realm of oppositional political struggle' (hooks, 1989, p. 15) which informed my practice. Responding, in doing so, to Giroux and McLaren's (1991) call to uncover and transform the systems of domination by 'rupturing disciplinary boundaries, decentring authority, and rewriting the institutional and discursive borderlands in which politics becomes a condition for reasserting the relationship between agency, power, and struggle' (hooks, 1994, p. 129).

This 'self' was also the one who believed, with Stuart Hall, when asked what he was most proud of in his life (here I confess remembering this from listening to him on BBC Radio 4 Desert Island Discs), that I was 'a good teacher' and a good 'enabler of other people doing things', especially those who did not come from a 'formal educational background'.[2] I sensed this space was my opportunity to begin that 'process of revision' (hooks, 1989, p. 15), which would not only draw on everything that had informed my own learning across the years but would also involve us in 'an unlearning' of the 'inherent dominative mode' which Williams (1958, p. 376) speaks so powerfully of.

I also decided I needed 'accomplices' in this struggle. One of these was Marjorie Mayo, Head of Professional and Continuing Education (PACE) – a Department with a reputation for radical thinking and commitment to the local community. Phil Mullen, from Community Music, Andy Porter from Digital Media for Social Change and theatre practitioners and educators Rachel Dickinson and

Sara Clifford made up the team. All of them committed to validating lived experience and implementing practice-based learning. Situating ourselves in PACE rather than an arts discipline, facilitated the battle with university regulations to ensure significant practical experience within professional and/or community arts as a practitioner and/or activist would be valued as highly as any first degree. It also enabled us to demand our students could take five years to complete the MA, instead of the usual one year full-time or two part-time, thereby making it accessible to those whom financial constraints and care duties might otherwise have excluded.

Turning to a text that has been my touchstone as arts practitioner, teacher, activist and writer for over 40 years, *Reclaiming the Margins* (hooks, 1989), I was resolute the curriculum would also embrace 'creativity and power' by being arts-based and experiential and reflect the inclusive, non-hierarchical and collaborative nature of the work itself. Our prospective students, many of whom identified themselves as 'other', or as belonging to what feminist theory defines as 'the periphery', along with the communities they chose to work with, would be our 'critical co-investigators' (Freire, 1970, p. 79) on this journey.

Our first cohort included an Afro-Caribbean woman storyteller, a number of community musicians with little or no formal music training, a theatre-maker and a psychologist from Brazil (women who worked together as carers in homes for the elderly), a Japanese Theatre of the Oppressed expert working in the Philippines, a Mexican documentary maker and a Romanian civil society activist. Each of them brought diverse lived experience, not only as artists and activists but also as workers (paid or unpaid) in sectors, including the care system, formal and non-formal education, social services, community development and counselling. I wanted them to recognise that experiences were as important to our shared conversations and process of 'unlearning' as any formal qualifications they might bring to the table. Freire's principle of praxis as 'reflection and action on the world in order to transform it' (Freire, 1970, p. 52), I determined, would be at the root of everything we did. We, the teachers, would be 'taught in dialogue with the students … jointly responsible for a process in which all grow' (1970, p. 56). Our 'classroom' would be not only 'the most radical space of possibility in the academy' (hooks, 1994, p. 12) but also a place where 'excitement' and 'fun' were an integral part of the process of learning (1994, p. 7).

Taking out a large piece of A3 paper, I began to map out an inventory of concepts, people and places that had influenced my practice over the years. Sadly, this piece of paper no longer exists and in attempting to reproduce it in any form, I am conscious of the impact the act of rethinking and rewriting (Reed-Danahay, 1997) will inevitably have on its content. I started, as I always do, with the doing, using an exercise I first led in 2000, when we brought artists together from across former Yugoslavia following the NATO bombings. I trace around my hand, writing on each digit in turn, beginning with my thumb, what drives me in the work, what I want to change, what I bring to that, what my challenges might be, one thing that has inspired me on this journey and in the palm, one thought I hold dear. It is the first exercise the students and I do together and one I still offer as a way of opening up spaces for dialogue and reciprocal exchange.

Rediscovering the original 'Indicative Reading List', I note it is headlined by *Teaching to Transgress* (hooks, 1994), *Deschooling Society* (Illich, 1971), *Pedagogy of the Oppressed* (Freire, 1970) and Dewey's (1939) *How We Think*. If, looking back now, I spot a remarkable absence of Gramsci or Bourdieu (rectified I hasten to add in later iterations), I might want to concur with Freire (1995, p. 63) that: 'I read Gramsci and I discovered that I had been greatly influenced by Gramsci long before I had read him. It is fantastic when we discover that we had been influenced by someone's thought without even being introduced to their intellectual production'. In one corner, I also scribbled names that were not part of that canon but were people who had helped me understand what transformative pedagogies might be. I reproduce them here, as a reminder of their generosity of spirit: Tony Harrison, poet and, for one year, my tutor at Newcastle and Dorothy Heathcote, drama in education expert, and Ljubica Beljanski-Ristic, leader of Stari Grad, Belgrade, who taught me reciprocity in action.

'Without practice', Freire proposes, 'there is no knowledge, but in order to use that knowledge we need to underpin it: with "a theoretical type of practice"' (cited in Horton & Freire, 1990, p. 98). While I wanted my students to feel confident in their practice, I also wanted them to be able to underpin it with rigorous critical thinking. Owen Kelly, in his pivotal book *Community, Art, and the State: Storming the Citadels* (1984), had argued one of the major failings of that movement lay in a reluctance to 'engage in serious theoretical debate of the sort needed to establish a political framework' which meant there was 'no shared theory and no shared language...to begin a discussion'. An absence he asserts, which allows the practice to 'be overlooked or neglected within official narratives' (Kelly, 1984, p. 53), an absence I have also suggested undermines its ability to resist the de-politicisation and co-option of the work by the cultural hegemony and mainstream institutions (Tiller, 2017).

Explaining the place creating that shared language played in developing the MA in *Hybrid lives of teaching artists in dance and theatre arts*, I touch on a delight in discovering Polanyi (1958) on valuing 'tacit knowledge' and Schön (1984) on the difference between reflecting 'in-action and on-action', alongside Dewey's (1939) thoughts on reflective thinking as a process which encourages open-mindedness (freedom from prejudice), wholeheartedness or absorbed interest, and responsibility in facing consequences (Tiller, 2014, p. 11). Combining the interdisciplinarity of the sources I reached out to, constantly driven by a 'need to learn as much as possible about the ways in which meaning is produced in and through these other contexts' (Kester, 2000, p. 5), and the hope that by enabling artists 'to draw on analytic resources from other areas such as critical theory, social history or environmental science', we might also connect them to other 'existing sites of political and cultural resistance' (p. 5–6).

Starts, False Starts and Restarts Three: July 2014

At the end of an academic year during which I have been undergoing treatment for breast cancer and am forced once again (I have already had cancer in 1988) to 'face the essentials questions of my own mortality' (Lorde, 2020, p. 21), my white, male, middle-class, Oxbridge Line Manager calls me into college for what he says will be a five-minute meeting.

Sitting poker-backed behind his desk, he proceeds to tell me that he and senior management have decided, during my sick leave, that in light of a large Departmental deficit and a need for more BA student fees, my MA is being withdrawn as part of a multi-stranded approach to reshaping the department's profile and ensuring its sustainability. A practice-based MA, which takes up time and staff resources, he suggests, no longer seeming a good fit for a Department which has decided to go in a more research-based direction. I fold my arms across my breast, in the protective movement that has become instinctive since my mastectomy and say nothing. He glances at his watch. I may, he proposes, want to think about a more traditional dissertation-based MA, which would involve a smaller team (me) and fewer contact hours, but even that couldn't be guaranteed. Then, as if to signify the meeting is already over, he stands up and holds the door open.

Forced to recognise that while progressive, radical, feminist and transformative pedagogy may form the subject matter of courses in the academy, it is rarely welcome in practice, especially when it actually seeks 'to make a difference to what happens in the institutional world in which it is located' (Hall, 1992, p. 284), I also stand. And, defiantly using what Childers identifies as the 'pit bull voice' – 'activated in all sorts of adult settings when class origins become apparent' (Childers, 2002, cited in Goode, 2019, p. 90) – I offer my resignation.

23 March 2022

In his introduction to *The Art of Listening* (2007), Back tells us that, despite being a wonderful writer, wordcraft did not come easily to sociologist C. Wright Mills, sharing a story of Mills complaining to a friend while writing *White Collar* that he just 'can't write it right' (Mills et al., 2000, p. 136). There is something wonderfully reassuring when I note Mills was writing this in 1949, the year of my birth. It is moments of self-revelation like this, that somehow connect with my own lived experience, that have so often drawn me to those like hooks, whose work I continually return to as my guides. 'Language is', as hooks herself insists, 'a place of struggle' (1989, p. 16). For many working-class women, that place of struggle has often been compounded by a need to confront the silence and inarticulateness imposed by the feeling one continually belongs on the margin. Revisiting the closure of the MA following my resignation, I recognise the care with which I worked, with my students and colleagues, to craft it as a space of radical possibility and resistance as well as struggle. A space which allowed me to learn and unlearn, look back and move forward and as such form the keystone of the arch that is my creative practice, holding and locking its disparate elements together.

If 'coming back to class', metaphorically, as well as literally, has forced me to re-confront the fears and anxieties imposed by moving 'out of one's space' (hooks, 1989, p. 15) as a working-class woman in arts and culture and academia, it has also set me off on a new journey. A journey which has given me permission, through re-engaging with the texts and actions which make up the decade my PhD focuses on, to take care of and craft that self in a more authentic way. If that process has proved painful at times, it has also reintroduced me to what Dissanayake speaks of as the *joie de faire* (Dissanayake, 1994), or joy of learning through making and doing which has always been at the centre of my practice as a socially engaged theatre-maker and pedagogue. The task of writing the PhD, and the act of claiming the situated knowledge (Haraway, 1988) which has been an essential part of that process, has begun to enable me not only to see myself anew but also to integrate these past experiences into that new self.

Holding on to hooks' (1989) invitation to see language and writing as part of a creative process where we can recover, reconcile, reunite and renew our past selves, I now dare to imagine that the act of writing this PhD thesis may become a space of knowledge production that will free me to share 'not just who I am in the present but where I am coming from', as well as enabling me to share 'the multiple voices within me' that are part of that (1989, p. 16). Knowing that I will have old and new 'accomplices' in this re-constitution of self, partly through my discovery of *Clever Girls* (Goode, 2019) and a group of women from a similar historical, social and cultural context, whose stories resonate so powerfully with my own, the journey is already beginning to feel more affirming this time round.

Notes

1 'Transmission' is a seven-year transnational programme, funded by DGV, the Directorate General for Employment, Social Affairs and Inclusion at the European Union. It developed creative training, mobility and employment opportunities for artists working in participatory contexts.
2 https://www.derekbishton.com/professor-stuart-halls-desert-island-disks/

References

Ahmed, S. (2017). *Living a feminist life*. Durham: Duke University Press.

Arendt, H. (1958). *The human condition*. Chicago: University of Chicago Press.

Back, L. (2007). *The art of listening*. London: Bloomsbury.

Bathmaker, A. M., Ingram, N., & Waller, R. (2013). Higher education, social class and the mobilisation of capitals: Recognising and playing the game. *British Journal of Sociology of Education, 34*(5–6), 723–743.

Bourdieu, P. (2019). *Habitus and field. General sociology, volume 2 (1982–83)*. Cambridge: Polity Press.

Bourriaud, N. (1998). *Relational aesthetics*. Paris: Les Presse Du Réel.

Childers, M. C. (2002). 'The parrot or the pit bull': Trying to explain working class life. *Signs, 28*(1), 201–220.

Cultural Policy Collective (2004). *Beyond social inclusion: Towards cultural democracy.* Scotland: Cultural Policy Collective.

Dewey, J. (1939). *How we think.* Retrieved from https://www.gutenberg.org/files/37423/37423-h/37423-h.html

Dissanayake, E. (1994). *The pleasure and meaning of making.* Retrieved from https://ellendissanayake.com/publications/pdf/EllenDissanayake-The_Pleasure_and_Meaning_of_Making.pdf

Freire, P. (1970). *Pedagogy of the oppressed.* New York: Continuum International.

Freire, P. (1995). Reply to discussants. In M. Figueiredo Cowen, & D. Gastaldo (Eds.), *Freire At the institute.* London: Institute of Education: University of London.

Giroux, H. A., & McLaren, P. (1991). Radical pedagogy as cultural politics: Beyond the discourse of critique and anti-utopianism. In D. Morton, & M. Zavarzadeh (Eds.), *Theory/pedagogy/politics* (pp. 152–186). Chicago: University of Illinois Press.

Goode, J. (Ed.). (2019). *Clever girls: Autoethnographies of class, gender and ethnicity.* Basingstoke: Palgrave Macmillan.

Hall, S. (1992). The question of cultural identity. In S. Hall, D. Held, & T. McGrew (Eds.), *Modernity and its futures.* Cambridge: Open University Prss.

Hall, S., & Massey, D. (2010). Interpreting the crisis: Doreen Massey and Stuart Hall discuss ways of understanding the current crisis. *Soundings, 44*(Spring 2010), 57–71.

Hanley, L. (2016). *Respectable.* London: Penguin.

Haraway, D. (1988). Situated knowledges: The science question in feminism and the privilege of partial perspective. *Feminist Studies, 14*, 579–599.

Heart of Glass and Battersea Arts Centre (2021). *Considering co-creation.* In Arts Council England Retrieved from https://www.artscouncil.org.uk/publication/considering-co-creation

Hey, V. (1997). Northern accent and southern comfort; subjectivity and social class. In P. Mahony, & C. Zmroczek (Eds.), *Class matters: 'Working-class' women's perspectives on social class* (pp. 140–151). London: Taylor & Francis.

Hoggart, R. (1989). Introduction to George Orwell, *the road to Wigan Pier* (p. vii). London: Penguin.

Hoggart, R. (1957). *The uses of literacy: Aspects of working-class life.* London: Penguin.

Hooks, B. (1989). Choosing the margin as a space of radical openness. *Framework: The Journal of Cinema and Media, 36*, 15–23.

Hooks, B. (1994). *Teaching to transgress: Education as the practice of freedom.* London: Routledge.

Horton, M. & Freire, P. (1990). *We make the road by walking: Conversations on education and social change.* Philadelphia: Temple University Press.

Illich I. (1971). *Deschooling society.* London: Penguin Books.

Kelly, O. (1984). *Community, art, and the state: Storming the citadels.* Stroud: Comedia.

Kester, G. (2000). Dialogical aesthetics: a critical framework for littoral art. *Variant Magazine Glasgow.* Issue 9. Special Supplement.

Kester, G. H., & Lacy, S. (2011). Seminar: The Oakland dialogues. *On the Edge Research.* Retrieved from https://ontheedgeresearch.files.wordpress.com/2011/11/seminar1_theoaklanddialogue.pdf

Kuhn, A. (1995). *Family secrets: Acts of memory and imagination.* London: Verso.

Lewis, G. (2009). Difficult dialogues once again. *European Journal of Women's Studies, 16*(1), 5–10.

Lorde, A. (2020). *The cancer journals.* London: Penguin Random House UK.

McIntosh, P. (1985). Feeling like a fraud. *Work in progress*, 18. Wellesley: The Stone Centre, Wellesley College.

Mills C. W., Mills K., Mills P. (2000). *Letters and autobiographical writings*. Berkeley: University of California Press.

Polanyi, M. (1958). *Personal knowledge: Towards a post-critical philosophy*. Chicago: University of Chicago Press.

Reay, D. (1997). 'The double bind of the Working Class Feminist Academic: The Success of Failure or the Failure of Success?' In P. Mahony and C. Zmorczek (Eds.), *Class Matters: Working-class Women's Perspectives on Social Class*. (pp. 19–30). London: Taylor and Francis.

Reay, D. (2017). *Miseducation: Inequality, education and the working classes*. Bristol: Policy Press.

Reed-Danahay, D. (Ed.) (1997). *Auto/ethnography: Rewriting the self and the social*. New York: Berg.

Schön, D. (1984). *The reflective practitioner: How professionals think in action*. New York: Basic Books.

Skeggs, B. (1997). *Formations of class and gender: Becoming respectable*. London: Sage.

Thomas, L. (2019). On be-(com)ing clever. In J. Goode (Ed.), *Clever girls: Autoethnographies of class, gender and ethnicity* (pp. 73–88). Basingstoke: Palgrave Macmillan.

Tiller, C. (2014). Training the reflective practitioner. In M. E. Anderson, & D. Risner (Eds.), *Hybrid lives of teaching artists in dance and theatre arts* (pp. 117–132). New York: Cambria Press.

Tiller, C. (2017). *Power up: a new direction*. Retrieved from https://www.culturehive.co.uk/resources/power-up/

Tiller, C. (2019). *Theatre matters: thoughts on torch*. Retrieved from https://www.heartof-glass.org.uk/thoughts-and-news/news/thoughts-on-torch

Tiller, C. (2020). *Care as a Radical Act*. Heart of Glass. Accessed at: https://www.heartof-glass.org.uk/news-and-resources/thoughts/care-as-a-radical-act

Tiller, C. (2021). Email to Jackie Goode, 22 December 2021.

Tiller, C. (2022). *Pitching In, Lessons on Sharing Power from Creative Civic Change*. In Creative Civic Change. Retrieved from https://localtrust.org.uk/wp-content/uploads/2022/04/Pitching-In.pdf

Walkerdine, V., Lucey, H., & Melody, J. (2001). *Growing up girl: Psychosocial explorations of gender and class*. Basingstoke: Palgrave.

Williams, R. (1958). *Culture and society, 1780–1950*. New York: Columbia University Press.

SECTION V

Place and Belonging

12

WALKING AS KNOWING, HEALING, AND THE (RE)MAKING OF SELF

Lauriel-Arwen Amoroso

Introduction

Over the course of my life, I have come to understand my relationship with the land and with 'place', in various ways. I had thought that through conventional ways of knowing, I could connect with the world and help others to do the same – I sought understanding through learning the names and functions of local plants and animals, I earned degrees in science and teaching and dedicated years to a career in environmental education. But there was something missing, something under the surface of the conventional ways of knowing I had been taught. I knew that much of my own learning came from places outside of books and classrooms and outside of my own intellect: a sensory and embodied way of knowing and being.

A new way of learning came through walks. Every walk I take changes me. It becomes a continuation of the narrative that is my life and becomes part of me: of my story. I have learned that, as humans, we are what we *do*. For me, walking seems to be the main way I connect with myself and the world around me – each walk becoming an embodied expression of self-in-relationship-to-place, and an active making and remaking of my life's narrative. They also lead to profound moments of awe. Like when I notice the first flowers blooming in spring; an intimate sensory experience of my own connection with the cyclical nature of the seasons. Or when I look up into the night sky and understand just how small I am in the universe. Or when I find a dead animal on the side of the trail and come to terms with the fact that all life is connected, and as one organism's matter decomposes it becomes nutrients for the continuation of other life. These are all moments of connection, aliveness, and ultimately of love. The more I walk, the more I understand walking as an act of love for being alive. Walking as making myself anew.

DOI: 10.4324/9781003309239-18

A series of walks in both rural and urban settings became the autoethno-graphic focus of my doctoral dissertation (Amoroso, 2021). In this chapter, I include accounts of several of these walks. Through reflections on these walks, recorded in my journal, I describe the way that the autoethnographic text that formed the core of my doctorate constituted the making of a new epistemology and a new self: a self connected to the land, to my body, and to a deep feeling of awe and aliveness. It also gave rise to the *un*making of a self raised with an inheritance of colonialism, epistemic hegemony, and a disconnection from embodied ways of knowing. The making of this new self through my reflective interpretations of my experience of these walks exposed the fact that Western structures of knowledge, which privilege objectivity, are inadequate to support holistic human growth and development. I was also brought face to face with the ways in which society is hostile to embodied experiential learning. Walking led to a process of healing for me by providing me with a deep connection to my *own* ways of knowing; and my reflections on them show how they also led to the (re)making of an identity more connected to the land and to a much more 'alive' self.

Honouring Land and People

I would like to acknowledge that in all of the places I walk, I am walk-ing on Indigenous land. Where I live, in Northwest Oregon, is the ances-tral homeland of many Indigenous tribes and bands, including the Chinook, Clatskanie, Cowlitz, Tualatin, Yamill, Tillamook, Atfalati, Multnomah, Clackamas, Kalapuya, and Siletz. The people of this region were forcibly removed from their land by European colonists and have endured hundreds of years of violence and oppression. I recognise that I am a descendent of those same colonisers and have a responsibility to address this historical and ongoing injustice. I also recognise the resilience of Indigenous communities and their intricate knowledge of, and relationship with the land (Kimmerer, 2013). I am also deeply grateful for the knowledge that Tribal community members have generously shared with me over the years, both in personal communications and in books and lectures. I know that this knowledge came about through living on this land since time immemorial and I recognise the tremendous gift this is to receive – especially since it is knowledge that my ancestors tried to erase.

Journal Entry: Walking and the (Re)Making of the Self

In the beginning, I was so young and such a stranger to myself I hardly existed. I had to go out into the world and see it and hear it and react to it, before I knew at all who I was, what I was, and what I wanted to be (Oliver, 2019, p. 4) (see Figure 12.1).

FIGURE 12.1 Author walking. Photograph by author

Journal Entry: Storying the Body

I like to think about my life as a book in which my stories are written into my flesh. A story that morphs and changes as new experiences rewrite past narratives. I like to know that I can learn to read my body if I am patient – if I slow down to its pace. The body has a language; each physical interaction with the world is a phrase born of memory. Bodies are perpetually engaged in an expression of their experience; they tell their stories in every movement. Pain, joy, depression, fear, excitement, wonder – all have stories written into the body. Stories that become lived, intentionally or not. My body often tells me to explore – it reminds me that my flesh has been shaped by experiences that challenge me to expand my notion of reality and to experience the unknown.

Written in my gut is three months at sea when I was 21, motion sick and tired of vomiting, but enamoured with the freedom that comes with sailing across parts of the globe – watching humpback whales breach as the sun rises behind an active volcano. The Caribbean wrote me a novella as I walked through a valley of bubbling mud pits on my way to the Boiling Lake; my skin covered in mineral deposits that had only recently pushed up from the insides of the earth to this moonlike surface. Parrots called in the distance. I was not *of* that place, but that place wrote a story that still shapes me today. A story that lives through me; perpetually desiring to be born into the world as an embodied narrative. I am no longer sailing through that time or place, yet within me remains a living, corporeal story.

These days, my body often tells me how I have spent too much time indoors – too much time sitting and looking at screens. My body hurts from immobility, while the algorithms draw me further into my couch. I can feel my flesh merge with the textiles of the furniture in my living room. *Am I just another accessory?* Sometimes I long for the meaning I found in the middle of the sea, but I am afraid to give up the comforts and ease of digital existence. These days, I seem to have replaced adventure with my smartphone. The freedom I remember has become a distant memory encased as two-dimensional images in a convenient handheld device. Looking into it, I am never *bored* and yet increasingly *so bored*. I have become a 'disembodied' story. The sway of the sea is a fiction now; so implausible that it sometimes feels like it never happened at all. I have so many stories to tell that seem to make no sense in a world where we mostly exist online. An online world where people want to *be seen* somewhere rather than to *be* somewhere. It seems to me that this disembodiment becomes a crushing existential pain that we desperately want to make disappear. So, we disconnect further. Shrink our existence. Live as if our bodies are not important; live for the *likes* and *followers*, not the fulfilment of bodily *sensation*.

No wonder entertainment industries are the largest corporations on Earth. Billion-dollar companies designed to keep us in a perpetual state of *disembodiment*. The stories written into our own flesh become transient, vicarious visualisations of other people's experiences – stories traced, not etched. Nothing in my body knows how to make sense of purely visual stimuli, experienced only on a screen and not in the flesh. What do my legs learn while watching a movie? What meaning does my low back make when playing a video game? What stories are being told while sitting mostly motionless, the right thumb rapidly moving across an artificially illuminated screen? The body becomes dislocated – storyless; cast aside.

I am a student and an educator. I have spent my life in the pursuit of knowledge, others and my own. Knowledge is both power and freedom. Or so I had thought. *But what is freedom when the body is a prisoner?* Sitting six to eight hours a day in a chair, bound by the rules of time and the expectations of meritocratic structures. *Is this liberation?* My body tells me that it is not. It rebels from the inside out. My stomach is always the first to protest: nausea and more nausea (but not the kind that comes from feeling the perpetual motion of a ship). I am often overcome by a desire to vomit my feelings of frustration and futility that mark most of these motionless days. Or to curl up under my desk and just go to sleep – maybe when I wake up, everything will have changed – maybe everyone else will have finally let themselves acknowledge the same pain, and together we can throw away the computers and the phones and the televisions and walk away from this world where all we do is sit.

I know that even when my mind tries to separate from my body, my body is always in the here and now – it can never be somewhere else. Disembodiment is ultimately an illusion. An *embodied* sailing across the ocean respects my body's contribution to the whole. Sitting, while passively engaging in a digital world, treats my body simply as a vehicle for my mind; a vessel of little consequence. As a digital participant, I am unintentionally rewriting my story, changing from being *part* of the natural world, to being *separated* from it. I need to find my way back to the motion of existence.

I have to remember that for me, to live and to learn is to *move*. My learning happens through movement. When I walk, my body and mind join in conversation; together they tell new stories. If I keep moving, new chapters unfold. I may see glimpses of meaningful self-expression: my body wants to interact and engage; it wants to tell *its* story.

Walk 1: The Camino de Santiago

I wake before dawn and make my way through twisting cobblestone streets. A few faint stars glisten above, and the half-moon sits on the eastern horizon, casting a warm glow across the still sleeping town. I came here alone, but there were dozens, if not hundreds of people who also woke at pre-dawn light to walk towards the mountains in the distance. I walk alone, yet in the company of other pilgrims, as we make our way to the edge of town. In front of me are green rolling hills, cast dark grey by the lingering shadow of night. The morning's light is slowly announcing itself, but it seems timid, the sunrise lasting for hours, as sharp blue hues give way to soft pinks; the landscape brilliantly painted before my eyes (see Figure 12.2).

As the morning turns into day, I make my way up into the Pyrenees. There are sheep and horses everywhere. There are giant *Lammergeiers* – the last of the European Bearded Vultures, the mountains providing them a refuge in an ever-urbanising world. The livestock wear bells that ring out across the steep valleys; a kind of metronome for my steps, counting out the journey's rhythm. The scenery is stunning – I am in awe of everything around me. The flowers seem more vibrant, the sky more blue, the valleys more lush, than any place I have ever been before. I want to roll in the grass, to be as close as possible to the landscape. I drink in the mountains and listen for the heartbeat of the earth. There are many plants and animals I don't recognise, but there are many I know: foxgloves, banana slugs, and Queen Anne's lace, all which make me feel at home even when home is so far away.

FIGURE 12.2 Walking the Camino de Santiago, Spain. August 2012. Photograph by author

As I walk, I ascend towards the pale blue sky above and fall prey to the optical illusions of the hills. Each bend in the road looks like the path to the final pass, before heading back down the other side. For hours, I feel my hope at making it to the top rise and fall, again and again. My body has never walked so far in a single day and gaining 4000 feet of elevation is more than I am ready for. Eventually, I give up hope that the pass will ever arrive, yet I continue to walk up, and up, and up for hours. The longer I walk, the less sure I am that I'm going to make it – my steps become painful, and my body slows down.

With each step, I feel my solitude, and a growing intimacy with the world – there is nothing else. My whole life, everything I have worked for, all my possessions, and everything that once seemed important dissolve into meaninglessness. I struggle to walk, yet feel myself come alive, connecting deeply to the world around me. This is all there is – and it's so beautiful. I'm not sure I've ever recognised such beauty before. Perhaps I've never been somewhere so alone, where I have no choice but to be in the present moment. And the present moment is breathtaking! I can feel the entirety of existence enter my heart, breathing life into my body. I am completely in love with life. Everything makes sense. *What if I had never come here? What if I never had this moment of understanding?* I shudder at the thought. This unmistakable, fully embodied acknowledgement of the present is what has called me here. I feel truly *alive*!

As I walk, my body continues to struggle. I start to go over and over in my mind what I'll do if I can't go any further. What will happen if my legs give out or my feet just stop working? I am in the middle of nowhere; at the crest of the Pyrenees Mountain surrounded by wilderness.

By the time, I finally make it to the top, my body is in shock. Still, miles remain – and 1500 feet of descent. Few others remain on the path; no one to pass me from behind. I'll be the last person on the trail at the end of the day and if I'm unable to continue there will be no one to find me and call for help. I have to keep going. The cramps on the bottoms of my feet make each step tortuously painful – my legs become as heavy as tree trunks; stiff and nearly immobile. The final three miles take me over two hours. I take a step and then rest. Take another and rest again. I cry as I walk – I've never felt so alone or unsure of myself in my entire life. *Who do I think I am, coming here?* I keep moving forward.

When the large stone church where I will stay the night comes into view beyond a densely wooded turn in the trail, I burst into tears. I've just walked over the Pyrenees, by myself, with a body that was in no condition to do so, yet I've done it all the same – I've pushed myself beyond any limits I'd known possible, and beyond my own comprehension, my poor tired body has given me one of the most difficult, beautiful, and meaningful lessons of my life – I am suddenly in love with my body. At this moment, she is the most beautiful thing in the world, and I realise that I need to learn to love and care for her unconditionally. She is perfect. She is me.

Journal Entry

My journey on the Camino continued for the next two weeks. The weather grew hotter and temperatures soared to over 100 degrees each afternoon. My body continued to struggle, and I found ways to show love and care and make amends for all that I had done to harm her in the past. In total, I walked about 175 miles across Northern Spain, completing about two-thirds of the walk. I took a train across the high plains, cutting off the middle of the journey, instead of walking that section, as the heat was just too much for my temperate, Pacific Northwest body to handle.

Before I left on my trip, I had assumed that I would be embarking on a grand adventure, but nothing quite prepared me for the profound ways in which I would change along the way. It was almost as if the experience of walking each day had interrupted old neuropathways, which had detached me from being truly alive – like I had been on autopilot, and I was suddenly aware of my surroundings – in control of my life for the first time. The sensations in my body felt novel. The way the land talked to me and told me stories of its own life felt like coming home, even though I was in a place I had never known. As I walked, I began to shed the parts of my identity that were just for show – I stopped wearing makeup – I became less concerned with sharing my thoughts and ideas with others – I no longer cared if my body didn't look 'just right' in the mirror. My feet and the ground I walked on demanded authenticity; they expected me to know myself. And it turned out that I was stronger than I knew. More capable – more full of love, and hope, and joy than I had ever thought possible.

Walk 2: A Poem

Oxbow Regional Park

The rocks are rough and pocked,
gray and white (perhaps basalt).
To my hand, they are familiar.
I know this river and these stones,
(I have been here before).
Another is dark,
smooth,
(It tells a different story).
I represent an infinitesimal moment in both their journeys
(They have seen millennia),
I am here for just a day;
I wish I understood my place
in this existence.
The rocks seem certain of theirs.

Walk 3: To Mt. Tabor and Back

Today is mostly overcast and relatively warm for mid-winter. In many ways, it is a perfect day to go for a walk. The kind of day that makes me glad I live in Western Oregon. Early season flowers bloom in yards across the city – Daffodils, Daphne, Witch Hazel, and Flowering Currant, to name a few – I can see, and smell, that spring is not too far away. Winter never quite arrived – temperatures stayed warm enough that on some trees, cherry blossoms began to emerge in late December and by January, there were trees in full flower across the city. It is now early February and as I walk from my house in inner NE Portland to Mt. Tabor and back again, I contemplate my relationship with the seasons and how walking connects me to this annual, cyclical change.

As I walk, I give most of my attention to the flowers. It was only a few years ago that I did not know them by name – shortly before that, I barely noticed they existed at all. Over the years, I learned to understand these flowers – they had stories to tell about the seasons, the soil, and the annual rainfall; they had stories to tell about who and what they were in relationship with and how that relationship unfolds over the course of the year. Yet it's hard to hear the stories of flowers over the noise of the city, the rivers of cars that have replaced the rivers of water that once made up this region.

Journal Entry: Rivers of Cars

Roads are a poor substitute for rivers – they transport cars, which are loud, aggressive, deadly, and take up more space than they deserve – unlike rivers which bring life and renewal as they wind through the landscape. Most of our cities are more dedicated to making sure people have a place to park than making sure people have a place to live; or that life itself has a place to flourish. We prioritise cars: where they park, where they get to go. There are *roads* everywhere – *parking* spots everywhere – '…large areas of the globe now consist of car-only environments…And they exert an awesome spatial and temporal dominance over surrounding environments, transforming what can be seen, heard, smelt, and even tasted' (Sheller & Urry, 2000, p. 746). To be a human in these places dominated by cars is to be secondary to *their* needs. On two feet, I cannot use the roads or the freeways to explore or travel. These are places just for automobiles. As Sheller and Urry (2000) observe, human movement in any other form is – if anything at all – just an afterthought.

Cars take life *away* instead of being life-giving. In the United States, over 100 people a day die in automobile crashes and 18 people a day are struck and killed while walking, by people driving cars. Before the COVID-19 pandemic, automobile crashes were the leading cause of death in the United States for people between the ages of 1 and 54 years (Center for Disease Control and Prevention, 2020). Additionally, one million vertebrates are run over every day in the United States. Yet none of these numbers captures the ways in which automobiles and automobile infrastructure have destroyed neighbourhoods, increased pollution, warmed our planet, and driven individuals and families into ever more dependent relationships with this machine (Sheller & Urry, 2000).

There is an illusion of freedom with the automobile (Urry, 2004). We can go most places we want when we want – but at what cost? At the expense of how many lives? With how much pollution? With how much debt? All externalities tied to each automobile that most people never see or consider – externalities that go beyond the thousands of dollars a year that it costs to participate; costs that we (as a society) subsidise – millions of dollars in healthcare costs, lost wages, grieving families, asthma, cancer, destruction of wildlife and habitat, climate fires, lost neighbourhoods, and forced poverty. Individualism tricked us into believing that having our own private transportation was worth the destruction of our communities; destroying our ability to walk out our front doors and just be. There is no walking anymore without coming face to face with the fact that we have lost our rights to roam (Malchik, 2015) – we have lost our ability to get around on foot safely and in peace.

Cars also breed impatience – urgently showing up at intersections and wildly racing down each road they encounter – all built specifically for them. A road that sits on ground that was once something else: forests, gardens, homes, community gathering spaces, and water – they embody the death and destruction central to colonialist, capitalist ways of living – they suck out empathy and replace it with entitlement (Sheller & Urry, 2000).

They impair the epistemological process of embodied inquiry on foot.

Cars are the opposite of free-flowing water.

Walk 3 Continued

I am glad to be on foot, despite the ever-present automobiles and everything they bring with them as they move through our shared space. You can't smell the flowers from the inside of a car or listen to the birds announce the coming of spring. I continue to walk and notice what's around me. I know this place and this route well as I have been walking these streets since I was a child – I used to visit my best friend at his apartment on Belmont Street when I was around eight or nine years old. Back then, this was a working-class, dingy part of town with boarded up businesses and cheap rent. I walk past the block where the Dixie Mattress Co. used to be. A business that never seemed to be open and made clear, with its Confederate flags, that only certain people were welcome. I hated that place and I was glad when it was finally gone.

Journal Entry: Race and Class in Oregon

I only now understand the history of race in Oregon, something that I was never asked to consider growing up as a white person – a history that seems a struggle for our state and city to accept and rectify. The streets I walk down have been shaped by interpretations of race; of who belongs where. Portland is not predominantly white by some random accident – walking its streets I am confronted with that racist past. The exclusionary zoning and red-lining[1] in Portland meant that these streets and neighbourhoods were not built for everyone and that legacy lives on today. The cost of living has sky-rocketed and automobile infrastructure has woven racism into the very fabric of this and most if not all other American cities (Sheller & Urry, 2000). Those in power (predominantly white, wealthy men) built freeways through traditionally Black neighbourhoods, often intentionally, 'to clear so-called slums and blighted areas' (Dewey, 2020). Now, in most of the neighbourhoods where one can walk, bike, or take the bus, the cost of living is so high that communities of colour, who do not typically have the same generational wealth as white communities, are pushed out of the inner core of the city into run-down suburbs, where driving is a virtual requirement of survival – to walk freely is not an option for many and the fact that this neighbourhood has sidewalks and crosswalks reflects policies rooted in race and class structures. Yet, even with the walking infrastructure present, few people seem to take advantage of the opportunity to move about in this way.

Walk 2 Continued

When crossing Belmont Street on foot, I am reminded of just how much has changed in the past 30 years. Old, once abandoned buildings have been knocked down to make way for new ones. Although some relics still stand if you know where to look – the stained-glass sunshine still sits in the window of what was once a pizza place and is now a fashionable, prohibition-themed bar. I see a few reminders of the past; even those seem to be fading.

Journal Entry Continued

Like the seasons, change is inevitable – the idea of progress, however, is up for debate. Brand new cars line the streets. I remember it was around 2012 when I first noticed shiny new cars rolling around SE Portland, a once rare sighe. It was with the arrival of those new cars that the act of walking began to feel more hectic in this city, drivers less patient. People used to walk and drive slowly here. Now, it seems like everyone is in a race to get somewhere important. Walking is just too slow for someone who needs to get to their jobs, to pay for their expensive new car and recently remodelled single-family house; a house where, just a few years ago, six working-class adults lived, before being evicted – to make room for the burgeoning tech class who came in droves with cash in hand and brand new automobiles.

Walk 3 Continued

Today, like most days, I encounter only a handful of people choosing to walk. I am alone in my endeavour and only find people on foot once I get to Mt. Tabor Park, which is surprisingly crowded.

Journal Entry Continued

I wonder why so many people in the United States feel that walking is an activity that can only be done in certain places? What would happen if we treated our whole city as a park, where walking was the central way of moving around? Imagine all these streets being turned into long, sprawling, horizontal parks – places to walk, play, and gather as a community.

I have a feeling that people in this country are missing something fundamental to the human experience. *Why don't we walk more? What could we learn if we did?* With my focus on exploring walking as a way of knowing, I am struck by how simple an act it is and yet how central it is to my existence. When I walk, I get to be in the world without expectation or agenda – my social conditioning seems to fade, as the movement of my body and my relationship with the world around me becomes what's important.

In the chaos of today's world, I secretly wish to myself that I could just spend my days walking. Everything makes sense when I walk, but the moment I stop, I once again face uncertainty.

Walk 3 Continued

As I make my way back home, I am reluctant to end my walk – thinking about walking is not the same as walking – writing about walking is not the same as walking. When I walk, I know myself and the world. Only by putting one foot in front of the other, moving through the world at a pace where I can interact with my surroundings, can I find the embodied knowing I am seeking to understand. Can walking help make the self I hope to be?

Walk 4: Northwest Industrial Area

I am taking the kind of walk that makes me uncomfortable (see Figure 12.3). I am alone in an industrial area with no one else in sight except for an occasional, anonymous, passing car. This is the area of town where industries process the earth's extracted 'resources': wood products, industrial waste recycling, vats of

FIGURE 12.3 NW Industrial Area, Portland, OR. February 10, 2019. Photograph by author

'Hot Molten Zinc', metal fabrication. Elevated freeways are suspended dozens of feet overhead and the endless drone of automobiles rushing from place to place surrounds me. This is a landscape of concrete – a perverse monument to human progress.

Who would voluntarily walk here? This is a place for manufacturing industrial products, not a place for people to spend time. The land these buildings sit on has been stripped of life and is now a place haunted with toxic detritus; walking through it feels like a dangerous act of defiance. *If a place is not fit for humans to be present, perhaps it is not a place that should exist at all.*

Journal Entry

The United States is filled with impassable, uninhabitable places – places so toxic that we cut them off from most of society. Cut ourselves off from places that were once alive and now are wastelands of our own making. *Who decided that it was ok to create such apocalyptic landscapes? What does it mean when humans cut themselves off from the land that gives them life?*

Walk 5: A Poem

Kilchis Point Reserve

I found a trail
 meandering through the woods.
  She told me what it meant to live.
   Her voice: soft and deliberate; the neon greens
    of spring, white fungus fruiting from tall splintered snags.
     The birds sing to me that this is their home -
      that this is my home: Salmonberry,
       spruce tips, skunk cabbage;
        a rainforest of wonders.
   These are the places
  where my heart sings,
 where I become whole.

Walk 6: Tryon Creek State Park

I spent a busy, cold, and beautiful day walking with a friend around Tryon Creek State Park. It's the first day I spot Indian Plum *(Oemleria cerasiformis)* leaves this season, which for me indicates the official beginning of spring in the Pacific Northwest (see Figure 12.4). This year it came much later than I am used to. Their brilliant green leaves are like glowing orbs, little harbingers of what's to come strewn across the understory of the forest – they always give me hope and remind me that winter will never last forever – they show me, and the rest of

FIGURE 12.4 Indian Plum leaves emerging in late winter. March 2, 2019. Photograph by author

the forest, that we can emerge from the darkness of winter in the company of others – that we can shake off our dark moods and introspective days to prepare for a new year. There are seeds to be sewn and dusty corners to clean. Only a fool would ignore the call to emerge. Now is the time to prepare for what comes next.

All of the other plants are still hiding; their buds firmly closed against the chilly March air. However, their turn will come when the time is right – there is no way to hide from the inevitable. I take comfort in knowing that everything is as it should be and that my own personal healing is a process resembling the seasons – there are always dark days before the return of the light, and I must watch for signs of my own approaching emergence, so that I don't miss *my* time to unfold.

Conclusion

For me, walking as an autoethnographic research method (Ingold & Vergunst, 2016) is more than just an inquiry into the self and my own ways of knowing, it is also a source of healing and a remaking of who I am at my core – the more I walk, the more I come to understand that walking exposes the many ways in which I have been denied knowledge; the knowledge of the seasons, of cycles, of movement, of connection and relationships, and of the very nature of being alive in the first place. I came to understand this as a form of epistemic injustice (Fricker, 2007), a way in which capitalistic and colonial structures have designed our economies, our education, our neighbourhood, and the ways in which we live as a society – to actively disconnect us from these ways of knowing, and from our fundamental humanity. Walking has helped me to reconnect to myself and the world. This connection, this renewed relationship, allowed me to understand the pain of being severed from my own ways of knowing and exposed a pathway towards healing. I have come to find that contemporary educational systems are not only narrow in their scope – of what they consider valid knowledge – they actively suppress certain forms of knowledge. They are structured to be episte-mologically oppressive; denying people their ways of knowing to connect with community, the land, food, the more-than-human world (Springgay & Truman, 2018), intuition, and true survival outside of the capitalist paradigm. Walking reconnects me to the ways of knowing that I was born with and helps me heal from the pain of being severed from this knowledge for much of my life. In a society where money, power, status, and success are lauded as our highest goals, I rarely find room for the slow, immersive, quiet ways of knowing that teach me to value the opposite of these goals. Walking teaches me about joy, strength, beauty, relationships, and connection – I learn in ways that nourish me, that make me feel alive, and that make me *me*.

Note

1 This refers to a practice, dating from the early 1900s, whereby several cities in the eastern and southern United States adopted racial zoning ordinances to create sepa-rate areas for Black and white households; these ordinances were overturned by the U.S. Supreme Court in 1917. While there is no evidence that local government in Portland attempted to explicitly regulate by race, many cities found workarounds to the Supreme Court decision and continued to intentionally segregate using other zoning tactics (see Hughes, 2019).

References

Amoroso, L. A. (2021). Walking as a way of knowing: an autoethnography of embodied inquiry. *Dissertations and Theses.* Paper 5651. Retrieved from https://doi.org/10.15760/etd.7523

Center for Disease Control and Prevention. (2020). *Road traffic injuries and deaths – A global problem.* Retrieved from https://www.cdc.gov/injury/features/global-roadsafety/index.html

Dewey, C. (2020). *Advocates rally to tear down highways that bulldozed black neighborhoods. Stateline.* The PEW Charitable Trusts. Retrieved from https://www.pewtrusts.org/en/research-and-analysis/blogs/stateline/2020/07/28/advocates-rally-to-tear-down-highways-that-bulldozed-black-neighborhoods

Fricker, M. (2007). *Epistemic injustice: Power & ethics of knowing.* Oxford: Oxford University Press.

Hughes, J. (2019). *Historical context of racist planning: a history of how planning segregated Portland*. Bureau of Planning and Sustainability. Retrieved from https://www.portland.gov/sites/default/files/2019-12/portlandracistplanninghistoryreport.pdf

Ingold, T., & Vergunst, J. L. (2016). *Ways of walking: Ethnography and practice on foot. Anthropological studies of creativity and perception*. Abingdon: Routledge.

Kimmerer, R. W. (2013). *Braiding sweetgrass: Indigenous wisdom, scientific knowledge, and the teachings of plants*. Minneapolis: Milkweed Editions.

Malchik, A. (2015). *Step by step, Americans are sacrificing the right to walk*. Aeon essays. Retrieved from https://aeon.co/essays/step-by-step-americans-are-sacrificing-the-right-to-walk

Oliver, M. (2019). *Upstream: Selected essays*. London: Penguin Books.

Sheller, M., & Urry, J. (2000). The city and the car. *International Journal of Urban and Regional Research, 24*(4), 737–757.

Springgay, S., & Truman, S. E. (2018). *Walking methodologies in a more-than-human world: WalkingLab*. Abingdon: Routledge.

Urry, J. (2004). The 'system' of automobility. *Theory, Culture & Society, 21*(4–5), 25–39.

13

WHERE THE RIVER FLOWS OUT TO THE SEA

A Story of Place-Making

Patrick Limb

Introduction

This chapter includes a previously published story of walks with my mother, shortly after she had received a cancer diagnosis (Limb, 2021). She wanted to return to Cramond, the village where we had first lived together in Edinburgh, the place where the river Almond flows out to the sea. In this chapter, the story appears first, followed by an exposition of how it was 'made'. The exposition shows how the writing of the story and the making of an annotated photograph album combined to constitute the excavation of the making of human relationships: with place and time; landscape and birds; between mother and son; between being ill and being alive; and between storytellers, as we supported each other 'remotely' during the pandemic lockdown, when physical human contact was restricted to online communications. It is an exploration, in other words, of the extent to which people make places, and places make people – and of how this happens. It examines the ways in which the taking of photographs and the fixing of words on a page can be both an aid to understanding of human relationships and an encouragement to develop/maintain an interest in the conscious act of looking. In literature, rivers, like the sea, are metaphorically rich. Each has an association with life and death. To add to that heft, there was once a ferryman at this place known as Cramond. What emerges is an appreciation of how interactions with strangers helped shaped my experience of the otherwise shapeless, fresh waters of a river, before they became lost in the salty waters of the Firth – and how in doing so they brought a degree of order, if not to a wild place, then to a wild time in my life.

DOI: 10.4324/9781003309239-19

The Story: 'Where the River Flows Out to the Sea'

This first Spring walk is like chancing on a found poem. Close to the water's edge, pale-pink inflorescences of butterbur nudge through. On the other side of the path, the last of February's snowdrops are jostled by swards of few-flowered leeks. Where clearer ground is found, yellow constellations of lesser celandines are strewn across the woodland floor. For me though, outshining them all, are the anemones.

Eager for light, their ghost-white flowers emerge before the broad-leaved trees stretch and unfurl their canopy of green. As they rely for spread on the slow growth of their root structure, not the distribution of their seed, anemones are looked upon as markers of ancient woodland. Over the course of a century, a cluster will range just half a dozen feet. By taking one step back, I see where they had grown when I walked the same banks as a child.

Even their name summons times past. The Anemoi were Greek gods of the winds; and of them, Zephyrus was the bringer of lighter breezes from the west. According to legend, to herald his coming in early Spring, they made a gift of anemones. For the Romans too, these windflowers, nodding on delicate stalks, were seen as a lucky charm: picking the first flowers of the anemones each year would ward off sickness.

What has called me back to the River Almond though is my mother's illness. Cancer came calling last summer. She felt the lump during lockdown. Waiting for the surgeon, fearing how it might grow and spread, she decided that she wanted to return to Cramond, the village we had first lived together in Edinburgh, the place where the river flows out to the sea.

★★★

To reach the river, I walk down Peggy's Mill Road. Peggy's had been the second of two upper mills, the first being Dowie's, closest to the old Cramond Brig (or bridge). The lower mills were known as Craigie, Fair-A-Far and Cockle. All five of them had drawn from the Almond as the river flowed onwards to the little natural harbour. After its demolition in the late 1960s, a few years after my family came to Cramond, all that was left of Peggy's were remnants of the mill lade, a floor slab and sluice gates held open by rust.

The promise of a new day is needed. I want to see the sun rising over the Firth. First light is already here (see Figure 13.1). Dawn-chorus is not just sound, but a transforming state of light. I hear thrushes, robins and blackbirds. Their songs are interrupted only by the occasional startlement of pheasants, suddenly caught up in an unarbitrated dispute.

Having passed an old fence that is no longer keeping anything in or out, I reach the edge of the river and stop. My arms go behind my back – I 'take in the view'. A reverent pause, not quite in the moment (but conscious of it). The lighter breezes from the west are passing through. Onwards, seawards.

FIGURE 13.1 Cramond Foreshore at low tide. Photograph by author

Made rich by shipping, Captain Salvesen of 'Inveralmond' resolved to give back, to encourage people to the sea. What he gifted was land – and steps to pass that land. Those steps offered passage over a rocky outcrop lying halfway between the Brig and the coast. Without them, there would be no continuous path by the river out toward the Firth. However, like all part-metal structures close to water, they have an inbuilt obsolescence. Every half century or so, the locals must decide to renew them, or to campaign to persuade the Council to do so. When I get to the Salvesen steps, the structure now seems so impermanent, so unkempt that I think the villagers and the councillors must have reached an impasse over who pays next. Later, I read that was about right.

How was my mother going to go this way? The steps are many and steep. As part of her convalescence, it would be good to encourage her this way – as if traversing the rocky crag, going seawards, would get her strength back up.

Onwards now to the Fair-a-Far Mill, long since made a ruin by the river in spate, unprotected even by its weir. Once I see the old Mill, I begin to remember what is coming next. From here, the path will lead to the row of white-faced cottages known as Caddell's Row. The path will narrow and straighten, mimicking the river before it opens out onto the little harbour, the ferryman's steps (see Figure 13.2) and the oldest parts of Cramond village.

Place-making may take a while for some. Others will never be home. But sometimes, somehow, places are in your bones. You recognise them first time you set foot, as if you had somehow met before. Rare those places that one really sees (and, you may tell yourself, see you) rather than those one just looks

FIGURE 13.2 The Ferryman's Cottage as seen from the steps. Photograph by author

at. Cramond is such a place for me. I quicken now and by the time I get to the headland, the combination of the rising sun and the ebbing seawater forge filigree on the sands.

In my childhood, two crossings could be made from the village. The first was a minute's journey by ferry across the stretch where river meets sea. The second was to Cramond Island by the causeway. When revealed by receding waters at low tide, it is slippery underfoot with strewn seaweed; the incoming tide reclaims the walkway. The old ferry is no more (time and tide not waiting even for the ferryman); only the crossing remains to Cramond Island.

★★★

Tidal islands like this one leave me feeling as though I have crossed from one border to another, a threshold to another realm. That is not what I want this morning. On the way back, I have flings of prospecting sandpipers for close company until, like quicksilver, they flee ahead. I learn afterwards that another collective noun for them is time-step. As I regain the mainland, I hear the beat of a swan's wing tips threshing the salt-water, seeking to get airborne and land where the ferry once crossed.

Later that day Mum and I walk back down Peggy's Mill Lane. Her arm is locked on mine, the under-part still tender from the biopsy. We turn to the

Salvesen steps but stop short of the first tread. There is a mallard dabbling by a boulder close to the largest islet. Mum sees it and tells me: 'Tasty bird. Not much eating on it though. You need one per person'. I laugh – a Frenchwoman who has lived longer in Scotland than France, remembering the meals of her childhood!

When the results of the biopsy come through, I am in England. All clear in the tell-tale nodes. A day later, there is a message from my mother. Without her realising, it is a photograph of roughly where I had paused, with the note: 'Lots of love from the river side xx'. For half a moment, I wonder whether this is from her or the Almond itself. A fortnight later another like message – this time of the largest islet, ringed by boulders and the caption: 'Mr and Mrs Mallard. This afternoon. Mr fishing, Mrs working on her tan plumage! Lovely walk xx'. I am touched. Perhaps she sees more than a meal for two.

★★★

A month later, I am back. Even with the biopsy, the big operation has still gone ahead – better safe than sorry, the surgeon feels. The train returns me to Edinburgh not long after my mother (as she puts it in her message just before surgery) has 'said goodbye to an old friend'. No visitors are allowed on account of the pandemic. In the hours before collecting her the following day, I decide to set off back down the Lane.

What a difference four weeks has made. Though the butterbur has lost its pop of colour and the celandines are dimmed, pockets of pink purslane have joined the anemones. Below the greening trees, the few-flowered leeks are slender alongside the ramsons that dominate with starbursts of white flowers. Both fill the air with garlicky scent; their conspiracy covers the woodland floor leaving little room for bluebells.

Two days later Mum and I head out. At the start of the walk, there is a scuttling on bark. Treecreepers! 'They look almost like mice', she says – skittering, as much as flittering. I like the description. This is a little different from the mother of my childhood. She generally patted her hands together on seeing beasts and birds, seemingly to encourage them to 'do' something. Given that she was a linguist, her conviction that they generally spoke but one language – the clap – struck me as strange. Here she is though, slowed to near stillness – and really watching. The pair are indifferent to our presence, which gives her long enough to notice how they hop, how their gently-curved beaks winkle out grubs cached in the bark. I hear their feet, tipped with long claws for clinging on, minutely clink across the surface of the wood; I hear a slight catch in Mum's breath.

★★★

The day to see the doctor again has come. I wake very early and head beyond the Salvesen steps. Mum has now asked me to produce a bird book of down by the river. Camera in hand, I go looking for the sentinel spirits of where the river meets the sea – the great cormorant and the Cramond swans. I see neither as I head downstream, an indication that the tide has not yet receded. At the harbour, first views across the Firth to the kingdom of Fife show a lead-weight of cloud, bearing down like Winter, on the woodland close by Aberdour. But the trees themselves seem autumnal, as the rising sun to the east burnishes the bark. Time seems out of joint.

Before stepping onto the seawall that leads to the causeway itself, I check the tide times. Too long to wait. My turn for home is stopped by sight of two mute swans arcing out toward the wide Firth (see Figure 13.3). Though by now they are high aloft, I hear the effortful whirr of their wing-beats. As they bank away, the underside of their white feathers is set aglow. I want Mum to see this – is she still sleeping or perhaps now awake with worries about what the doctor will say? – and I take a photograph.

By the time I hear the cormorant, it is well past me, tracking straight up river at altitude. The mid-river air is like an avian superhighway. Mallards, with occasional bouts of flight, dash up and down, no great height above the surface before skidding to a halt. Higher up, the heron charts a lonely, lugubrious course. But loftier still goes the great cormorant. This one does not deviate until it settles on a tall tree on the far bank. Only a forbidding cloak of black feathers to be seen. I can't even make out the plague-doctor beak. Mum messages me to ask: 'Are you

FIGURE 13.3 Two mute swans arcing out toward the wide Firth. Photograph by author

ok? Xx', I reply '3 mins away' – it was nearer 10 minutes but, well, sons! In comes another text: 'I was worried you might have been ambushed by some birds'. In a way she was right.

★★★

The news from the doctor is good. No more growths found. We emerge from seeing him and the radiographer (always one more doctor to see) to a rainbow that is not a bow; more a colourful smudge foregrounding the Pentland Hills. Mum smiles and I take some more photos, now of her. She looks straight back to camera, a protective mask in one hand; and in the other her fleece held up to cover the surgeon's work.

On the last morning before I return southbound, the causeway is fringed with algae and there are tiny, dark periwinkles littered under foot like ball bearings. I have come to take more photos for the book. The last page will show the steel-eyed cormorant diving in the stretch of the Almond before the weir at Fair-a-Far, where there is the map by the Mill that reads: 'You are here'. Never truer words.

Place-Making through the Crafting of an Autoethnographic Text

Though a response to my mother's illness, the makings of the story above go back to before anyone knew she was unwell. I was attending an event at Five Leaves Bookshop in Nottingham. The author Julian Hoffmann was on a tour to speak about his new (2019) book, *Irreplaceable*. Its full title was *Irreplaceable: The Fight to Save our Wild Paces*. Engagingly, generously, he began his talk by quoting another writer, Alan Gussow: 'The catalyst that converts any physical location – any environment if you will – into a place, is the process of experiencing deeply' (1971, p. 26).

The word catalyst immediately caught my attention. Though no chemist, I had a vestigial recollection that a catalyst is something that causes activity between two or more persons or forces without itself being affected; a making without being unmade. Julian asked his audience what places for them had been claimed by feelings. Too slow or reticent, I did not put my hand up but found that I wanted to give my answer the following day.

Without explanation as to where it depicted, but doffing my virtual hat to Mr Hoffmann, I posted on Twitter an Edwardian postcard showing bonneted ladies in the Cramond ferry and asked that question again: 'What place for you has been claimed by feelings?' Answers came in. One referenced Ted Hughes' (1979) *Remains of Elmet*: 'Moors/Are a stage/For the performance of heaven./ Any audience is incidental'. Another replied: 'Mine exists mostly in imagination, since it combines forest meeting the sea'. A third spoke of Snowdonia, 'where I have spent at least a week every year, where my family came from, where we have built our own memories': private memories, accreted over generations, placed into the public domain. Yet another spoke of how, conversely, she more often found her feelings claimed by place. I liked that too. It spoke to the old conundrum of whether people make places or places make people; and if the answer is both, what may be the catalyst that converts them into something other than, even more than, just themselves.

That said, one reply struck me in particular. It went like this: 'Place-making may take a while for some. Others will never be home. But sometimes, somehow, places are in your bones. You recognise them first time you set foot. Belonging'. This moved me to reply: 'Yes, as if you had somehow met before. Rare those places that you really see (and you may tell yourself see you, somehow) rather than those you just look at'. Without further record, I wrote this exchange into a booklet I keep on which there is embossed 'Not my story to tell' – and forgot about it until my mother's illness took her back to Cramond. Without remembering where those words had come from, that exchange, as quoted, found its way into *my* story.

The Cramond ferry crosses the River Almond shortly before the point where, with a final rush (steady or urgent, according to season), that river flows out into the sea. The woodland bordering the river is an ancient one, the river valley still more. The river valley was forged by a glacier that millennia before had forced its way out into the Firth of Forth. What I was calling to mind, with that antique postcard, were my own first memories as young boy, my oldest memories.

I could remember the ferryman having a jaunty, blue cap. When I later got in touch with his grandson (once more by Twitter), he told me that his grandfather wore it because he had some sort of mark to conceal, a shrapnel mark, a legacy from fighting in the Second World War that he preferred to hide. His boat was single-oared and could only cross either side of high tide. One would ring the bell and wait, according to his whims and how many prospective passengers were assembled. As a young boy, I knew nothing of Charon – the ferryman across the river Acheron (or Styx), that divided the world of the living and the world of the dead – but this ferryman made an impression on me.

During the pandemic, a diagnosis of cancer led my mother to move back to this place where the river flows out to the sea. Childhood memories were now summoned and sharpened by the combined effects of a condition that risked ending a life-giver's life; and a virus that, in killing so many, had prevented travel. I had not been North of the Border, to my home from home Edinburgh, for months and this was the first time in years I was looking at the tumbling waters of the River Almond. What I was now going to was a place on the edge: one where physically land meets sea; one where emotionally old securities risked being overthrown.

It is perhaps no surprise that places away from the safe centre of things can be productive of making. In an elegant Introduction to their important contribution to writing about archipelagos, Allen, Groom, and Smith (2017) suggest the questions that are posed by exploring what lies at the margins:

> What level of detail has escaped the eye looking out from the centre? What sits precariously on the outer edge of perception or cultural memory? What new encounters become possible the closer we get to the edge of the known landscape?
>
> *pp. 2–3*

Such questions do not admit of easy or narrow answers but call for both looking closer – and further away – than one might ordinarily. Whilst at one level I did not *want* to be where I found myself, I sensed that mapping out the peripheries of this place would make something of me and I would make something of the place. So it proved.

Returning to those banks was quite the giddy rush. I was self-conscious standing there ('My arms go behind my back – I "take in the view". A reverent pause, not quite in the moment (but conscious of it)'). That said, an idea quickly formed that I should make something of these moments. My mother's fatigue was such that she slept past the dawn chorus so I recorded it – to bring her the birds, to bring her the sounds of a new day. I brought her too photos of the sun rising over the Firth, igniting the tops of the forests on both sides of the Forth. By going seawards, with the tide low, I could cross over to Cramond Island, another realm of sorts, before the rising tide reclaims and remakes the Island. It was now a walk too far for my mother after a fall the year before. During the confinements of the 2020 lockdowns that had reduced her world to three rooms, the other side of town, she had tripped over a trailing wire. Though bones healed, confidence less so.

She also wanted me to make something of all this ('Mum has now asked me to produce a bird book of down by the river'). For both of us, albeit unspoken, it seemed important not only to mark the time that was literally marking her, but also to repudiate the reduction in fortunes that had brought us to this point. Put more abstractly, this would be a buffer against, a rebuff of, the risk of things being unmade or altogether undone.

I would create the antithesis of a *memento mori* (a remembrancer that we all have to die) – rather, a *memento vivere* (a reminder to live). It would record sightings on our walks together between those two bounds that we could manage together: between the Brig and the steps leading seaward. It would encourage her to do them alone; when she could not lean on my arm, she could at least see through my eyes. It would perhaps, between its covers, bring some form and order to these moments (and places) we were both passing through. This was not so much a wild place as a wild time, in the sense of having all the potential for being strange, unmanaged, even (worse still) unmanageable.

Walks were taken alone and together – the former to bring back images beyond easy reach; the latter to record *our* beat. Particular sightings were looked for, including the 'priest heron' and that sentinel spirit of the River, the great cormorant. Both revealed themselves and I took these sightings to be a good sign. Other moments were unlooked for, like when spotting (or, in truth, first hearing) the treecreepers. Usually one does not see the thing expected or half-hoped for, but something else – a taking by surprise, even on a local safari. And that's something she and I came to enjoy. I was glad to know the names of those little birds straightaway. Maybe it's a male thing that we like to have a territory, a place where we can talk with some kind of assuredness. In all events, the names of birds sighted were given and learned – son teaching parent, an encouragement to learn more.

Other thoughts, however, were not imparted, until now. Though my experience of it was vicarious, to me odd perceptions emerged. I became fixated by how tree-roots on the one hand split boulders in the high-sided banks while, on the other, somehow held the great rocks they had fissured together. They reminded me of how Christopher Hitchens had spoken of his cancer in an interview. He declared that what so affrighted people about cancer was:

> … the idea of there being a live thing inside you, a sort of malignant alien that can't outlive you but that does in a sense have a purpose to its life which is to kill you and then die, it's like an obscene parody of the idea of being pregnant. In fact, I always feel sorrier for women who have cancer than men, for men hosting a life of any kind is hard to think about but for women it must be a harder, grotesque nasty version of being a host to another life.
>
> *Paxman interview (2010)*

As well as making a book of photographs, I next decided to write about the process of compiling it, about this place that was once more claimed by feelings, strong feelings. Was this once more about the bringing of order? Shorn of their digital trimmings, cameras are still at heart just a device to capture light. I now wanted that light to shine on my writing. I shared the essay in draft with a group that I had joined in lockdown, fledgling memoirists. Drawn together by a course called 'Excavating the Self: Reading and Writing Literary Memoir', we started meeting in October 2020 – that is to say, we have never met. By force of circumstance, all contact has been online. But, over the course of the succeeding months, that remoteness led to a peculiar intimacy, all of us then being starved of little contact beyond our respective bubbles. Trust was quickly built. Through their contributions, the scribblings became writing. Through that contact (and excavating), I discovered that my perceptions were not so odd but all too typical of how cancer charges the ordinary, both in terms of place but also time. One person within our group spoke from experience of how narratives get quickly interwoven: the ferryman, the birds, the landscape, with each one (as she put it) 'time-hopping', giving that sense of past and present existing simultaneously which seems to happen so intensely when dealing with cancer. Waiting for results is a weird liminal space when one is intensely aware of human mortality and the part chance plays in all our lives. Again, coastlines particularly lend themselves to having this quality. There is a paradox implicit in them as no coast follows a linear course. As with the Latinate origins of the word – 'Limen' meaning threshold – they pass one through a transition between two states, be they of a landscape, an ecosystem or even lives. Though reading images and situations through that lens is pretty universal, that makes their impact no less personal.

In all of this, the landscape played the fullest part. In my case, at least, it became a way of self-discovery. I think there is that impulse: one is perhaps trying to find out something (with, for me, the added charge of walking next to the river of my childhood) or maybe in the course of such walks, an experience. There is something that one discovers. On the other hand, there is a contrary impulse to get away from oneself, just to get out of one's own skin, taking away current and pressing preoccupations. At the risk of stretching metaphor too far, was that dichotomy reflected in a river bounded by its banks on the one hand and then those waters just flowing out into the boundless brine? There was a sense of satisfaction, fixing on a page something that would be recognised by my mother in her new state of hyper-locality – her reduced beat would be broadened. And then, hopefully, recognised by others.

Conclusions

In ancient Rome, a 'genius loci' was the protective spirit of a place. If this place where the river gives out to the sea has a genius loci, it is surely water. The one *constant* is water in perpetual motion, be it the current of the Almond or the back-and-Forth tides. Just as the place is *made* by water, so also water encouraged taking these walks and writing the story of those walks. In her wonderful 'Sea Poem' Alice Oswald (2005) posed questions about 'what is water in the eyes of water' to which her response, in first part, was that it is 'loose, inquisitive, fragile, anxious'; and of the sound of water she wrote of how 'you can hear the sea/ washing rid of the world's increasing complexity,/making it perfect again ...' In a Guardian podcast about the river Dart, the same poet said: 'I like the idea of water as a kind of rememberer or recorder of whatever goes on beside it. It is kind of reflector, it reflects images and somehow records signs' (Guardian, 2012). How true, how perfectly true.

In deference to them, the last word here to excavations of what those ancient Romans left behind. The 'Cramond Lioness' is a Roman-era sculpture recovered in 1997 from the mouth of the River Almond at Cramond in Edinburgh. The sculpture, which turned out to be one of the most important Roman finds in Scotland for decades, was discovered by the ferryman who replaced the one with the jaunty hat. It depicts a bound male prisoner being killed by a lioness. The upper torso and head of the prisoner are shown, with the giant beast behind him, sinking her teeth into bone. In the version of my story published earlier by Little Toller Press (and here), of necessity, I edited out an image of it. But the sculpture, now housed in the National Museum of Scotland, speaks to the truth that finds can be made by 'excavating' turbid waters, as much as by excavated earth and silt. My mother, a lioness of sorts, remains well.

References

Allen, N., Groom, N., & Smith, J. (Eds.). (2017). *Coastal works: Cultures of the atlantic edge.* Oxford: Oxford University Press.

Guardian. (2012). *Literature and landscape podcast: Alice Oswald on the Dart River.* Retrieved from https://www.theguardian.com/books/audio/2012/jul/13/1.

Gussow, A. (1971). *Sense of place: The artist and the American land.* New York: The Seabury Press.

Hoffman, J. (2019). *Irreplaceable: The fight to save our wild places.* London: Hamish Hamilton.

Hughes, T. (1979). *Remains of Elmet.* London: Harper Collins.

Limb, P. (2021). Where the river flows out to the sea. *The Clearing,* July 15. Dorset: Little Toller Books.

Oswald, A. (2005). Sea poem. *Woods etc.* (p. 3). London: Faber & Faber.

Paxman, J. (2010). *Newsnight interview.* Retrieved from https://www.youtube.com/watch?v=LIVEsa2g4ag, beginning at 2 minutes 35 secs.

14

MAKING MISTAKES

Learning through Embarrassment when Curating Indigenous Collections in UK Museums

Jack Davy

Introduction

There are times when a non-Indigenous curator who works with 'Indigenous' museum collections learns their trade through embarrassment. 'Indigenous' collections, formerly known as 'ethnographic' and before that 'tribal', are collections formed from living cultures (as opposed to archaeology), and gathered from the material cultures of what used to be called 'primitive peoples'. This category was so named because our predecessors in the nineteenth century thought that by examining the material cultures of hunter gatherers and people at the sharp edge of expanding colonialism, we might gain insights into our own European prehistory (for example, see Pitt-Rivers, 1906). The idea was that by comparing peoples at roughly the technological advancement which we presumed our Iron Age or Stone Age British ancestors to have, we could gain insights into how those people lived and how their societies were organised. As Aaron Glass has put it, objects 'acquired novel meanings that privileged Euro-North American categories and ways of knowing over their local significance' (Glass, 2010, pp. 181–182), creating 'false and reductionist spaces' and 'closing off countless other stories and routes of understanding' (Yohe, 2016).

This approach is nonsense of course – technology is relative rather than absolute and humanity does not live on a sliding scale of civilisation or historical progression but rather a shifting quilt of adaptive practices we call tradition. Moreover, the specific political, geographical and organisational structures of a society rely on far more complex and diverse sets of factors than simple technological position. The colonial museum construct which this idea birthed is still however very much the framework within which these institutions operate – hence the nebulous and implicitly racist 'Indigenous' category itself, separated conspicuously from European history, fine art and other supposedly more

DOI: 10.4324/9781003309239-20

advanced categories of material culture, once explicitly termed high art (see Auger, 2005; Errington, 1998).

In general, these collections were not formed under the ethical conditions museum acquisition policies require these days. Though comparatively few objects in these collections were acquired by the legal definition of theft, the vast majority of them were extracted from peoples undergoing colonialism – simply if reductively defined here as the diminution by state oppression of political, social, economic or cultural independence. These conditions necessarily unbalanced the exchange, whether by gift, sale or other means, in favour of the acquirer, who was able to utilise their higher authority to obtain artefacts on terms which we would today acknowledge as unethical and exploitative.

A non-Indigenous museum curator working with Indigenous collections is therefore more in the position of an assessor sifting through the looted salvage from a burning building, than a scientist preserving and curating intact culture. This is the historical legacy and responsibility of contemporary curation, to examine how we use what has survived to tell other peoples' stories in profoundly European institutions. Sometimes, the only way to do it is by getting things wrong and having the assurance and humility to listen as people tell us in no uncertain terms that we have made a mistake, as we squirm internally with embarrassment. How we listen and respond to this embarrassment defines how and whether we learn from our mistakes, and that is the key to scholarly autoethnography in the ethnographic museum institution.

Part 1: 'A Very Anglo Thing to Say'

To illustrate this problem, I'll go back to the earliest part of my career when, in 2009, as a 25-year-old novice collection manager at the British Museum, I was on the team tasked with providing approximately 400 objects for a Haida delegation of 30–40 artists, students and heritage workers from the Haida Nation, an Indigenous Canadian people from the islands of Haida Gwaii, which lie off the northern coast of British Columbia.

The delegation was travelling as part of a project later described in the book *This is Our Life* by Cara Krmpotich and Laura Peers (2013), an effort to examine best practice in the encounter between Indigenous American groups and museums in the UK. The delegation would be presented with a table laden with historic artefacts and asked to go through them one at a time, explaining their function and history to non-Indigenous researchers standing by with clipboards to note down any impressions.

As a junior collections manager, I was not a researcher and therefore not tasked with this transcription task. Instead my role was to produce objects, remove them at the end of the sessions, and to answer questions from our guests about storage, use in the museum, provenance and documentation. This enabled me to have chats with the guests which were more 'off-the-record' than the established researchers, who had done extensive background research which I, as a technician, had not.

The result was a number of awkward conversations, of which one stands out. I was discussing a beautiful hardwood club, probably 150 years old and perhaps 18 inches long, with a delegate, a middle-aged Haida woman who worked as a heritage worker. The club is carved with a beautiful formline seal design, the animal delineated in bold incisions down its length. Clubs exactly like this from the Haida and Tlingit people formed some of the basis of Claude Lévi-Strauss's theory of the anthropology of art. Lévi-Strauss's theory on this point posits that unlike Western art, in which decoration is a corollary to the scientific principles of an artefact's production (or its affordances that give it function), to Indigenous peoples the design is often central to its function – thus the seal design (which Lévi-Strauss calls a 'sea monster') is not a pretty pattern, but an integral part of what makes the club effective at its purpose (Lévi-Strauss, 1966 [1962], p. 26).

Knowing nothing of this then, I chatted amiably but carelessly with the visitor, commenting that the club looked too small to be used for seal hunting. Then, in an ill-advised joke, I commented 'well, maybe a baby seal' referencing the ongoing controversy in Canada over Indigenous harvesting of baby seals (see Randhawa, 2017). The visitor gave me a cool look, and then very politely said, 'you know, that's a very Anglo thing for you to say'. It was in fact so very polite that I completely failed to recognise at the time that her words were actually a cutting condemnation, in reference to my display of casual ignorance about something which mattered so much to her she was willing to travel nearly five thousand miles (4,688 to be precise) to see it, and over which I had, apparently inexplicably, been given authority. To my recollection, I happily continued the conversation, and the rest of the visit, stumbling in my ignorance, no doubt, into many other clumsy and offensive mistakes.

The club of course was not for killing seals – the seal design was not indicating the animal hunted, but the essence, the spirit, of the animal best adapted to hunting fish. It is a fish club, used to belabour and bludgeon halibut hauled into an open canoe. The seal design makes the club good for killing fish because seals kill fish. It doesn't kill seals and certainly doesn't kill baby seals.

What I, a White male British museum staff member, had stumbled into was what Kwakwaka'wakw curator Gloria Cranmer Webster (2013) has identified as the dissonance between what museums and museum staff expect to learn from Indigenous objects and experiences, and what Indigenous objects and people are willing to tell them. She identifies this with a story, first told by Lévi-Strauss, as follows:

> I would like to tell you a story about a very noble American woman anthropologist, a princess among her people, who got her PhD and became curator in a Canadian museum. One of her white colleagues who was studying those marvellous chief's rattles of the North Pacific Coast, beautifully carved and painted with elaborate designs, was puzzled by one specimen. He turned to her and asked: 'How do you read this rattle?' and she answered 'We don't read them, we shake them.'
>
> *Lévi-Strauss (1985, p. 5); see also Cranmer Webster (2013, p. 165)*

The point of this story is that the White curator, identified elsewhere as Wilson Duff, is expecting to be able to understand the rattle by reading, as if it were a book, and expecting Cranmer Webster to translate it for him. Cranmer Webster's response articulates that such a reading is impossible – it's a rattle not a book and it cannot be read, only shaken. Moreover, simply shaking the rattle will do nothing. One can only learn the meaning and purpose by shaking the rattle within the context from which it comes, and only if one is sufficiently versed in the traditions within which the rattle and the ceremonies in which it participates originate. Without all that context, the rattle is essentially orphaned and becomes just a White tool of aesthetic pleasure, no longer an instrument of ceremonial importance unless it is returned to its original context.

This was the lesson that a naïve museum technician had yet to learn in 2009 when he began working with the Haida visitors. And slowly, and partially, learn it I did. Though not all at once, nor on any sort of systematic basis. I worked with other visiting groups, and other artists. I became familiar with the huge emotional importance the visits had for them, importance which I, as a White English museum professional, could observe but never perhaps fully experience – never able or permitted, (nor was it appropriate for me) to 'shake the rattle'.

I recall the Inuinnait visitor (from 5,371 miles away), who discovered that the markings on a harpoon collected in 1843 were the same as his own grandmother's tribal tattoos and who excitedly compared photographs, not having any tattoos of his own – family tattoos were prohibited for the Inuit people for much of the twentieth century. He requested that he be allowed to handle the harpoon directly – since this visitor, like all visitors these days to the collections, is required to wear blue nitrile gloves before handling objects. They travel halfway across the world to find an impermeable barrier fractions of a millimetre thick between them and their heritage. Learning from my earlier mistakes and growing in confidence, and in clear defiance of the British Museum's strict requirements, I let him take the gloves off and wield the harpoon as his distant ancestor who once owned it must have done, brandishing it above his head.

I also recall the Plains visitors viewing ceremonial headdresses who, when given similar permission to break rules and handle the artefacts, proceeded to take things further than I had agreed with them, put the fragile garments on and perform an impromptu dance around the viewing room, to the consternation of myself and the other 'Anglos' present. These visitors to the collections were indirectly and inadvertently, through my mistakes and embarrassment, teaching me about how they interacted with their heritage, which in turn taught me to be a more sympathetic curator and manager. So far, so autoethnographic. Yet this is only the start of this process.

Part 2: 'Research Is a Form of Healing'

In 2013, I left the collection manager role to start a PhD with the British Museum's Collaborative Doctoral Partnership Programme. I was now something of a veteran in engaging with Native American visitors to the Museum's collections – I knew the right terminology, I fancied I understood something about the experience the visitors were expecting and tried to facilitate it for them – going so far as to supply special foods, to permit smudging and prayer ceremonies and to break the rules on handling which applied to other visitors because these people were not just any other visitors, but people with a deep and abiding emotional connection to the works they viewed. The truth is that I still had no idea what that experience was like.

Over the next four years, I studied the ways in which miniaturisation operates within the material culture practices of the Indigenous peoples of the Pacific Northwest, conducting fieldwork and interviews with artist from four communities in Washington state and British Columbia. This thesis demonstrated unequivocally that Native artists embedded their miniaturised objects, now in museums, with complex layers of emotional meaning, and that their descendants today travel in search of this meaning with emotional intent and ambition too often thwarted by institutional obstruction and confusion.

Nika Collison, curator at the Haida Gwaii Museum and participant in the 2009 delegation, described this process of travelling to find ancestral works in European museums, as she had done as part of the 2009 delegation, in her *Canada Seminar* lecture at Oxford in 2016:

> There is a practice in our culture called 'putting a string on' someone. For example, during the times of arranged marriages, a family of a very young girl might endow a great deal to the family of a young boy, effectively 'putting a string' on that child, ensuring the two would one day marry, and move forward in life together.
>
> I like to think Charles Edenshaw and Bill [Reid, prominent Haida artists] put a string on their work, binding us to something that is so much more than art. Binding us so that we'd come together in the future, when the time was right.
>
> *Collison (2016)*

During and following my PhD I worked at the Horniman Museum, part of the team developing the new World Gallery there, and as part of my responsibilities was tasked with developing a children's interactive exhibit as part of the Northwest Coast displays. The basic plan was already in place – three masks on cedar pillars which would tell traditional stories. The only problem was sourcing those stories – I now knew that you couldn't just get anyone to tell any story – the story had to come from a particular community, pertaining to a particular cosmological figure and most importantly, had to be told by a person with authority, position and above all the permission to tell it.

Eventually we commissioned and paid a young Kwakwaka'wakw artist and activist named Sierra Tasi Baker, then resident in London, to produce the stories. This was much more than a commission to read the stories. It was a lot more than just to write them. Rather, Tasi Baker was in fact employed as an intermediary between the Museum and the Kwakwaka'wakw; before the stories could be read, before they could be written, they had to be approved. This required Tasi Baker to discuss the museum's requirements, find appropriate stories from the collected stories of her people – stories which they hold as a form of communal and strongly protected property.

The community was receptive but laid down conditions which had to be negotiated via Tasi Baker. There were specific requests that caused clashes with museum best practice and even accessibility legislation. For instance, the community by tradition do not permit these stories to be written down in order to protect them from theft. However, the museum has a responsibility to its hearing-impaired visitors to ensure that they too can participate in the interaction. Eventually an abridged compromise was agreed.

Navigating these competing priorities took time and skill – skill that the museum staff did not and could not possess. We were forced to acknowledge and adapt to the limitations not only of our expertise, but also our lack of ability as British curators to even access the information required to conduct the negotiations, let alone tell the stories themselves, to which of course we had no right without the permissions Tasi Baker negotiated before she ever started recording.

These stories in fact cannot be read any more than the rattles – they can only be experienced. We were, in the more literal sense of the word, embarrassed by our inability, reliant on Indigenous support to effectively utilise our collections. But Tasi Baker considers this situation a strength, not a weakness of the process, suggesting at interview that it is precisely this sort of collaboration which produces the best work:

> I think the more that researchers start shifting towards realising that they're helping to change the narrative, and shift the narrative, and understanding that they are agents of reconciliation, I think that researchers will realise that their work opens up quite a bit more. The more they realise that research is a form of healing. I think that would be really amazing if academics could figure that one out.
>
> Davy & Baker (2018)

Part 3: 'A Dismal Display'

Indeed, the consequences of not 'Figur[ing] that one out' were made apparent the year after the new gallery opened. Though the interactive installation was well received, a neighbouring case which was not supported by an Indigenous curator came under heavy criticism. The case in question was that depicting the material culture in the Horniman collection belonging to the Plains peoples of the American Midwest. Centred on a buckskin suit, eagle feather war bonnet and hunting rifle, it struck a more inanimate and warlike pose than the stories-centred neighbouring Northwest Coast case, at once portraying a fixed and stereotypical aspect of Plains culture which did not go down well with Indigenous visitors.

Taylor Norman of the Oklahoma Cherokee, then a School of Oriental and African Studies (SOAS) student, now a member of the Oklahoma State Bar specialising in Indigenous heritage law, who visited the gallery in person, called it a 'dismal display':

> ... a stereotypical presentation of Plains cultures - entrenched entirely in the Indian War era without recognition of how these cultures see personhood, giving or connection with the land ... even in this well-intentioned attempt, the museum manages to erase women, along with amicable aspects of Plains culture unconnected to war and violence, and any description of who, most importantly, Indigenous people of the Plains are today ... The omission of these factors suspends the museum's attempt at telling truths just short of being actual truth-telling because visitors are still largely left to maintain the false and/or stereotypical assumptions stemming from Hollywood portrayals ... one relying on this display to educate could infer that Plains Natives are extinct given the limited time frame and subject matter. I need not launch into a discussion about the harm this causes.
>
> *2019, p.19*

Norman later noted at interview that:

> ...it was honestly shocking to me. I think the most shocking part of that is the mannequin in the middle holding the gun, just because it feels so violent. It feels violent, and it also goes with a theme I have been seeing – they focus exclusively on warrior societies.
>
> *cited in Davy (2021, p. 6)*

Thus, I was forced to confront that a project which I had worked on, without intending to do so, had caused offence to Indigenous visitors through a lack of understanding and a lack of intimate knowledge required to sensitively depict and portray Native heritage in the museum setting. Having been part of the team which installed this case, all experienced curators with the best of intentions, I was, once again through the medium of embarrassment, forced to confront my own biases and preoccupations, and to question whether I and the institutions for which I worked were equipped or even permitted to tell other people's stories without their consent – because in deciding that we could, we demonstrate that we should not have. And in doing so, have caused harm.

Part 4: 'Varying Nations Crowded into a Rail Car'

In 2017, I was appointed as a Senior Research Associate at the University of East Anglia on a project entitled *Beyond the Spectacle: Native American Presence in Britain*. The project was intended to explore the range of visits and interactions that Native Americans coming to Britain had experienced over the last 500 years and involved extensive archival research, which I supplemented with a series of interviews with contemporary Native American visitors and residents in Britain, including artists, students and academics.

The results painted an interesting picture of the limitations British society can place on Indigenous visitors, including their treatment as exotic ambassadors, not only for their own communities but also for the entire system of North American colonialism. Frequently these impositions were uninvited and unwelcome, placing the visitors in a highly uncomfortable position.

I routinely offered the visitors my own expertise with their collections in UK museum collections as a thanks for their participation in the research, providing tours of institutions, of reserve collections, setting up meetings with curators and providing advice on cultural engagement with the UK museum sector. I tailored these experiences to what I anticipated the visitors were hoping to experience, and what their existing expertise levels were in engagement with museum collections. This brings us to my most powerful example of learning through embarrassment: an embarrassment so extreme and significant that it fundamentally changed the way I think about museums and museum collections in Britain.

In the summer of 2018, as part of my work with *Beyond the Spectacle*, I made the acquaintance of a woman named Madeline Sayet. Sayet, a playwright of the Mohegan people of Connecticut, had previously studied for an incomplete PhD programme in the UK, and so was of great interest to my research as an Indigenous person engaged with British academia and heritage. We exchanged emails, spoke several times over Skype, and built the amicable professional relationship and rapport so essential to the development of effective research. Indeed, I was starting to believe that we were becoming friends of a sort. In October 2018, Sayet informed me that she was travelling to the UK and I offered her, as I had done with others, the opportunity for a guided tour of the British Museum.

I took this seriously – I had (and have) the greatest respect for Sayet, whose work in the theatre had won her many plaudits, including being named one of Forbes '30 under 30', and recipient of the White House Champion of Change Award from President Obama. Based on our conversations about her experiences in the UK while studying for her PhD, and her familiarity with the limitations of museum service in Britain, I anticipated a conversation between peers soberly and carefully dissecting the weaknesses of the institution and the wider sector. I had miscalculated badly.

For two hours, we toured the museum, discussed its history, its collections and its immense cultural impact. We discussed individual Native American objects and collections, how the museum placed, interpreted and used those objects, the histories and biographies of the displays, and broader issues of representation and repatriation across the institution. It was a frank and honest discussion based, I thought, on the peer-to-peer conversations we'd been having online.

But I had forgotten the dynamics of the contact zone. This was Sayet entering a world in which I was ostensibly comfortable, and she was profoundly not; where I held an ill-defined and unspoken authority which she did not. And I got it wrong. Very wrong. Exactly how wrong I wasn't to find out for some time. After we parted, I emailed Sayet to say thank you and continue our correspondence. She did not reply. I tried again a few weeks later. Still nothing. I told my research superiors that I must have made a mistake, spoiled the relationship, but even then I did not understand the mistake I had made.

Months later I saw that Sayet had been booked to give a performance at Shakespeare's Globe on the South Bank, and I persuaded my entire team to book tickets. I contacted Sayet and told her, and she wrote back to say that she was looking forward to seeing me and that 'just FYI the section based on our conversation at the British Museum is not actually a reflection on you. It is not you - it is just the info and context of that conversation as is useful to further the storytelling of the questions of the piece' (Sayet, 2019a). Inwardly alarmed, I assured her that I was thick-skinned.

And then for the performance itself: I was seated in the front row at the Globe Theatre as Sayet recounted her life in Britain, and in extended detail, her tour of the British Museum by an academic who is dismissive of repatriation claims from Indigenous Australians, and who propels Sayet through the Gallery heedless as she is left, 'looking at a mash of mislabelled indigenous objects, like varying nations crowded into a rail car – a continent facing genocide over hundreds and hundreds of years - wide expanses of geography thrown together in cases without specific acknowledgement' (Sayet, 2019b, p. 30).

The academic is also dismissive of the treatment and repatriation of human remains: 'No, if we start giving back human remains, well they don't know where that would lead. They might have to give other things back'. In the end, Sayet is only 'sorry I have nothing to offer the spirits crowding the building, mashed up against friends, enemies, and strangers who don't understand them. I am scared to close my eyes and listen to the howling and pain around me ... I wander away into an exhibit on clocks and stare at it for a while – to cleanse my body of all the stolen stories, and objects of violence in this place. I want to go home' (Sayet, 2019b, p. 33).

As these words fell before the packed house, I have never in my life wanted to disappear into a gaping hole in the ground as I did in that theatre. Regardless of Sayet's assurances that I was not personally responsible, but rather representative of a wider system of museum colonisation, the impact was immense. My embarrassment was not just about being so publicly exposed as part of a harmful system to which I had devoted my career, but it was also that I had misunderstood the situation so badly in that one encounter, which had provoked that measure of pain in someone I respected. It was that it made me, on reflection, reconsider all of my interactions with Indigenous peoples in museum spaces over the previous decade, not just those embarrassing or awkward interactions, but even collegiate ones, such as those Tasi Baker referenced.

I realised with shock that I had to reconsider my entire approach to how I communicated with Indigenous visitors. I had already been toying with the idea of writing an article on the subject of Native visitors to museums in Britain. Now I knew that I had to do more. It was not enough to simply record visitors' experiences or produce simple critiques. I needed to make a difference, to address a problem and ultimately attempt to compensate for the embarrassment I endured during Sayet's excellent play, which in 2022 toured the US, taking Sayet's experience to thousands of theatregoers.

That seems perhaps an indulgent way to frame my efforts to introduce new approaches and critiques to the sector, which is in dire need of long overdue and substantial change. Embarrassment, and redemption from it, wasn't my primary goal of course. My intent was to use my experience, my relationships and my skills as an academic and curator to shine a light on a genuine and serious problem – the deficiency of Indigenous representation in the UK museum sector and the harm that it causes, harm demonstrated by Sayet's play.

But embarrassment was the moment that I learned something, the precise point when realisation tipped from 'I am part of the solution' to realising with shock that 'I am part of the problem'. And indeed that I may always be, by virtue of my race, my gender, my nationality, my upbringing and my profession. I will always problematise relationships between Indigenous objects in museum collections and their interpretation in that space – objects which Cranmer Webster (2013) makes clear are not meant for men such as me to 'read' or 'shake', and whose presence in the museum is, to them, alien and uncomfortable.

So I *leaned into embarrassment*. I spoke to Native American visitors and scholars and asked them what they thought of the displays, the labels and interpretations, and what we, what I, had done wrong. For example, Kimonee Burke of the Narragansett told me that the British Museum displays, for which I was on the 2011 redesign team, were:

> ...missing a lot ... I had an issue with how they had selected what they considered to be relevant groups from North America, considering there were like 600 tribes. It seemed like a weird selection and an oddly grouped selection to address their objects with little to no explanation of how they got them and little to no explanation of what they were. I think for me it was kind of confusing ... I don't really know how they curated the display, who chose the objects or how they wrote the blurbs.
>
> *Davy (2021)*

I did. Not alone or with primary responsibility, but I did. The experience was humbling, as the displays I had worked on were picked apart, the criticisms made of the difference between observing and writing on a subject and people who actually lived it. And that is ultimately the lesson here.

Conclusion

We have to learn from our embarrassments to listen, to understand, and to accept that we may need to defer to other people with deeper knowledge than ours on a cultural level. We must use this learning to build new curation models which are not about asserting authority, but rather designed as catalysts among peoples, objects and audiences, with a focus on Indigenous-led knowledge and communication. To get there I had to be embarrassed repeatedly, to be remade as a curator from my upbringing and training, into someone capable of empathetic deferral and an acknowledgement that there are systems of understanding closed to me by design.

As evidenced by scholars like Norman (2019), Tasi Baker, Sayet (2019b) and Cranmer Webster (2013), Indigenous curatorial thinking and heritage management have long considered these problems and have designed solutions. It is incumbent on non-Indigenous curators to stop gatekeeping the collections of living peoples and to be embarrassed when they do. Instead we must develop models which promote funding and communication networks to facilitate Indigenous curation of collections and displays. We have to use that embarrassment to reshape our sector and fundamentally change our approach. Embarrassment changed me, and embarrassment must change how our museums work, or embarrassment will continue, and it will get much, much worse.

Curators make and remake the world, marrying theory with imperfect collections to try and present a respectful and educational display. They in turn, as I have demonstrated, are remade by the collections and people with whom they work. This is a complex responsibility, requiring engagement with numerous stakeholders and it is prone to error – indeed error is an important part of the making process for a curator. Making errors, especially embarrassing ones, and being corrected, is a key part of how curators working with ethnographic collections learn, and in turn how they inform the remaking of the institutions within which they work.

My hope is that by documenting my embarrassment in this autoethnographic self-reflection, and demonstrating how it contributed to my development and 'remaking' as a curator, I have been able to illustrate the role that saying and doing the wrong thing have played in my career. I hope too to spare curators who follow from making the same mistakes, and to enable them to learn to listen, to defer at the start of the process and to work to improve access and interpretation for all.

References

Auger, E. E. (2005). *The way of Inuit art: Aesthetics and history in and beyond the Arctic.* Jefferson & London: McFarland & Company Inc.

Collison, N. (2016). An unbroken line: Haida art and culture. Lecture presented for the *Canada Seminar* University of Oxford: Lady Margaret Hall., 12 February 2016.

Cranmer Webster, G. (2013). The dark years. In C. Townsend-Gault, J. Kramer, & Ki-Ke-In (Eds.), *Native art of the Northwest coast: A history of changing ideas* (pp. 265–269). Vancouver & Toronto: UBC Press.

Davy, J. (2021). *Native Americans in British museums.* Cambridge: Cambridge University Press.

Davy, J., & Baker, S. T. (2018). *Research is a Form of Healing.* Beyond the Spectacle Blog, University of Kent. Retrieved from https://blogs.kent.ac.uk/bts/2019/01/11/research-is-a-form-of-healing/

Errington, S. (1998). *The death of authentic primitive art and other tales of progress.* Berkeley: University of California Press.

Glass, A. (Ed.) (2010). *Objects of exchange: Social and material transformation on the late nineteenth-century northwest coast.* New York: Bard Graduate Center.

Krmpotich, C., & Peers, L. (2013). *This is our life: Haida material heritage and changing museum practice.* Vancouver: University of British Colombia Press.

Lévi-Strauss, C. (1966). [1962]. *The savage mind.* Chicago: University of Chicago Press.

Lévi-Strauss, C. (1985). Introductory address. In D. Eban (Ed.), *Art as a means of communication in pre-literate societies* (pp. 1–16). Jerusalem: The Israel Museum.

Norman, T. (2019). *Bridging the divide: re-evaluating native American displays in the British Museum and Horniman World Gallery.* Unpublished MA thesis, SOAS.

Pitt-Rivers, A. (1906). *The evolution of culture.* Oxford: Clarendon Press.

Randhawa, S. (2017). Animal rights activists and Inuit clash over Canada's Indigenous food traditions. *The Guardian,* 1 November 2017. Retrieved from https://www.theguardian.com/inequality/2017/nov/01/animal-rights-activists-inuit-clash-canada-indigenous-food-traditions

Sayet, M. (2019a). *Personal Communication.*

Sayet, M. (2019b). *Where we belong.* Play performed at Globe Theatre, 17th June 2019.

Yohe, J. A. (2016). Unanonymous native women artists. Paper presented at *Evidence and Discovery in (Re)theorizing Native American Art and Material Culture.* 115th AAA Annual Meeting, Minneapolis, 17 November 2016.

CONCLUSION

Jackie Goode, Karen Lumsden and Jan Bradford

Autoethnographic Crafting in Pandemic Times

As indicated in the Introduction to this edited collection, we wanted to feature different forms of 'crafting' of (material, biographical and cultural) autoethnographic artefacts by practitioners using a variety of materials and media. We wanted to include but move beyond writing ('graphy') as the main practice in autoethnography. We also wanted to draw from different academic disciplines and non-academic practitioners. This has enabled us to explore and expand what constitutes autoethnographic 'making' as research method.

The variety of making processes and practices represented proved as rich and illuminating as we had hoped. What was initially striking was how much the pandemic and the constraints it imposed on our lives figured in these accounts, bringing the ways we make ourselves and wider culture into sharper focus through completely altering the way we experience *time*. As Stephanie Shelton (2021) writes, when quarantine started in response to the spread of Covid-19:

> I found time slipping away. Trying to trace and track time was like trying to hold onto water: messy remnants marked my efforts, but my hands remained empty. Clocks, which had seemed so faithful suddenly held little meaning ... The linearity of the day was no longer a line but a scribble that looped, broke, and collapsed on itself.
>
> *p. 824*

Many of our contributors echoed this in the ways in which they framed their simultaneous crafting of self and culture in the context of time 'collapsed on itself'. Aidan Teplinsky is 'waiting for the world to change back to normality' after losing his job and social networks. Both he and Jackie Goode find

DOI: 10.4324/9781003309239-21

themselves 'stuck'. Mark Price draws on the image of the Möbius strip as a symbol of time experienced in a looping, self-referential way, disturbing orientation in space and place: 'On hold', 'Locked-down' and 'Zoomed-out', so that he 'lose(s) track of time'.

Patrick Limb's mother's illness confronts him with life's unpredictability. He marks time in decreasing measures: a river valley forged over *millennia*; anemones spreading over the course of a *century*; historical remedies gathered *annually*; his needing the promise of a *new day*. Watching attentively now, his mother slows to *near stillness*; altogether, 'Time seems out of joint'. Two major ruptures − 'a condition that risked ending a life-giver's life; and a virus that, in killing so many, had prevented travel' had put it out of joint. 'Time-hopping' (Shelton, 2021) narratives get interwoven 'giving that sense of past and present existing simultaneously'.

Building on Heidegger's (1971) ideas and those of Merleau-Ponty, Ingold (2000) offers the notion of 'dwelling as building' − a perspective through which 'the forms of building arise as a kind of crystallization of human activity within an environment' (Ingold, 2000, p. 186). Perhaps it was the slowing down of time to 'near stillness' and the intermittent confinements to home that allowed *us* to 'dwell'. Perhaps in the very particular temporal context in which we found ourselves, we are trying to 'build'/craft new selves and cultures in and through dwelling.

The Selves We Are Crafting

Before we comment on the variety of *processes and practices* which contributors engaged in when making our autoethnographies, we consider what is revealed about the kind of 'selves' being crafted. For Probyn (2003), the *body* is 'a site for the production of knowledge, feelings, emotions and history, all of which are central to subjectivity' (p. 290). Jacquelyn Allen-Collinson (2013) illustrates this in a visceral way in her field notes on running, as she records how:

> …a few minutes into my stride the navy-dusk wind is cutting away the work smog, sloughing off the grey skin of the working day. I am cleansed. I am back. I am back in-body after yet another day of attempted body denial and enforced focus on the headwork. Quads surge forward, muscles strong and bulking, pushing against tracksters, abs tighten and flatten against the chill wind as I begin to up the pace… Power surges through me, I feel butch, lean, mean and honed, and very much woman.
>
> *p. 281*

Reflecting our focus on making-methods that go beyond the practice of writing, an *embodied, sensory* self is very much in evidence among contributors; sight, sound, smell, touch, movement are all in play.

For Clare Daněk, scents, saliva-wetted fibres, crumbs, cat hairs and the detritus of household existence are all captured in the quilt of her stitch journal. Mark feels the weight, curves, form of the figure he is transforming. Aidan's shirt becomes the meeting point of all the threads that connect the individual with the realities of being working-class, while his compositions are sonic representations of how he and his peers experience working-class bodies. Edgar Rodríguez-Dorans discovers that grief is physical, as his choreography puts together music, collective memory and bodily movements. David Méndez Díaz explains that in their ensemble dancing, Edgar's company *felt* each other through the text, choreographies, gossip, laughs and experiences shared. Rommy Anabalón Schaaf acknowledged embodied experiences 'as a fundamental part of knowledge production' while Javiera Sandoval Limarí's hands are moving restlessly, feeling the softness of her yarn, feeling her blanket's warmth. For Lauriel-Arwen Amoroso, bodies tell their stories in every movement of her walking: pain, joy, depression, fear, excitement, wonder as she 'drinks in the mountains and listens for the heartbeat of the earth'. For Patrick, the dawn chorus is not just sound but 'a transforming state of light'. He hears tree-creepers clink across the surface of the wood, the effortful whirr of swans' wing-beats, the slight catch in his mother's breath. He is 'claimed by feelings'.

Furthermore, bodies are *connected* to other bodies. They exist and acquire meaning in social spaces: 'the body cannot be thought of as a contained entity; it is in constant contact with others ... subjectivity [is] a relational matter' (Probyn, 2003, p. 290). Hodgson (2022) shows how even individualistic activities ostensibly focussed exclusively on 'the self' and solitariness, like retreat-going, can be not only sites of what Mason (2018) calls 'potent connection', encompassing sensory and kinaesthetic affinities, but can also unexpectedly produce collective forms of often intense sensory and atmospheric experiences which he frames as 'mystery-work' (p. 207). Among our contributors, such connected *social selves* were very much in evidence. Mark, for example, speaks of 'encountering myself through and within relationship with others, human and non-human'. Rommy and Javiera's autoethnographic crafting practices intimately connect daughters to mothers. As Gauntlett (2011) observes, making *is* connecting.

Given the pandemic times, connections were often made digitally, manifesting our *digital selves*. As he wrote about place-making, Patrick sought others' experiences on Twitter. He expresses a need for the restoration of some sort of order and certainty and reaches for these through the crafting of narratives that tell a much larger story than one with a sovereign individual as sole protagonist. Clare comments on a need for order too. As she struggles with the external impositions of doctoral study, she is 'stitching myself into being in ways over which I alone have control'. But she too needs connection. Her engagement in digital interactions is a way of 'disrupting the solitary experience of doctoral study'. Her daily stitch journal, initially created as a distraction from the PhD, over time becomes 'a means of creating connection and community' and a way of testing whether her making has validity. Chrissie Tiller is seeking validation in this way too: 'through sharing my practice I was proving my credentials and establishing my right to inhabit this space'. And Karen Lumsden, Edgar, David and Joanna Neil all connect with audiences as their making activities become performances.

There are risks in making such connections, however – we become *vulnerable selves*. Joanna risks seeing aspects of herself and her practices that might not be attractive. On the other hand, like Clare, she is alienated by the consciously constructed but inauthentic 'outward-facing self' that some others seem to project on social media. Simon Denison also acknowledges the vulnerability inherent in experimenting: 'It can reveal to us aspects of our presuppositions and values – our unconscious or conscious biases and commitments – which, on reflection, we might prefer to distance ourselves from, or modify'. But there are rewards too. Javiera explains: 'Sharing the intimate space where *The Blanket* was created was a way for me to show my vulnerability … connecting with the grieving vulnerable side of myself', but through this she was also making new connections that were not visible when analysing in a more conventional way. Simon discovered 'fresh ways of thinking about pictures, ourselves, and our relation to the world'. Disclosing the partiality, the flaws, the very humanness of the researcher may risk undermining 'the "authority effect" in critical writing', he observes, but the reward may be greater authenticity: 'A practical consequence of engaging in the self-reflexive process outlined here is that we critics might start to produce a more authentic type of critical writing'.

For some, the search for an *authentic self* also became evident through *acts of resistance*. Chrissie, Clare, Karen, Joanna and Simon all set their crafting of selves within institutional contexts, revealing a distinction between a private (authentic) and a public/professional (performative) self. Released from institutional constraints post-retirement, Jackie Goode rejects a 'hand-me down proforma' form of writing with a prescribed destination in mind, in favour of an autoethnographic writing of the self that involves 'striking out, sloughing off that straitjacket, writing "in the buff", making connections, tracing and presencing absences ….' And Clare cites De Certeau's (1988) *'perruque'*, in which the worker finds small ways to subvert his or her work experience. Her stitch journal offers such an escape route.

Other forms of resistance appear in opposition to oppressive regimes of gender, class and 'race'. For example, Chrissie shares a process of reconnecting with an earlier self:

> The 'self' who, like my mum, is well practised at 'giving a good talking' to the other one. This is the 'self' who grew up among the women on a Leeds council estate, was schooled in class-consciousness and feminism in the '70s and '80s, and has built a lifetime's practice informed by feminist, transformative, pedagogy.

It is often *intersections* of class, gender, sexual-orientation and 'race' that informs resistance. Rommy reflects on how her mother learnt to become a woman and taught *her* to be a woman in particular socio-economic circumstances.

Jackie strives to recapture the child she remembers 'out alone in the world …
befriended by it' before she learns as a girl/woman 'to be vigilant when out
alone'. Lauriel sheds parts of her identity that are 'just for show', like make-up.
In reflecting on their collaborative crafting of a digital performance, Edgar
and David become protagonists in their own stories, as gay men. Moreover,
Lauriel, Jack Davy, Rommy and Javiera are all resisting the legacy of ancestors whose colonising led to the privileging of 'Western ways of knowing'. In
Panya Banjoko's chapter, resistance is palpable. She writes not only against the
historical injustices of the transatlantic slave trade but also the current injustices
of racial profiling by the police, inadequate social provision, racial inequalities
in health services, the Black attainment gap in education and the additional
layers of discrimination experienced by Black women. Her chapter powerfully
portrays an *activist self* through whom she explicitly aims to remake history
and culture. She is both 'an activist appealing for justice and reparation' and 'a
dreadlocked Rasta woman performing poetry on television'. Finally, what is
implicit (and sometimes explicit) in all of these accounts is the figure of a *storied
self.* The way our stories appear 'in conversation' with each other is considered
in more detail later.

What do these coexisting agentic and constrained making selves reveal about
how we understand the theorisation of 'the self'? Skeggs (2014) argues that ideas
about personhood emerged via the power to consolidate the interests of specific
groups. For her, the very notion of a self refers to *middle-class* subject formation –
the formation of 'subjects of value'. This conceptualisation of the self as a bour-
geois product of 'possessive individualism' underpins her theorisation of the role
of 'proper personhood' in legitimating only certain subjects, therefore – a status
which is reliant for its definition on an 'improper self'.

In their use of 'collective biography', Davies et al. (2006) echo this conceptualisation of the constitution of the self when they identify the operation of a quest
for social *recognition* in one of their author's stories, showing how this is accomplished in interaction with others. It is clear from our contributors' accounts of
making 'selves' that even while forced under pandemic conditions to become
'lone actors', social selves are being crafted within the connections they make
with others. In making a self *in connection*, as Butler (cited by Davies et al., 2006,
p. 89) says, 'the "I" neither precedes nor follows the process … but emerges only
within and as a matrix of … relations themselves'. Our contributors' embodied,
social, contingent and resistant selves demonstrate this.

The particular details of specific subjects are interesting, Davies et al. (2006)
suggest, only insofar as they can be used

> to make visible the ways in which bodies/emotions/desires/memories
> become the inscribed (and reinscribed) public/private, inner/outer, depth/
> surface to be read against the grain of dominant/humanist discourses and
> practices. In this process, who or what one is may become undecidable.
>
> *p. 100*

While Davies et al. focused on *writing* as a constitutive act, all our authors' making-materials and methods of crafting of selves are shown to be a necessarily ongoing process with an as-yet 'undecidable' product. Like Davies et al.'s participants, we too:

> ... can be read as both rational, competent, humanist individuals and as subjects in process who are working and worked on to appropriate themselves within a particular culture, in a particular moment and within particular relations of power.
>
> *2006, p. 100*

Elsewhere, Davies and Gannon (2006) suggest that:

> The self both is *and* is not a fiction; is unified and transcendent *and* fragmented and always in process of being constituted, can be spoken of in realist ways *and* cannot; its voice can be claimed as authentic *and* there is no guarantee of authenticity.
>
> *p. 95*

Jackson (2010) also offers a way of bridging the conceptual divide between the self as self-consciously fashioned and narrated – and subjectivity as precarious and unstable. In revisiting what she refers to as the often over-simplified and distorted versions of GH Mead's theorisation of the self, in conjunction with his work on time, she highlights the temporality, reflexivity and sociality of the self. Mead's approach, she argues, allows for human agency while insisting on the sociality of the self, it eschews any notion of a fixed or core self while avoiding an overly fragmented and decentred view of the self, and, while conceptualising narratives of self as symbolic constructions, it acknowledges the actuality of past events and experience.

Gordon (2008[1997]) captures these contradictions in what she calls 'complex personhood', in which:

> ...the stories people tell about themselves, about their troubles, about their social worlds, and about their society's problems are entangled and weave between what is immediately available as a story and what their imaginations are reaching towards.
>
> *p. 4*

Our collection shows authors' multiple 'selves' straddling these conceptual divides as they 'reach towards' something, allow it to unfold, try to bring it into being. Ingold reminds us that this conceptualisation of making is 'not the imposition of preconceived form on raw material substance, but the drawing out or bringing forth of potentials immanent in a world of becoming' (2013, p. 31). We turn below to look at the 'how' of this model of self- and cultural-production – at the collapsing of boundaries between thinking and making in our processes and practices.

Processes and Practices of Making

In her study of knitting, Jones (2022) makes connections between: the power of textiles to be used as communicative resources; Ingold's taxonomy of lines (2007) which elaborates a 'correspondence' between maker and the material world; and Saito's (2017) work on everyday aesthetics. In doing so, she not only wants to overcome the privileging of written over visual forms of communication (Dissanayake, 2000), as we have sought to do, but also to '(re)open ways of understanding (this) craft as a meaning-making practice in its own right' (p. 1). The links she makes can be applied equally to autoethnographic craft(ing), as evidenced by our meaning-making practices, the selves we are in the process of making and the material and symbolic texts and artefacts we have produced.

For example, we can see Ingold's dynamic, unfolding and entwined 'correspondences' – what he calls a 'meshwork' (2007) of historic, social, cultural, political, material, affective and aesthetic factors – even when authors' favoured medium is writing (and performing written texts). These authors are still making with bodies and minds, intertwined as they are in space/place and time. Jackie pauses on her detective trail to watch squirrels, look at trees, sky, feel the sun, make tea, run her fingers along a shelf of books, leaf through one. Karen is 'grasping' at something in her writing and manifests it in the public performance of her script. But perhaps Ingold's 'correspondences' are most clearly illustrated in chapters by Clare, Joanne, Rommy and Javiera.

Clare wants to 'get her hands dirty', 'think with her hands', 'express herself through material engagement rather than via words'. The tiny steps of the stitching process – 'slicing, piercing, pinning, cutting' invite parallels with surgical actions performed on the human or animal body: 'I am thus able to create and recreate myself through these appliqued actions, stitching myself into being …'. In sharing her work on social media, she is mindful that stumbles, glitches and failures are vital parts of an 'improvisatory process'. She cites Ingold's (2013) 'following the material' and Brown's (2021) 'unfolding', combining skill and adaptivity in the ongoing situation as she 'unfold(s) into her experience of doctoral research while simultaneously constructing a new identity'. Gauntlett (2011) observes that:

> …people mess around with materials, select things, experimentally put parts together, rearrange, play, throw bits away, and generally manipulate the thing in question until it approaches something that seems to communicate meanings in a satisfying way. This rarely seems to be a matter of "making what I thought at the start", but rather a process of discovery and having ideas through the process of making. In particular, taking *time* to make something, using the hands (gives) people the opportunity to clarify thoughts and feelings, and to see the subject-matter in a new light.
>
> *p. 4*

Joanne is heavily invested in just this form of experimentation in her quest to make the familiar unfamiliar. She wants to 'examine *how* artists reflect on their work, what making the work *feels* like, and how they *make sense* of what they are doing *both in the making and over time*'. She experiments with different devices. There is a lack of confidence and a self-consciousness, she consciously crafts in the editing of the film, she reflects on 'the co-ordination of body and mind', she comes to see that repetition and iteration are important in her making, she sees bits of herself she isn't used to seeing: what her face is doing when she is drawing, what the materials she uses look like as they make contact with surfaces: the textures, absorbency, sound they made, the flow and relationship between her movement, the material and the mark. 'The making of the work became its own reflexive methodology', as she sought a space where practice and research were inseparable, a space 'where the barriers between making, performance and reflection are collapsed'. Opening up publicly (in a conference performance) helps her dismantle the boundaries between making, presentation, performance and reflection. It feels 'like slipping into the spaces "in-between", in order to discover the "cracks and erasures" in the process of making'.

Rommy and Javiera are also exploring what insights their creative acts of knitting/sewing and drawing are helping to unlock. They become very aware of what their hands are doing, and 'the particularities of the time and space created to think with them'. Intimate, painful, mysterious dialogues with the shadows of their mothers, through their artistic creation, unfold a different understanding of their data and of themselves as researchers. Javiera is literally and symbolically 'knitting these different parts of my world and my research, finding new connections' as she begins to 'think differently, with my whole body' – connections that were not visible when analysing in a more conventional way. '*The Blanket*, then, became method'. Sewing her tree allows her to discover 'one continuous history and not a fragmented self'. For Rommy, like Joanne, watching the video of her hands (drawing the portrait of her mother) becomes 'a meta-reflection'. The knowledge they produce with their hands, whether knitting/crocheting, sewing or drawing, offers conclusions that were not visible when engaging with their ethnographic data via a more traditional analytic approach.

Crafting 'In Conversation'

We have seen how 'conversations with others' are integral to our authors' making practices. We see them in conversation with the past, with digital and face-to-face audiences, with their co-authors, with their students, with those who are lost for whom they grieve, with family members and friends, with nature and with themselves – younger selves, future selves, professional selves, 'imagined' selves.

In *The Tidy House* (1982), Steedman shows the identificatory/resistant work little girls are doing through their creative writing at school, as they 'story themselves' as gendered and classed subjects. They do this by drawing on the *cultural discourses* available to them, the subjectivities/'destinies' with which they are surrounded in their families and wider neighbourhood settings – in their case, discourses that encouraged them to story themselves as subjects destined to keep 'a tidy house'. Bennett (2007, p. 33) refers to the 'material practices' that eventuate cultural production. It may be the availability of both Steedman's 'available cultural discourses' and Bennett's 'material practices' that accounts for the fact that, although written independently, our contributors appear mysteriously to be 'in conversation' with each other. This is revealed in the form of a number of common themes that appear: *liminality, waiting and 'stuckness'; haunting, grief and loss;* and the nature of *storytelling* itself.

Liminality, Waiting and 'Stuckness'

Mark explicitly evokes the shape shifting, 'fluid liminality' which he experiences betwixt teacher and student, researcher and writer, thinker and dreamer; while waiting for his mother's medical results, Patrick finds himself in 'a weird liminal space' when one is 'intensely aware of human mortality'; Aidan writes of the 'suspension' of his self in a liminal space between working and inactivity, translating this state into suspension in harmony – musical notes leading to unsatisfying chromatic dissonance, while a steady pulse keeps time slowly moving. The feeling of emptiness he experiences when struggling to find a goal in the constant shifting between different pixelated panes of glass becomes a measure of 'stuckness' in the related composition, 'each moment bringing the recognition I was hollow when staring between the TV, my phone and laptop'.

At the same time, autoethnographic making offers some the potential for freedom and liberation. The waiting involved may be waiting for 'the right time', the point at which something will finally 'surface'. For Jackie, reading acts as a stimulus. But it too comes to a halt. Karen wonders (in dialogue with Jackie's chapter): is it lockdown? Is it because *we* feel physically and mentally stuck, so that our activities – writing – reading – become 'stuck' too? The tension between 'movement' and getting 'unstuck' is at times palpable. Further, 'getting going' after the two-year pandemic and consecutive lockdowns is a gradual and piecemeal process as we emerge from our shells, discard them, find ourselves again: picking up the pieces of what was before, sifting through the remains, recrafting and remaking our futures.

Some authors (e.g., Mark and Karen) also employ notions of 'becomings' and '*un*becomings'. Karen employs the image of a pendulum, signifying a backwards and forwards movement, in contrast to the traditional linear narrative that others also reject, with its connotations of a privileged 'onwards and upwards' pattern, of a 'progressive' journey. In place of this, we read about 'going back', 'reversing', 'returning' and 'reflecting'. Where these appear, it is less a question of 'unravelling' or 'losing the plot' and more an act of deliberate resistance, as authors interact with and make sense of the past – past selves, past 'others'. In this reading, then, 'stuckness' is a halt or a pause in a stretched-out productive process, a moment that allows thinking to move from a well-worn path to an elsewhere that allows 'dreaming', 'dwelling', 'imaginings'.

Haunting, Loss and Grief

At points, there is the very real sense in our chapters of the authors doing what Panya refers to as their 'life's work'. We are haunted by what was, what is and what could be, for us and others, and we grieve for what and whom we have lost. Haunting and loss come through for authors (e.g., Jackie, Mark, Karen, Clare and Joanne) who reflect, to varying extents, on their academic careers and identities. For Jackie, there is a diffuse sense of loss, a preoccupation with nostalgia and how it is interpreted, reflections on absences and a noting of the concept of redemption. O'Brien (2018) observes that:

> ...the specific obsessions with a working-class past...are symptomatic of a crisis of belonging and self. The past, its presence felt as a spectral form, is a way of trying to deal with, or seek solace from, the contemporary moment.
>
> *p. 1407*

Mark is moving on from his long-term academic career and this involves 'loss too; and vulnerability. Things would be, can be, never the same'. For Karen, lived experiences, feelings and echoes of imposter syndrome haunt her throughout her career, reminding her that academic identity is unstable.

Edgar and David's chapter features themes of loss and haunting very prominently as they grieve the loss of a friend through death and celebrate his memory collectively but 'remotely', via performances on Zoom. Patrick highlights places that are haunted by the people who lived in them, who carry a trauma that is psychically and socially transmitted across generations, leaving scars. Loss is also implicit in Panya's and Jack's chapters. Jack reflects on the loss of cultural artefacts by nations subjected to colonial domination and the appropriation of these artefacts by British museums, while Panya reflects on what has been lost for her people through centuries of racial injustices. She mourns this loss at the same time as recognising the remnants that remain, evidenced in her own personal experiences and the poetry and exhibitions based on them.

Avery Gordon writes that haunting is '... the domain of turmoil and trouble, that moment (of however long duration) when things are not in their assigned places, when the cracks and rigging are exposed ... when disturbed feelings cannot be put away' (2008[1997], p. xvi). As suggested earlier, it may be Covid-19 and lockdowns that led to these 'disturbed feelings' bubbling up to the surface, forcing us to confront ourselves (and others) in an age of uncertainty. The pandemic forced us to 'hold up a mirror to our society' (Lupton, 2020) and to 'raise new questions, generate new knowledge, and re-evaluate our existing ways of knowing' (Pruulmann-Vengerfeldt, 2020). As Marris (1996) points out in relation to uncertainty:

> Traumatic events which rob us of the attachments and purposes around which the meaning of life has been organized – like bereavement or losing a career – provoke an anxious, intense and often despairing search to recover a sense of meaning. We experience that search as grieving…
>
> *p. 117*

Storytelling

Rebecca Solnit (2014) writes that stories are 'all in the telling'. They are:

> …compasses and architecture; we navigate by them, we build our sanctuaries and our prisons out of them, and to be without a story is to be lost in the vastness of a world that spreads in all directions like arctic tundra or sea ice.
>
> *p. 3*

The 'stories of making' that are shared in this collection are personal, embodied, interactional, relational; they unfold in changed times and in different locations. The narratives that 'become' and 'emerge' are woven-sewn-cut-glued-mended out of the 'brokenness' of selves – as well as out of hope – and sometimes we see the cracks that have been filled in (Jackie and Mark both referencing the Japanese practice of 'Kintsugi').

A number of authors challenged conventional modes of *temporality and chronology* in storytelling. As we have seen, authors flit between past and present, sit long in particular moments, moments that cannot be written as quickly as they happen or are experienced.

Some contributors contemplate *whose* stories are being told, and how. For example, Lauriel-Arwen writes of honouring the land she walks on, acknowledging and expressing gratitude for the gifts of knowledge and understanding she has received from its rightful owners – knowledge her ancestors tried to erase. Jack problematises the 'complicated transactions' engaged in by museums in the acquisition of the objects they display. He complicates for us the stories they tell as he unveils certain transactions as unethical and exploitative and offers the hope that curators who come after him will learn from his mistakes.

Karen provides an example of how stories can be told via managerial audit tools like the 'Performance Development Review'. She too offers alternative stories and shows us how they can be crafted and told, not only how we 'perform' the appropriate 'self' for that context but also how we can craft and stage a more authentic self, existing 'in the shadows'.

Jackie notes that on the bigger political stage we are also in desperate need of new stories to tell about ourselves as individuals and as a country, in order to make a more sustainable future for all. But she questions the capacity of those impacted most by austerity and precarity, whose 'imaginative capacities' may have atrophied, to fantasise a new reality before they too are allowed to mourn what has been lost. She hears a slightly patronising tone in Stewart's (1988) anthropological quoting of others' vernacular speech and contrasts this with more compassionate renderings of others' communities. She cites Garner (1997) as 'storytelling at its finest' as he captures 'the cadence, the music' of vernacular vocabularies through the image of a line of men 'rhythmically moving in concert as they cut corn with scythes' (p. 57). The way anthropologists and ethnographers could echo this much more respectful rendering of 'others' is beautifully illustrated by Javiera's description of her fieldwork visit to a Haitian evangelical service:

> Every attempt (to write about it) looked like a caricature of an exotic culture because I was trying to explain them, the exotic racialised 'other' … I was trying to explain to a Western audience the daily faith of a racialised community from the Global South. I desisted and instead I decided to reflect and write about myself in the service, how I embraced being in a religious celebration, joining the joy of the parishioners and how I decided to talk to my mother in the service, as it was in her funeral the last time I went to a church. In the writing I described our conversations and how I felt connection and support from a community that welcomed me, the other, in their sacred practice.

Finally, our authors seem to be in agreement that this storytelling that is 'doing the work of making selves' is an ongoing, unfinished and unfinish-able affair. Of his seventh piece, Aiden says: 'I don't want this to be the end of the collection'. He wants to hold the future open in the hope that it will bring better times for him and his working-class peers than those he has experienced in the past. Panya's poems 'are an ongoing process of revision with no clear end in sight'. Clare refers to a self that continues to 'unfold', from an identity of 'novice' stitcher into an 'amateur' one (perhaps also holding the possibility open for the amateur stitcher to morph into something else?) For Mark, too, there's no clear destination: 'Where does this process of dreaming, of becoming, take me?' he asks, when 'everything is in process; both being and becoming'. His citation of the concept of *limbotopia* to represent a narrative without end or closure echoes Jackie's getting to the 'for a time' end of her crafting of an autoethnographic artefact and her citing of Steedman's (2001) assertion that 'there is no – there cannot be an – End, for we are still in it, the great slow-moving Everything'.

Autoethnographic Making as Research Method

If authors have elaborated the processes and practices through which they are 'making selves', how might this constitute a research method? As we said in the Introduction, we regard it as crucial that autoethnographic approaches mine 'personal experience' *in order to* throw light on wider social and cultural issues and relations; that they make connections between the individual and the social, between the self and culture, between the personal and the political and between private troubles and public issues. Have our authors made such connections? Have we shown ways in which we are engaged in 'making culture(s)' as well as making selves?

Karen, Chrissie, Clare, Joanna and Aidan are all engaged in refashioning higher education to make it a more inclusive, less 'disciplining' institution, one that offers a space for a variety of approaches to epistemology, pedagogy and artistic practice. Clare's and Karen's contributions further highlight the *myth* of academic privilege – showing that the time they have to sit back, to 'philosophise', to 'think/make', is far from the reality. The performance targets that Karen focuses on are just one example of how academia is increasingly constituted by disciplinary technologies.

We saw at the beginning of this chapter that despite negative feelings of 'stuckness', it was during a period when time slowed down, sometimes to a point of stillness, that authors crafted the autoethnographic artefacts brought together in this collection. In response to the neoliberal academy where the focus on generating 'products' and 'outputs' is a constant pressure, with no time for reflective making practices, there have been calls for a 'slow academia' (Berg & Seeber, 2017). In relation to autoethnography, Sparkes (2018) observes that it is:

> … at the will of the body, often involving unbeknown yet-to-be told stories that circulate within us at the pre-objective, enfleshed, multisensory and carnal level, not yet ready for language to take its hold. When the body is ready to release its story, it lets us know in subtle ways so that we can accept its gift and engage in the somatic work of crafting a tale for the telling to self and others.
>
> *p. 267*

On the other hand, critics have suggested that 'slow academia' is itself a form of privilege, as untenured colleagues and those on temporary contracts are not in a position to 'stretch out' the time they take for writing, researching and crafting. Perhaps this paradox provides further potentialities for the imaginative crafting of a different kind of higher education institution – for the autoethnographic making of a new academic self and a new kind of inclusive 'academic work' produced through a research method fitted to resistance.

Patrick and Lauriel-Arwen demonstrate the ways we are connected to the natural world – to landscape and to non-human living things – showing how place(s) make us just as we make place(s); reminding us as they do so of our responsibilities to care for our natural world. Edgar and David are creating spaces in which hitherto untold gay men's stories are told, heard and seen. Authors' remaking of culture(s) is variously described as cathartic and healing. Mark is reaching for a place of 'relational intersubjectivity and interbeing', where we breach the spaces between the Self and the Other(s) – a place that provides 'an affordance to dream again'; just as Jackie seems to be searching for new stories of re-enchantment. Simon offers us a way to *look, see* and *critique* differently. Others, in one way or another, *demand* reparation and healing: Rommy, Javiera and Jack through practices aimed at bringing a postcolonial world into being; Panya as she challenges a racist status quo through her powerful poetry.

A number of contributors echo Aidan's 'pieces' in their use of metaphors of fragments, assemblages, patches, collage, quilts etc. Stanley, Salter, and Dampier (2013) explain how a process of actively gathering these together (even if, as Jackie put it, the picture on the lid of the jigsaw isn't immediately intelligible) constitutes the 'bringing into being' of *'cultural assemblages'*. They also highlight the importance of showing 'the work of making it':

> Cultural sociology has greatest import not as the development of a particular area called culture but as a means of focusing reflexive analytical attention on 'the making of the cultural' ... Cultural practices involve their own often implicit knowledge-claims, with cultural production encompassing what Mukerji (2007, p. 50) calls the 'time-making activities' through which cultural forms eventuate ... seeing these in terms of cultural genealogy, around the production of epistemic knowledge both within society and within cultural sociology, raises the important elements of process, time and historicity ... Bennett's (2007, p. 33) ideas about 'the work of making it', the material practices that eventuate cultural production, and 'the work it does', organized by cultural knowledges and competencies, usefully emphasize that both are constituents of cultural assemblage.
>
> *Stanley et al. (2013, p. 288)*

We have seen the ways in which processes and practices of crafting selves and cultures are inescapably interwoven with/through and dependent on external social relations and macro forces and released, in our case, in response to the social/structural factors of the Covid-19 pandemic and lockdowns; oppressive regimes of class, gender and racism; institutional constraints that prescribe conventional forms of epistemology but proscribe innovative forms of pedagogy, artistic practice, art criticism and professional curation, in favour of the disciplining of 'proper' neoliberal subjects; and the need to negotiate major life transitions such as retirement and threatened mortality. Making ourselves in the face of these challenges is shown to be an inquiring, exploratory, practice-based, messy research method in which it is important to recognise that we are not aiming for a final 'polished' product (or in fact, for anything 'final' at all). Process and product are inseparable, even when using the most conventional medium of all – writing. In *Body Work*, Melissa Febos describes her essays as 'attempts to describe the ways that writing is integrated into the fundamental movements of my life: political, corporeal, spiritual, psychological, and social' (Febos, 2022, p. ix). Finally, whatever material or media they chose, authors were also willing to face the inherent challenges of autoethnographic making: to recognise that it is a research method that makes us *vulnerable*.

What of the Future?

The fact that vulnerability is integral to autoethnographic making means that an ethic of care is important. The sociologist Les Back (2016, p. 114) calls for generosity in academia, not just as a matter of 'being nice to others', but also as a 'survival strategy' or 'a prophylactic against the corrosive aspects of intellectual cruelty' which are part of the neoliberal university. Moriarty argues that:

> … rewilding academia can and will provide a potential antidote to neo-liberalism, helping those scholars who feel wounded by its effects to adopt different approaches to pedagogy and research that will help them to feel nourished and replenished.
>
> *2020, p. 4*

Barbara Grant suggests one means of addressing the toxic and harmful structures and practices of neoliberal academia is via the concept of 'a thousand tiny universities'. According to Grant, we can challenge these forces which are out of our control on the ground level by taking perspectives from within our smaller 'tiny' worlds and effecting change wherever we can (Pfaendner, 2018). Can autoethnographic (re)making become a part of this wider 'rewilding', remaking project?

Of course, a number of our contributors are practising outside higher education institutions. Perhaps it is fitting then that autoethnography has been described as a 'blurred genre' (Bretell, 1997; Sparkes, 2018). Clifford Geertz (1980) also draws attention to 'genre blurring' and mixing in postmodern scholarly work. He argues that as a result of this, it is difficult to situate authors within particular disciplines and to classify their works (Bretell, 2007). The chapters in this collection draw attention to a reluctance to be categorised or classified, a desire for a method with the capacity to reach into a variety of creative spaces, practices and contexts, a desire to experience the 'joie de faire'. We go beyond merely blurring disciplinary boundaries or forms of writing, by also blurring the boundaries between autoethnographic research undertaken inside the academy and writing/making/performing selves and culture(s) beyond its symbolic and material walls, in spaces where storytelling includes writing, poetry, exhibitions, art, artefacts, digital media, craftwork, fiction, dramatisation and film. And we do it from inside and outside ourselves. As Frandsen and Pelly observe, through autoethnographies:

> … we witness power struggles and contextual complexity that can be best understood from a position of both 'being wrapped up in it' (experiencing it) as well as 'being outside of it' (reflecting upon it, writing about it, theorizing it)
>
> *2020, p. 252*

It is our hope that through the sharing of our autoethnographic crafting of selves and cultures, readers will gain insight into how this 'crafting space' is itself one of intellectual inquiry, debate and reflection and be encouraged to consider their own autoethnographic making processes and practices. In describing, explaining and reflecting on our processes and practices, we have shown what Stanley et al. (2013) called 'the work of making it'. What 'the work it *does*' is, remains to be accomplished, as readers hopefully (re)make *their* worlds, in part at least by engaging with this collection.

References

Allen-Collinson, J. (2013). Autoethnography as the engagement of self/other, self/culture, self/politics, selves/futures. In S. H. Jones, T. E. Adams, & C. Ellis (Eds.), *Handbook of autoethnography* (pp. 281–299). Walnut Creek: Left Coast Press.

Back, L. (2016). *Academic diary*. London: Goldsmiths Press.

Bennett, T. (2007). The work of culture. *Cultural Sociology*, *1*, 31–47.

Berg, M., & Seeber, B. K. (2017). *The slow professor*. Toronto: University of Toronto Press.

Bretell, C. B. (1997). Blurred genres and blended voices: Life history, biography, autobiography and the auto/ethnography of women's lives. In D. Reed-Danahay (Ed.), *Auto/ethnography: Rewriting the self and the social* (pp. 223–246). Oxford: Berg.

Brown, A. (2021). The mark of the researcher's hand: the imperfections of craft in the process of becoming a qualitative researcher. *Management Learning*, *52*(5), 541–558.

de Certeau, M. (1988). *The practice of everyday life*, trans. S. F. Rendall. Berkeley, CA: University of California Press.

Davies, B., Browne, J., Gannon, S., Hopkins, L., McCann, H., & Wihlborg, M. (2006). Constituting the feminist subject in poststructuralist discourse. *Feminism & Psychology*, *16*(1), 87–103.

Davies, B., & Gannon, S. (2006). *Doing collective biography*. Berkshire: Open University Press.

Dissanayake, E. (2000). *Art and intimacy: How the arts began*. Washington: University of Washington Press.

Febos, M. (2022). *Body work: The radical power of personal narrative*. London: Penguin.

Frandsen, S., & Pelly, D. M. (2020). Organizational resistance and autoethnography. In A. F. Herrmann (Ed.), *The Routledge international handbook of organizational autoethnography* (pp. 252–268). London: Routledge.

Garner, A. (1997). *The voice that thunders*. London: Harvill Press.

Gauntlett, D. (2011). *Making is connecting: The social meaning of creativity, from DIY and knitting to Youtube and Web 2.0*. Cambridge: Polity.

Geertz, C. (1980). Blurred genres: The reconfiguration of social thought. *The American Scholar*, *49*(2), 165–179.

Gordon, A. F. (2008[1997]). *Ghostly matters: Haunting and the sociological imagination*. Minneapolis: University of Minnesota Press.

Heidegger, M. (1971). *Poetry, language, thought*, trans. A. Hofstadter. New York: Harper & Row.

Hodgson, J. (2022). Potent connections, mystery-work and the relational nature of retreat-going. *The Sociological Review*, *70*(1), 199–214.

Ingold, T. (2000). *The perception of environment: Essays on livelihood, dwelling and skill*. London: Routledge.

Ingold, T. (2007). *Lines: A brief history.* Oxon: Routledge.

Ingold, T. (2013). *Making: Anthropology, archaeology, art and architecture.* Oxon: Routledge.

Jackson, S. (2010). Self, time and narrative: Re-thinking the contribution of G.H. Mead. *Life Writing, 7*(2), 123–136.

Jones, S. (2022). Knitting and Everyday Meaning-Making. *Textile,* Online First. https://doi.org/10.1080/14759756.2022.2092967

Lupton, D. (2020). Contextualising COVID-19: Sociocultural perspectives on contagion. In D. Lupton, & K. Willis (Eds.), *The coronavirus crisis: Social perspectives.* London: Routledge.

Marris, P. (1996). *The politics of uncertainty.* London: Routledge.

Mason, J. (2018). *Affinities: Potent connections in personal life.* Cambridge: Polity.

Moriarty, J. (2020). *Autoethnographies from the neoliberal academy: Rewilding, writing and resistance in higher education.* London: Routledge.

Mukerji, C. (2007). Cultural genealogy. *Cultural Sociology, 1,* 49–71.

O'Brien, P. (2018). 'Takes you back even if you were never there originally': Class, history, and nostalgia in Gordon Burn's The North of England Home Service. *Textual Practice, 32*(8), 1405–1423.

Pfaendner, B. (2018). A thousand tiny universities – my impressions from HERDSA. *TECHE.* Retrieved from https://teche.mq.edu.au/2018/07/a-thousand-tiny-universities-my-impressions-from-herdsa/

Probyn, E. (2003). The spatial imperative of subjectivity. In K. Anderson, M. Domosh, S. Pile, & N. Thrift (Eds.), *Handbook of cultural geography* (pp. 290–299). London: Sage.

Pruulmann-Vengerfeldt, P. (2020). The ways of knowing the pandemic with the help of prompted autoethnography. *Qualitative Inquiry, 27*(7), 812–819.

Saito, Y. (2017). *Aesthetics of the familiar: Everyday life and world-making.* Oxford: Oxford University Press.

Shelton, S. A. (2021). Entangled time hops: Doomsday clocks, pandemics, and qualitative research's responsibility. *Qualitative Inquiry, 27*(7), 824–828.

Skeggs, B. (2014). Values beyond value? Is anything beyond the logic of capital? *The British Journal of Sociology, 65*(1), 1–20.

Solnit, R. (2014). *The faraway nearby.* London: Granta.

Sparkes, A. C. (2018). Creating criteria for evaluating autoethnography and the pedagogical potential of working with lists. In L. Turner, N. Short, A. Grant, & T. Adams (Eds.), *International perspectives on autoethnographic research and practice* (pp. 256–267). London: Routledge.

Stanley, L., Salter, A., & Dampier, H. (2013). The work of making and the work it does: Cultural sociology and 'bringing- into-being' the cultural assemblage of the Olive Schreiner letters. *Cultural Sociology, 7*(3), 287–302.

Steedman, C. (1982). *The tidy house: Little girls writing.* London: Virago Press.

Steedman, C. (2001). Something she called a fever: Michelet, Derrida and dust. *The American Historical Review, 106*(4), 1159–1180.

Stewart, K. (1988). Nostalgia – A polemic. *Cultural Anthropology, 3*(3), 227–241.

INDEX

Note: Locators in *italics* represent figures.